Practising EU foreign policy

MANCHESTER
1824

Manchester University Press

Practising EU foreign policy

Russia and the eastern neighbours

BEATRIX FUTÁK-CAMPBELL

Manchester University Press

The right of Beatrix Futák-Campbell to be identified as the author of this work has been asserted by her in accordance with the Copyright, Designs and Patents Act 1988.

Published by Manchester University Press
Altrincham Street, Manchester M1 7JA
www.manchesteruniversitypress.co.uk

British Library Cataloguing-in-Publication Data
A catalogue record for this book is available from the British Library

ISBN   978 0 7190 9589 4   hardback

First published 2018

Typeset
by Toppan Best-set Premedia Limited
Printed in Great Britain
by CPI Group (UK) Ltd, Croydon, CR0 4YY

There is no essence of Europe, no fixed list of European values. There is no 'finality' to the process of European integration. Europe is a project of the future. With every decision, not only its zone of peace, its institutions, its political, economic and social order, but also its very identity and self-determination are opened for questioning and debate.

(Biedenkopf *et al.*, 2004: 12)

Contents

Acknowledgements

Studying practitioners is not new in International Relations (IR). The field of IR has always focused on practitioners, especially for information and data. However, the arrival of the practice turn changed the focus, and made the practitioners the focus of analysis, rather than just mere information providers. This so-called practice turn originates from scholarly works that were done in different disciplines such as philosophy, sociology, and social psychology for decades now. They have inspired many IR scholars, but a more focused discussion on how to introduce practice theory to IR has only been done more recently. The literature on this topic is ever growing, which is a testament to our changing analytical interest in practitioners as well as the persuasive nature of the theory.

Yet, I found it intriguing that in this emergent literature the discussion on the methodologies that we ought to develop to study practitioners is rather limited. In the other disciplines, where practice theory was established, methodological discussions went hand in hand with theory development. While practice theorists in IR agreed to promote methodological pluralism, most scholars stuck to applying Bourdieu and his concept of *habitus*, and therefore focus exclusively on the conduct of practitioners, bar a few exceptions. Duvall and Chowdhury (2011) already drew attention to this, and critiqued the lack of application of discursive approaches among practice theory scholars.

My training in conversation analysis, discursive psychology, and ethnomethodology, plus my practitioner background led me to engage in this limited methodological discussion, and to develop a conceptual model that aims to bring those who merely focus on conduct and behaviour with those schools who focus on discourse and linguistic approaches. EU foreign policy and EU practitioners seemed an ideal option, and focusing on Russia and the other eastern neighbours is equally apt, considering the developments in Russian foreign policy.

This book is the work of years of pondering about the EU as a foreign policy actor that I began at the Europa Institute in the Edinburgh Law School and continued at the University of St Andrews. During my research and since, a number of other scholars were kind enough to read and comment on my work. Among them I am most indebted to Rick Fawn, Karin Fierke, as well as Ben Rosamond and John Anderson who provided very engaging and intellectually stimulating discussions throughout the process. I am also grateful to Sanjoy Banerjee who generously encouraged me and gave comments on the analytical chapters, as did Sue Widdicombe and Clair Haggett as well as Eric Laurier with whom I established the Scottish Ethnomethodology, Discourse, Interaction and Talk (SEDIT) research group (www.sedit.org.uk) at the University of Edinburgh. SEDIT has been a turning point for my engagement in contemporary discourse analysis. Besides SEDIT, Alexa Hepburn and Jonathan Potter have been instrumental in my methodological training. They provided a tremendous source of intellectual and personal inspiration. I learned a great deal from them, and they will have a deep and lasting influence on my thinking as well as on my own professional attitude. They are truly inspiring. I am also most indebted to Celia Kitzinger, among many things, for training me in conversation analysis. Other members of the academic community who generously helped along the way include, with apologies to those unintentionally left out: Tony Lang, Nick Rengger, Andy Williams, Michael J. Boyle, Michelle Burgis-Kasthala, Jeffrey Murer, Torsten Michel, Wojtek Ostrowski (and others at the School of IR in St Andrews), Lene Hansen, Antje Wiener, Thomas Christiansen, Anne Farbe, Imogen Sudbery, Emmanuel Schon-Quinlivan, Thomas Moore, Annika Bergman Rosamond, Luke March, Andrew Farrer, Elizabeth Stokoe, Sally Wiggins, Bregje de Kok, all colleagues and PhD students, whom I worked with while I was a Marie Curie Research Fellow at PF7 Project 'Power and Region in a Multipolar Order' (PRIMO), and my colleagues at the IR research group at Leiden University. Many thanks to each of them for their invaluable intellectual and often personal contributions, and to my anonymous reviewers.

Tony Mason at Manchester University Press was also instrumental in initiating turning this project into a book. I am indebted to him for his patience. I am also grateful to my research assistants Christian Schwieter, Tuure Niemi, and Joe Cotton who not only helped with copy-editing but were also instrumental in clarifying my arguments and pushing me to adapt my often highly technical writing style.

Without the generous Economic and Social Research Council (ESRC) scholarship, along with the various travel, training, and workshop grants from University of York Department of Sociology Bursary, Professional and Personal Development Fund University of St Andrews, Centre for Russian, Central and East European Studies (CRCEES) Fellowship and Russell Trust Award, University of St Andrews, my research would have not been possible. I am very appreciative of this support.

Finally, I would like to acknowledge and thank all those practitioners who participated and made this project possible. I am most indebted to Robert Cooper who was instrumental in the data collection process.

Further thanks have to go to Pat and Jane Harkin, Sabine Rolle, Pete Davis, Fr Hugh Purcell, Jane Feinmann, Naomi Hunter, Elena Pollot, and Andrew Thomson whose friendship and support meant a great amount to me, and still does.

My profoundest gratitude goes to my parents, and to my husband Craig, who not only introduced me to poststructuralist philosophy and social psychology but has been a wonderful partner for many years. For his love, support, and stimulating chats I am most grateful. I dedicate this book to him, and to our firstborn Xa.

Abbreviations

CA	conversation analysis
CEECs	central and eastern European countries
CFSP	Common Foreign and Security Policy
CIS	Commonwealth of Independent States
CMD	Category Membership Device
DIR	Discursive IR
DPM	Discursive Practice Model
EEC	European Economic Community
ENP	European Neighbourhood Policy
ENPI	European Neighbourhood and Partnership Instrument
EP	European Parliament
EU	European Union
Inv	interviewer
IR	International Relations
MEP	Member of the European Parliament
OMC	Open Method of Coordination
R	researcher
TEU	Treaty on European Union [Maastricht Treaty]
TFEU	Treaty on the Functioning of the European Union [Lisbon Treaty]
TUC	turn construction unit

Introduction

In considering EU foreign policy in practice, this book argues that a specific focus on practitioners' (diplomats, bureaucrats, and public officials) interactions can offer insight into the way EU foreign policy is practised. An assessment of the practices of practitioners through a new type of data set and a new discursive framework demonstrates the significance of European identity, collective interests, and the role that normative and moral concerns play for EU practitioners when they consider EU foreign policy in the eastern neighbourhood. It also highlights that these four concepts are interlinked when they consider the policy, despite the commonly accepted understanding, even by practitioners, that the EU is a normative power in global affairs. These findings are relevant not only for understanding current developments in EU foreign policy, but also for allowing scholars, as well as practitioners, to move away from considering the EU exclusively as a normative power but perceiving it as a more complex power with a collective 'European' identity, collective understandings of European norms that are linked to collective moral concerns that at the same time all link to collective European interests. Currently there is a lot of discussion regarding the EU becoming a resilient, or pragmatic power. Only time and EU actions will tell what these terms mean in practice. However, this book is a testament to the fact that practitioners have always considered EU foreign policy beyond the normative. In this introduction I begin by providing some context for the book, followed by an explanation of, and rationale for, its theoretical and methodological approach, as well as an outline of the rest of the book's structure.

The EU, including its earlier formations, is a major economic and political actor in the region. It was so even before the collapse of the Soviet Union, and has retained this status after the resurgence of Russia as the other main regional power. The EU is a complex actor with twenty-eight member states,[1] all of which have bilateral relationships with Russia and the other eastern neighbouring states, despite the common EU policy in the regions. This situation is the result of some clever manoeuvrings from President Putin, specifically in the energy policy he supports which is Russia's de facto foreign policy in the region. Ukraine, Belarus, and Moldova's geographical location between the EU and

Russia make them interesting for both regional actors. For Russia, they are directly within the Russian sphere of influence: historically they belonged to Soviet Union, and before that to the Russian Empire. For the EU, they offer a chance to exercise normative power in the region and to create a safe, secure, and stable neighbourhood where countries are more similar to EU member states. Ukraine's struggle to decide which regional actor's sphere of influence it would rather belong to creates an issue. This is no easy decision. Being caught between two regional actors both of whom want to assert themselves through their relations with Ukraine only problematises this decision. While Ukraine is particularly important because of its size, history, and the energy transit pipelines delivering Russia gas and oil to the EU, the region as a whole became strategically important after the last EU enlargement in 2004 and 2007. Ever since, more and more studies consider the eastern neighbourhood of the EU as a collective region to study. The development of the Eastern Partnership in 2009 is also a testament to recognising the eastern neighbourhood as a collective which shares specific concerns. However, no one has yet examined how EU practitioners, who are directly responsible for policy developments in the eastern neighbourhood, consider this policy domain.

This leads to the theoretical reasons behind this study. Focusing on practices and practitioners is not entirely new. The practice turn in International Relations (IR) was initiated by Vincent Pouliot in his PhD thesis, which was later published in 2010 as *International Security in Practice: The Politics of NATO–Russia Diplomacy*. This was followed by a volume entitled *International Practices* in 2011 edited by Emmanuel Adler and Vincent Pouliot. By Adler and Pouliot's own admission, the practice turn focuses on the practices of IR, rather than just the theoretical approaches that explain it. Inherently, it aims to combine theory and practice. However, the practice turn is still a relatively novel way of considering IR, despite McCourt's (2016) rash claim of already being the new constructivism; and only more recently have attempts been made to apply it to EU foreign policy. This means that the theoretical implications of the practice turn are relatively understudied, and hence offer many opportunities for further research in both IR theory and EU studies.[2] Furthermore, since most of the scholars who engage with the practice turn predominantly use policy documents, non-recorded elite interviews, news items, or autobiographies to investigate these practices, there is an opportunity to use different methods. This leads to the final reason behind this study: methodology.

Suppose we turn to different kinds of data to trace these practices, such as transcripts of conversations where practitioners openly discuss specific policy focuses? Through this new direction, our focus changes from what is being said, to what these practitioners achieve through their talk. Or, put differently, our focus turns to the social action of talk, and their impact on policy development. Using verbatim data from practitioners is practically unheard of. Diplomats rarely go on record, for many reasons, ranging from personal reservation to security. By using verbatim transcripts of conversations and by focusing on the sequential organisation of talk, this study offers an innovative way of analysing practitioners and their practices. To be clear, the aim is not to expose each individual position of the EU practitioners' participating in the study, or to link them to their respective member states' positions, or to check whether they truly represent EU positions. Rather, this study seeks to understand how these practitioners make sense of the policy. Therefore, their anonymity and confidentiality is not compromised by the transcripts. This is crucial. While it would be possible to draw such comparisons, it would have been impossible to have the practitioners on record. What these transcripts do reveal, however, is that there is a distinctly collective understanding of this policy area, to which practitioners ascribe regardless of their nationality, rank, or the EU institution they work for. This shared understanding revolves around four concerns: identity, normative and moral concerns, and collective interests. As I argue, there is already an indication that EU practitioners are perceiving EU foreign policy more as a multifaceted power than official documents would allow it to be until the new EU Global Strategy (EU HR/VP 2016) comes into force.[3] In addition to this very specific understanding of this policy area, the transcripts show the way in which the EU approximates itself to Russia as the other power in the region. They also identify that EU practitioners predominantly still view the EU as a normative actor, or what Manners coined a normative power.[4] Finally, the transcripts reveal several excellent negotiating techniques that EU practitioners possess, either through training or experience. But, at the same time, the transcripts suggest that practitioners ought to be more careful and reconsider using specific discursive formulations that link the EU to moral authority in its eastern neighbourhood. Implying moral authority can potentially be dangerous and could harm EU interest in the long term, especially if the EU does not deliver on, for example, augmented support and closer cooperation with Ukraine in order not to aggravate its relations with Russia.

As a result, this book establishes a strategical link between theory, methodology, and practice. I argue that by paying attention to the social action of talk, that is, what EU practitioners achieve through interaction, we have a better understanding of foreign policy practices. These interactional accounts also offer us a clearer insight into how practitioners manage key IR concepts such as identity, normative, moral, and collective interest concerns. Furthermore, they allow us to observe how these four notions are dependent on each other during policy development rather than any one taking priority over the others. Building on poststructuralist IR theory and on discursive psychology's theory of social action, I show that this interdependency is a significant step for poststructuralist IR theory as well as IR practice theory. I put forward a new analytical framework to capture practice, namely Discursive International Relations (DIR), which includes a new conceptual model the Discourse Practice Model (DPM) to help to recognise specific practices through identifying social action, fact, interest formulations, and agency. DIR also serves our understanding of EU foreign policy development and helps us to establish the kind of actor, or power that the EU is.

To demonstrate this, the book focuses on EU foreign policy vis-à-vis its eastern neighbours, namely Russia, Ukraine, Moldova, and Belarus. It argues that the practitioners who develop EU policy with respect to these countries distinguish these neighbours as European; in contrast to southern neighbours, or even Turkey, a candidate state. While they acknowledge the normative role that the EU plays in the eastern region, and its vocational or moral responsibility to do so, practitioners also remain acutely aware of the collective EU interest in the region, particularly in the security of energy supplies. As a result, this book reveals a dual impetus in which closer ties with eastern European countries is not merely a matter of moral concern, or of clarifying issues of identity for the EU, but also of protecting the EU's own interests. In short, these notions are connected and exist in parallel to each other, when practitioners consider EU foreign policy, rather than favouring one notion over the other. This book also argues that, in understanding European foreign policy towards its eastern neighbours, practitioners draw upon dichotomised categories combined with various discursive devices that effectively work to fragment 'European' identity and to dilute the EU's moral authority in the region, if the focus at the end is seen to be on EU collective interests. This will have implications for practices of EU foreign policy.

Structure of the book

This book is split into two parts: theory and practice. In Part I, I develop the theoretical and methodological framework to study foreign policy practices through practitioners' interaction. Chapter 1 examines the ways in which practitioners are studied. I begin by a general examination of the practice turn, starting with Theodore R. Schatzki, Karin Knorr Cetina, and Eike von Savigny's (2001) renowned edited volume *The Practice Turn in Contemporary Theory*. In this distinguished collection of essays, I focus on the more general approaches on the use of practice theory by Schatzki, Turner, and Rouse to the more specific ones such as Lynch's contribution that links language, practice theory, ethnomethodology, and conversation analysis (CA). Lynch's argument serves as the theoretical base for the contribution of this book to the practice turn. Next, I focus on the application of practice theory in IR and more recently in EU studies. Although there is a clear divide between conduct and more linguist-based approaches, both groups focus on practices and social action, hence the division is methodological rather than theoretical. Furthermore, this division presents a clear research gap that this study addresses through its focus on identifying the social actions achieved through practitioners' interactions.

Following on from this, Chapter 2 outlines the new methodology used to study social action of practitioners' interaction. I propose a new framework DIR and the application of the DPM. DPM has four main features: social action, fact/interest formulations, agency, and IR practice, and focuses on the speakers' communicational practice and interactions. This chapter also considers data collection and the methodological and ethical implications of using recorded elite research interviews.

Part II of this book focuses on practice. Each chapter centres around one particular topic such as identity, norms, moral concerns, and collective interests, and I examine these concepts through verbatim transcripts of talk from a large data set collected from EU practitioners. To the corpus, I apply the DPM and build these four collections by focusing on the social action achieved by practitioners in interactions. In Chapter 3, I introduce the different constructs of the category of the 'European'. The two main patterns that emerge from the corpus are EU practitioners differentiating between 'European' neighbours (e.g. Ukraine), potential neighbours (such as the South Caucasus and Kazakhstan), and non-European neighbours (including Morocco, Egypt, Algeria, and, significantly, Turkey). In drawing up criteria for outlining what is European (or the category entitlement of the 'European'), practitioners draw on geography, culture, history, economics, and heredity accounts of European civilisation.

In Chapter 4, I consider the ways in which EU practitioners account for the normative role and power of the EU in the eastern neighbourhood. There are four dominant patterns that emerge from the data. These are: what practitioners actually understand by norms; the reasons behind neighbouring countries wanting to emulate the EU model; what practitioners identify as specific concerns over non-compliance; and the ways in which practitioners perpetuate a very EU-centric view of the world. Chapter 5 examines how EU practitioners justify their vocational interest in the region through: claims of moral duty; communicating the 'right' message; identifying neighbours who have different moral concerns and recognising when it is morally wrong to be involved in a country. In the final analytical chapter (Chapter 6), I demonstrate that practitioners not only consider identity, norms, and the EU's moral obligation in the regions but also collective security interests. Their pragmatism surpasses the common expectation and ways that the EU has been perceived. The corpus revealed many different collective EU interests in the region such as migration, terrorism, organised crime, and the environment, but energy security seems to prevail. The three main patterns emerging from the data are: the ways in which they identify energy interests as the collective EU interest in the eastern neighbourhood; their claims to future plans for managing the collective EU concerns over energy supplies; and, finally, the ways in which they justify collective EU interest in the region through moral concerns and the vocation attributes the EU has for the eastern neighbours.

In the Conclusion, I reflect on the main findings of the book and the theoretical and methodological contributions that these findings make to IR practice theory and EU studies. I also consider the practical relevance of my research for EU practitioners and for their practice.

Notes

1 This will change to 27 as soon as the EU and the UK agree on an exit deal following the Referendum held in the UK on 24 June 2016, and the invoking of Article 50. It is beyond the scope of this book to cover the impact that Brexit will have on EU foreign policy. The only remark I would like to make on the topic is that losing UK military capabilities will have minimal impact on future EU military competencies, especially concerning the EU becoming more pragmatic also about using its military capabilities. If anything, the UK leaving the EU will only give way to further developments in EU defence.

2 More on this, including a review of the literature, in Chapter 1.

3 The EU Global Strategy deliberately opts for not describing the EU as a specific type of power. Having said that in her foreword, High Representative/Vice-President Frederica Mogherini draws attention to the fact that the EU cannot only rely on its soft power, and nor should it be exclusively considered as a civilian power, since the EU has more capabilities including military and defence competencies. Furthermore, the language used in the EU Global Strategy indicates that the EU wants to be seen as more pragmatic, or, more precisely, apply principled pragmatism to its external relations. The trouble at the moment with this concept is that it is unclear what it actually means. The EU has to face up to the changing nature of the global order and how it wants to fit into this new order.

4 This is the case despite the fact that most of the EU practitioners who participated in the study had not heard of, read, or been taught the concept of normative power. They could not, for example, name Ian Manners or any other scholar engaged in the topic.

Part I

Theory

1

Studying practitioners' practices

Practice theory is a diverse and constantly evolving body of ideas regarding the nature of social action, transcending a variety of disciplines in the social sciences. In this chapter, I trace the evolution of the practice turn, from the seminal work *The Practice Turn in Contemporary Theory* (Schatzki *et al.*, 2001) to a more recent application in the field of IR (Pouliot, 2010; Adler and Pouliot 2011) and EU studies (Adler-Niessen, 2016). In the process, I illustrate the different debates and discussions that have guided the path of the practice theory towards an application within IR and EU scholarship. I particularly emphasise the importance of Raymond D. Duvall and Arjun Chowdhury's contribution to the field, which highlights the emergence of two distinct approaches that the practice turn facilitates, namely the focus on behaviour/ conduct on one hand, and the discursive/linguistic on the other. While the former seems to have found greater support in the discipline of IR, I argue that the ontological foundations upon which the practice turn rests allude to the utility and even necessity for a discursive practice approach, and this book serves as a contribution to the linguistic approaches within the practice turn.

Practice theory in the social sciences

While the scholarly impulse to attribute primacy to practice over other traditional structure agency dichotomies to make sense of social action has existed for a while (see for example Bourdieu, 1977; Wittgenstein, 1958; Giddens, 1991 or the ethnomethodology and CA literature),[1] it was Theodore R. Schatzki, Karin Knorr Cetina, and Eike von Savigny (2001) who first sought to produce an overview of the state of the practice turn from philosophical, sociological, and scientific perspectives.

In the introduction to the volume, Schatzki identifies general agreement among practice scholars in terms of equating practices to 'arrays of human activity' (2001: 2). Beyond this definition, it is generally agreed that social phenomena such as meaning, power, language, knowledge, or science can be understood as elements of the field of practice, where practice is the 'nexus of interconnected human practices' (*ibid.*). Another fundamental element of practice theory is the embodied quality of practice, where social action is seen as a productive force of the character of the human body itself. This social action, in turn, is founded upon a shared understanding of skills or tacit knowledge that is instilled in social life.[2] In other words, the practice turn advocates primacy of practice over social agents as the unit of analysis to explain social action. Schatzki illustrates this notion by focusing on post-humanist approaches, as they do away with the centrality of the human mind as the source of social phenomena. In general, practice theorists accept this decentralisation of the human, and see the human mind as constituted by practices, not vice versa.[3] However, most practice theorists still seek to explain practices from a human perspective. While they distance themselves from human agency as a point of departure for understanding social action, most shy away from incorporating the nonhuman into their investigations, which would call for a redefinition of the term social itself. Based on this ontological foundation of the practice turn, Schatzki concludes that 'the social is a field of embodied, materially interwoven practices centrally organised around shared practical understandings' (ibid.: 3).

It is this precise notion of the 'shared practical understandings' that Stephen Turner further investigates in his contribution to the same volume. Turner argues that '[p]ractices without sharing … are habits – individual rather than shared' (ibid.: 120). This 'sharing' of tacit knowledge is so fundamental to the social action in which practices operate, since it is vital to know how this 'sharing' can take place. This is where language comes in. Language is the key social phenomenon that allows the constitution of practices in the first place. This also implies that language ought to be considered as a productive force within a practice theory framework; in other words, there is the need for a discursive practice approach in order to fully comprehend how social action takes place. Turner takes a similar position when he claims that '[a]ny account of practice that fails to account for language will be defective' (ibid.: 121).

Ethnomethodology is one of these accounts of practice that attributes fundamental importance to language. Returning to the social phenomena listed above, ethnomethodology avoids considering these topics as if they were ontological entities by themselves. Rather, these topics are analytically broken down into their constitutive parts, which reveal these social phenomena to be the sum of local practices (Lynch, 2001: 131). Michael Lynch understands discourse from this perspective as 'a practically organised phenomenon: a coordinated assembly of what is said, and by whom, in particular circumstances' (ibid.). This reconceptualisation of macro phenomena into their constitutive micro practices is what makes ethnomethodology so useful to practice theorists. Conversation analysts, who developed their approach from ethnomethodology, highlight another fundamental problem of social inquiry in general, that is the gap between methodological instructions (the blueprint of what a practice should look like) and the actual enacted practice itself. The best example of this problem is the analysis of absences or the substance and relevance of something that did not happen. Harvey Sacks (1992) argued that by focusing on these absences and by placing them in their local contexts of 'contingently relevant events', we can uncover not only how the absences were managed but also what these absences accomplished (e.g. power, personal stake).

The existence of this gap implies a tacit knowledge or shared understanding that Schatzki already referred to and upon which Vincent Pouliot later based much of his take on practice theory. This problem, which Lynch (paraphrasing Polanyi) terms the 'hidden, unconsciously mastered rules' (2001: 140), is countered by conventional methodologists through utilising a rigidly formal methodology in line with the scientific method to describe these enacted practices. The problem here is that the practices that these investigations seek to unravel through their formal methodology impose 'theories, models, hypotheses, heuristics, protocols, and the decision rules' (*ibid.*) externally onto the situation and the practitioners. This excludes from the investigation the highly localised and contextual tacit knowledge that informs the practitioners and their practice. In turn, conversation analysts do not attempt to impose grand theories or identify deterministic internal mechanisms within their observations, but rather utilise an approach that seeks to unravel the 'machinery' that gives rise to the specific characteristics of the given conversation (*ibid.*: 140). The observed practitioner's use of specific discourse can then be extrapolated and observed in other situations, unbound by the context and present agents of the initial situation. While this reliance on replicability is, in and it of itself, criticised by scholars of the sociology of scientific knowledge, it seems like the only viable means to access the particularity of enacted practices. The problem here is that the gap between theoretical methodology and enacted practices cannot be overcome through a generalisable methodological approach. As Lynch puts it 'any abstract account of the logic of practice immediately reiterates the problem' (*ibid.*: 146). Rather, the logic of practice needs to be approached as the product of highly localised and tacit knowledge shared between practitioners.

However, it is precisely this non-generalisability and reliance on unidentifiable shared presuppositions of the practice turn that leads Stephen Turner in his 1994 book to criticise the use of practice as a unit of analysis in explaining social action as 'pseudoexplanatory' (Rouse, 2001: 189). Rouse counters this criticism by introducing two different concepts of practices: practices perceived as *regularities* and practices understood as *normative*. Practice theorists conceiving of practices as regularities rely on a fixation of meaning in order to be able to identify reoccurring patterns between different practices. In this case, there is a difficulty in unravelling temporal continuities when these are based on implicit, inarticulable shared understandings. Explicating the knowledge that is implicit in enacted practices is a problematic endeavour. According to Turner, these regularities are only visible 'against a background of other practices' (1994: 191), and therefore lack objective explanatory value. However, Rouse introduces the normative way of thinking about practices that deviates from the quest to identify regularities and continuities. Rather than practices being shared in the sense that they rely on continuous tacit knowledge (despite being difficult to identify these objectively), practices are shared among actors if the action invoked through this practice is considered as correct or appropriate because they are perceived as being in accordance with other, pre-existing practices. This approach allows for an inquiry into the embeddedness of practices within a given context without relying on the problematic objective identification of underlying regularities and continuities. The conceptual detour by Rouse reframes practices not as the product of underlying causal links, but rather understands practices within their discursive context. Hence the perception and interpretation of practices by other practitioners is what lies at the heart of the normative investigation (*ibid.*: 195).

Practice theory in IR

The different conceptualisations of practice theory explained in *The Practice Turn in Contemporary Theory* explicitly highlight the importance of focusing on discursive practices as a means to access the underlying forces that guide social action. While many of the themes and conclusions of Schatzki *et al.* fall on fertile ground a decade later in the discipline of IR through the edited volume *International Practices* (Adler and Pouliot, 2011), the acknowledgement of the role of the discursive, however, seems to not be backed up by scholarly application in IR. Rather, the authors further engage in the philosophical considerations regarding the normative role of practices. In their introduction, Alder and Pouliot define practices as 'socially meaningful patterns of action which, in being performed more or less competently, simultaneously embody, act out and possibly reify background knowledge in and on the material world' (*ibid.*: 6). This focus on competency is a new development, but it may be traced back to Rouse's (2001) discussion of seeing practices as normative action. Additionally, it links well with the role attributed to so-called communities of practice, a domain of knowledge where agents come together and create, share, and maintain knowledge about what is considered *competent* performance (*ibid.*). This concept seems to be of particular analytical strength, as it is consistently referred to in other contributions throughout the volume.

Beyond this discussion, Adler and Pouliot identify four traditional dichotomies in social science research which they believe a practice-focused research agenda could transcend, namely materiality/meaningfulness, agency/structure, reflexivity/habitus, and continuity/change. The penultimate one may be considered as a version of bodily performance (or conduct/behaviour) vs discursive performance (or language). Indeed, Adler and Pouliot posit that it is necessary to 'conceive of discourse as practice and to understand practice as discourse' (*ibid*.: 14). Yet far from transcending this chasm, most contributors in the edited volume seem to understand practice as a behavioural, rather than discursive performance. Having said that Adler and Pouliot promote a methodological pluralism (*ibid*.: 22), as they understand practice not as an 'ism' but rather as a point of convergence where different theories, and thus different onto-epistemological assumptions, can be united. The only ontological commitment required is that practices are the key units of social life. This is a shift away from the initial conceptualisations of practice theory by Schatzki *et al.* who maintain that practice scholars 'are generally suspicious of "theories" that deliver general *explanations* of why social life is as it is' (2001: 14). It is perhaps this broadening of the methodological basis of practice theory that obscured the general utility of a discursive approach for practice theorists.

Friedrich Kratochwil, on the other hand, argues for a more precise onto-epistemological position. His view can be broadly considered as postpositivist, as he categorically dismisses the possibility of an 'absolute standpoint' that conventional onto-epistemological approaches seem to advance (2011: 38).[4] He begins by discussing the use of the terms practice and pragmatism. Through drawing links between the two, Kratochwil puts forward three key points that could be summed up as reasons for a more practice-based research agenda in IR. First, the ultimate goal for practice theorists is to replace these grand theoretical reflections with an analysis of actual actions of practitioners (*ibid*.: 47). His second point focuses on the constitutive role of the researcher within the research process. By doing so, he questions the traditionally accepted role of the researcher as a neutral observer, allowing the practitioner to be equally involved in the research process. This move opens up the possibility of exploring 'communities of practice' as the site of knowledge production and how this eventually leads to specific conceptions of competent practices (*ibid*.: 47, 50). This move is also in line with another strong argument for the practice-based framework that is made by George Herbert Mead (cited by Kratochwil), who notes that the social sciences should not simply investigate agential action in response to stimuli. Rather, the very complexity of social action is exposed in the 'inhibition of an automatic response' and in the orientation of the response towards the other (*ibid*.: 49). This also suggests that a distinction should be drawn between practice as unreflective habits and practice as performance. Evidently practice theorists focus on the latter, but the question remains whether the analysis of the performance should be based on signs, gestures, and the *habitus* of practitioners as outlined by Bourdieu (also Bueger and Gadinger 2015: 450), or whether it should be more linguistically based. For Kratochwil, practices should not be treated as 'things' but as 'significations' that can be understood through an 'analysis of semantic fields' where the practice itself is operating in a sphere of particular meanings of discourse.[5] He quotes Doty, to reiterate that while there is a degree of autonomy in this sphere, practices develop a life beyond the sum of their 'intentions, will, motivations or interpretations' (2011: 57), therefore transcending both agency and structure. This clearly shows the necessity of a discursive practice approach, as it allows scholars to move away from treating practices as observable causal regularities, and to conceptualise practice as 'socially-meaningful patterns of action' (Adler and Pouliot, 2011: 6) which is embedded in Rouse's normative framework.

In addition to Kratochwil, Janice Bially Mattern also calls for a discursive practice approach, which she refers to as a 'mediated discourse analysis' (2011: 83) in her application of practice theory to the realm of emotions. At its core, her argument is that because of the complexity and different levels of operation, emotions exceed the capabilities of traditional levels of analysis. This leads to an ontological particularly in which emotions, similar to practices, occur at the nexus of the varying levels of analysis: sociality, materiality, structure, and agency. This further means that emotions are *not* reducible to their components but are rather suspended between different ontologies (*ibid.*: 71). Bially Mattern puts forward a convincing account of *emotions* as a type of practice, based on Schatzki's definition of practices as competent, socially meaningful, bodily performances (*ibid.*: 76). Her first argument here is that emotions 'do not happen; they are done', based on the complex interplay between physiology and psychology (*ibid.*: 77). Second, emotions are both competent and socially meaningful. They are competent because they are learned through the constant interaction of the biological system with environmental stimuli, and meaningful because different social settings affect the way emotions are both performed and perceived. This leads to her last point that emotional practices generate agency because the individual embodiment of emotions is a unique experience based on the varying influences of different social contexts that are carried into the next context. On the basis of these three points, Bially Mattern suggests that research into emotional practices requires an 'anthropological empirical research method' (*ibid.*: 82). This is where the *mediated discourse analysis* allows the researcher to encapsulate the entrainment of the practitioner within a social context, conceptualising emotions from an emic perspective without losing sight of the 'suspended' ontology of emotions.

Even with these theoretical defences of a discursive practice approach, however, none of the remaining nine contributions to the volume that apply practice theory to their research explicitly focus on the discursive formation of practices and their enactment within discourse. This is only to be expected, given the theoretical basis of some of the contributions such as the English School (Little), institutionalism (Morgan), or neoclassical realism (Ripsman). The onto-epistemological convictions of these theories are difficult to reconcile with the discursive approach. However, even Hansen's (2011) contribution, which differs from all the other analyses in that she explicitly negotiates a poststructuralist perspective with the practice turn, treats practice from a behavioural rather than a discursive perspective.

This imbalance is also observed by Raymond D. Duvall and Arjun Chowdhury, who argue that the meaning of a given practice is not fixed but often contested, thus problematising the emphasis on *competent practices*. They show that there is a greater need to focus on how given practices correspond to certain signifiers that may be interpreted differently by different audiences because *meaning* is discursively constructed. They use the concept of 'sender' and 'recipient' here, where a given practice may be interpreted differently by the recipient than originally intended by the sender (*ibid.*: 2011: 345). To advance analysis in the practice field, they suggest a greater focus on change over time through historical analysis, and on the linguistic structures that are at play in seemingly competent performances. All this points to the problem of perceiving the meaning of practices as stable: the authors argue that an emphasis on Bourdieu's *habitus* gives a misleading sense of stability to the actual polysemy of language (*ibid.*: 348). In addition, they emphasise the need to assess the relationship between practice and signifiers, in which practices can either ground or subvert a given signifier and thus change the meaning of fundamental concepts of the international order, such as sovereignty (*ibid.*: 350). In general, their contribution can be considered a strong critique of the prevalent emphasis on habitus and behaviour in practice theory, which neglects the problematic nature of how meaning is negotiated in discourse. Despite Duvall and Chowdhury's insights, a similar emphasis on conduct over discourse is found in the special issue of *Cooperation and Conflict* entitled *Diplomacy in Theory and in Practice*.

Diplomacy in theory and practice

In their introduction, Vincent Pouliot and Jérémie Cornut look at how diplomatic studies may be negotiated with a practice-based research agenda. They assert that 'what diplomats of all stripes do, and the ways in which they perform their trade, is taken to be basis for explaining world politics' (2015: 303), which mirrors the ontology of practice theory where conduct constitutes the key unit of analysis. Based on this assumption, they identify a research gap in the social sciences: although '[d]iplomacy is all about human intercourse' (*ibid.*: 307), the everyday practices have often only been analysed from the technical, reductionist views of rational choice, bargaining, and utility maximisation. A key point of convergence of practice theory and diplomatic studies should thus be the 'focus on concrete enactments of human performance' (*ibid.*: 298). Discourse, however, is not explicitly mentioned in this regard, and neither was it applied as an analytical framework among the other contributions within the special issue. Nevertheless, Pouliot and Cornut offer some reflections on the methodological foundations of practice theory. Similar to Adler and Pouliot, they shy away from a brute empiricist framework because, quoting Kuus: '[t] he task is not to construct checklists of actors and cause ... but to think about diplomacy as a structured terrain of practices which make certain practices more likely' (*ibid.*: 309). In general, they argue for an emic, ethnographic approach through which the micro-processes of the everyday that give rise to the social can be reconstructed and atheoretically catalogued (*ibid.*: 302–3).

Practice theory in EU studies

Similar to the previous methodological reflections on the practice turn in the social sciences, Pouliot and Cornut's onto-epistemological position could facilitate a discursive practice approach. Yet, as I argued above, most contributors to the special issue focus on the behavioural, physical aspect of practice. This is best illustrated by the contributions of Christian Lequesne and Merje Kuus, who both specifically focus on their investigations on the EU as a site of diplomatic practice.

Lequesne looks at the European External Action Service (EEAS) through the 'practice lens'. His main argument is that the clash of actors from different backgrounds (EU Commission or national ministries of foreign affairs) has resulted in the perception of the *other* possessing specific practices, which are often unsuitable for the other actor's way of doing things (2015: 358). However, Lequesne similarly points to the importance of cross-dialogue, where the experience of certain actors based on former working partnerships can facilitate cooperation between different institutions inside the EU. Furthermore, Lequesne argues that it is specifically this diverse *background knowledge* that produces informal and formal 'rules' that guide the interactional practices between institutions. More generally, he seems to suggest that institutions are not only the sum of rational calculations by their specific practitioners, but rather the sum of the *background knowledge* of its practitioners. This reverses the logic of institutionalism where 'the agents' backgrounds ... shape political institutions' as opposed to vice versa (*ibid.*: 364). By doing so, Lequesne also calls for a greater ethnographic and sociological approach to the study of diplomacy and IR more generally, as well as an acute awareness of the historicity of institutions. Another important point is that in his theoretical framing, Lequesne sees Bourdieu's *habitus* 'as a dynamic, not static disposition of agency behaviour' (*ibid.*: 362); this is a very different interpretation from that of Duvall and Chowdhury.

Merje Kuus also looks at the EU as a site of practice. She particularly draws attention to the importance of context and spatiality in studying diplomacy, understanding that 'backgrounds of knowledge' do not transcend space and time, but are intrinsically woven into the fabric that constitutes a location. For her this calls for 'the need for context-sensitive empirical studies' of practice (*ibid.*: 371), that does not take 'geopolitical imaginations' such as state-centricity as its point of departure, but rather looks at where practices are sited beyond the nation state. Following this understanding of practice, Kuus utilises the interviews she conducted with EU practitioners in Brussels to explore the importance of 'symbolic power' in diplomacy, particularly after the expansion of the diplomatic corps following EU enlargement. Her findings suggest that beyond the perceived *lateral* differences among diplomats, there are certain hierarchical ranks that are expressed through specific cultural or national traits. These hierarchies are 'more stable and deeper-rooted than professional skills' (*ibid.*: 376), and embody a social capital that is expressed through dress, but also through what Kuus calls 'ease' that is the product of 'deep socialisation'. This socialisation does not occur at Brussels, but rather at the schools and other sites of upbringing, as she claims '[i]t is a practical mastery that cannot be transmitted solely through instruction and prescription' (*ibid.*: 374). In a way, this mirrors the dichotomy of rationality vs practicality that Adler and Pouliot refer to, in which imitated or recently learned behaviour cannot substitute for a lifelong process of socialisation in an elitist surrounding. These are the powers that operate 'beyond formal institutional structures' (*ibid.*: 378), and that can only be exposed through a close examination of practices and their background, not by conceptualising practice as a mere performance of a set of learned skills.

Another recent addition to the practice literature within EU studies is that of Rebecca Adler-Nissen. Her article 'Towards a practice turn in EU studies' (2016) reviews recent EU scholarship that, as she argues, centres around practice as their main unit of analysis. Her rejection of dualisms mirrors previous attempts to portray practice as a point of convergence where the dichotomies of agency–structure, individual–institutional, and free will-determinism are transcended. Similarly, she dismisses grand theorising, and her focus on how social phenomena are constructed from the bottom-up is in line with the previously reviewed practice literature, both in its concrete application in IR (Adler, Pouliot, and Cornut) and its more general theorisation in the social sciences (Schatzki *et al.*). In their application to EU studies, these methodological implications call for a greater focus on everyday practices, how these practices come together into social processes such as EU enlargement, EU integration and Euroscepticism, and the different ways in which they are perceived by different stakeholders. Adler-Nissen's assessment of how power is negotiated within social interactions is particularly interesting. For her, these instances are not led by predefined capabilities or recourses, but are context specific. Furthermore, a practice approach can unravel these instances and can offer us a better understanding of how power is negotiated (*ibid.*: 96). This is in line with her discussion of the need for a 'relational ontology' in interpreting the EU. Doing so would allow scholars to open up EU-specific processes to investigation and not take them as unproblematic, predefined entities (*ibid.*: 94).

Adler-Nissen's dismissal of constructivist EU scholars' focus on discursive practices is interesting on two grounds. First, she claims they disregard the existence of tacit knowledge of practitioners (Schatzki's 'shared understandings' or Adler and Pouliot's implicit 'background knowledge') that underpins their practices; and, second, they predominantly focus on the intended development of EU integration and fail to account for the unintended ones. Adler-Nissen therefore sees the constructivist focus on discursive practices as distinct from practice theory. By contrast, this book argues that discursive practices is vital part of practice theory.

The aim of this chapter was to offer a review of the state and development of practice theory in IR scholarship, EU studies, and social sciences in general. From a methodological point of view, it can generally be assumed that an ethnographic, emic approach is favoured over grand theorising (Bueger, 2014; Bueger and Gadinger, 2015: 457). Rational choice theory in particular is criticised for its deterministic quality. Although the onto-epistemological foundations of practice theory are not clearly defined (particularly Adler and Pouliot shy away from any methodological prescriptions), the general emphasis on a bottom-up approach and the use of postpositivist methods would theoretically accommodate a focus on the discursive production of meaning as a cornerstone of practice theory. Yet, while there is explicit reference to the importance of discursive practices (Schatzki, Turner, Lynch, Rouse, Adler and Pouliot, Kratochwil, and Mattern), there is little to no application of a distinctly discursive practice approach in IR and EU studies. Rather, the practice scholarship is mainly concerned with notions of habitus and conduct: a behavioural interpretation of practice. Nevertheless, this disregard for the importance of discourse in producing the social meaningfulness that defines practices (Adler and Pouliot) has not gone unnoticed. In this regard, Duvall and Chowdhury's 'sympathetic critique' of the practice turn in IR is a useful point of departure for practice theorists interested in the discursive negotiation of meaning that underpins social action in general. To bridge this gap and to offer a specific discourse-based methodology to study the practices of practitioners is the purpose of the following chapter.

Notes

1 Both ethnomethodology and CA form a big part of the analytical framework put forward in this book, and they will both be examined in the following chapter.

2 This aspect of the practice theory is particularly stressed by Vincent Pouliot, which will be explored later in this chapter.

3 This indicates the utility of a focus on the discursive within practice theory as opposed to a focus on the behavioural, since discourse, as a unit of analysis can be detached from the social agent more easily than conduct, which is almost by definition linked to the agent's physical performance.

4 Losing sight of ontological and epistemological commitments have also been echoed by Bueger and Gadinger (2015: 450) as potentially leaving practice theory open to the type of criticism Ringmar (2014) pointed to.
5 Bueger and Gadinger (2015: 453) also acknowledges the need to focus on interactions as one of their six commitments of International Practice Theory. For them, these interactions are not necessarily limited to communication between the members of a particular group, but also to formalised interaction with a computer during training.

2

Studying social action in interaction

For more than two decades now IR theorists have been applying various forms of discourse analysis. Some focused specifically on its theoretical applications, some on its analytical applications, and some tried to bridge the two. This diversity was almost intentional, or, more precisely, the promotion of more structured methodological and research design standards was rejected by scholars such as Ashley and Walker (1990), Campbell (1996), and Milliken (2001). For those focusing on EU foreign policy, there has been a recent attempt by Carta and Morin (2014) to bring together the different discursive approaches applied in the field. While this edited volume demonstrated the vitality, dynamism, and variety of the analytical frameworks utilised, it yet again confirms the appeal and the strength in pluralism.

Furthermore, some of the discursive literature in IR overlap with the scholarship that focuses on foreign policy practices. This is not surprising, given the specific intentions by the scholars behind the practice turn to deliberately create an interparadigmatic research programme to promote methodological pluralism (Adler and Pouliot, 2011: 3). Nevertheless, there seems to be a division developing in the practice turn between those who focus on the language practitioners use by building on scholarship inspired by Michel Foucault, and those, who focus on practitioners' conduct, that is, 'what practitioners do' in line with Pierre Bourdieu's work. In this book, it is argued that it is instrumental to combine both. However, by focusing on the linguistic resources used by practitioners and on way they construct their social actions allows us to understand and explain specific foreign policy decisions, or their practice. To do so, I put forward a new discursive framework called DIR. DIR shares the same philosophical roots as some constructivist and most poststructuralist discursive approaches applied in IR, but it also combines features of discursive psychology (Edwards and Potter, 1992), CA (Davies and Harré, 1990; Sacks, 1992) and ethnomethodology (Garfinkel 1967; Lynch *et al.*, 1983) in order to combine discourse and practice. But, before offering an explanation of DIR, it is important to discuss how the above-mentioned disciplines influenced it.

Methodological influences: ethnomethodology and CA

In his attempt to break away from the traditional sociological approaches, Garfinkel (1967) developed a radically new method for data analysis that focused on the examination of intersubjective social accomplishments. Ethnomethodology focuses on the methods and practices that members of society employ to make sense of takes the world they live in (Garfinkel, 1974; ten Have, 2002), these could be for instance how queues are formed (Livingston, 1987), juries come to decisions (Garfinkel, 1967) or the way laboratories work (Lynch *et al.*, 1983). This understanding of accomplishment and personal accountability offers a greater acknowledgement of human agency and knowledgeability in the production of social action rather than traditional sociological approaches (Hutchby and Wooffitt 1998).

However, while in close parallel with the verbal interactive analysis similar to the turns of talk in CA, ethnomethodology is primarily oriented with the analysis of the mundane or institutional discursive accomplishments of social actions made *in situ*. That is, social actors produce utterances that are imbued with culturally shared expectations and understandings as a way of being considered skilled members of a particular cultural group. Next, I draw attention to three relevant aspects of ethnomethodology that directly define context at the local level within this study, namely, indexicality, reflexivity, and the documentary method of interpretation.

The notion of indexicality highlights the word or description being indexical, that is, the sense people make out of an utterance and subsequent social action by relating it to the precise context in which it occurs. In short, people index the details of the exchange to a specific and contingent situation relevant to members of society's intelligible accounting practices (Garfinkel, 1967). Through indexicality we make sense of the uniqueness of any interactive activity or event, and draw our consideration to the ways in which one accomplishes properties of social action. There is a similarity here with CA, which principally focuses on the sequential organisation of talk. At this micro level, social action and social facts are simultaneously context specific, thus, a speaker's utterance is constructed and designed with regard to the social actions that immediately precede and follow it (Heritage, 1984).

Indexicality is closely linked to the notion of reflexivity. Both concepts are concerned with the instant and continual recognition of sense-making in interaction. Thus, the event, or the self, become the object. This notion of reflexivity suggests that descriptions are not mere representations, but rather they are doing something; they are part of being implicated in a practical activity. Descriptions are not used simply for their own sake but they are part of an indexical interactive sequence. When a description is recognised and occasioned, then it becomes part of a social action. The focus is on the inferences and attributions of the actions they perform; thus, they are never viewed as a neutral telling of facts. On the contrary, descriptions are constructed to counteract activities such as justifications or criticisms (Edwards and Potter, 1992). In short, formulations and their inferences are not neutral theoretical outlines, but rather concise context-specific outcomes relating to future actions. Therefore, the inferences made are based on intelligible, culturally shared, taken-for-granted understandings, expectations, and norms of the phenomena being discussed.

The final ethnomethodological notion on the reworking of description and factuality is the documentary method of interpretation. Its aim is to establish how factual evidence is drawn from a social experience and cohere to a specific pattern.[1] An identified pattern is then utilised to act as a model for producing results in new facts that are gathered within another situation.

In order to verify this hypothesis, Garfinkel (1967) carried out a controversial experiment. He asked his students to talk, via a telecom system, about their personal problems with an anonymous psychotherapist, placed behind a screen. They were asked to put questions to the therapist, in which he or she could only answer yes or no. The students were unaware that the answers were random and not authentic, nevertheless the findings demonstrated that they were intelligible to the students and there was a pattern to the advice they received. In doing so, the students relied on their mutual, collectively shared, normative expectations, and intelligible understandings of the specific situation. Consequently, the capacity to produce order out of the information made available (even if it is senseless) demonstrates that no accurate truth claims, but rather only subjective notions exist. The answers from the therapist in the experiment made sense only in the context of the experiment and not beyond, suggesting that the students relied on their intelligible, culturally shared expectations and understanding, to present themselves as competent participants of the study. Furthermore, the experiment illustrated how people create their own social meaning from the information provided and relate it to specific contexts within their talk.

For instance, take the normative principles deployed in the opening sequence of a phone conversation (Example 1). In this sequence, the speakers, Nancy and Hyla attend to a typical opening of a verbal interaction of reciprocating 'hi's and 'how-are-you's'. This is achieved by a number of explicit actions, demonstrating the 'indexical', 'reflexive', and 'documentary method of interpretation' sense-making qualities of mutually intelligible social actions *in situ*, as it is argued above.

Example 1 – (from Schegloff, 1986: 114)

```
01          ((ring))
02 Nancy:   H'llo:?
03 Hyla:    Hi:,
```

04 Nancy: -<u>HI</u>::.
05 Hyla: Hw<u>a</u>ryuhh=
06 Nancy: =Fi:ne how'r you,
07 Hyla: Oka: [y,
08 Nancy: [⌐<u>Goo</u>:d,
09   (0.4)
10 Hyla: ˙mkhhh[hhh
11 Nancy: [What's doin,

Based on the ethnomethodology principles discussed above, Example 1 demonstrates that the objective order of social interaction is ongoing, accomplished through the practical and concerted social actions of the participants themselves. There is a continuous momentary production maintaining order in the social interaction. By adopting indexicality, reflexivity, and the documentary method of interpretation, a sense of structure emerges as a practical accomplishment of everyday communicative and interpretive processes of a typical opening to a phone conversation.

Conversation analysis was developed from these specific ethnomethodology principles by Harvey Sacks. However, CA principally focuses on the way specific social actions are accomplished through the sequential organisation of talk-in-interaction (Sacks, 1992; Schegloff, 2007). It is built around three main assumptions. The first is mundane talk, in which talk reveals certain structures orientated to by the speakers. It is important to note that the structures are independent of the psychological motivations of the speaker. The second assumption is sequential organisation, which takes into account how utterances cohere. The context that shapes the speaker's action is made conditionally relevant through references in the preceding sequence of talk. The context of a following action is contingently formulated with every action performed. The third assumption is the empirical grounding of analysis in recognising the first two assumptions within a fine-grain analysis of transcription of talk (Atkinson and Heritage, 1984).

Hence, analysts investigate the participants' fine-grain orientations and understandings of participants, acknowledging the indexical and reflexive nature of their talk. Moreover, conversation analysts are committed to basing their claims on practices, on the organisational features (such as repair, turn-taking, sequence organisation, word selection) and on what is going on in extracts from actual interactions (Schegloff, 2009). They rely on video or audio recordings of everyday, real-life activities, and latterly also on institutional activities. Consequently, CA is described as data driven. The focus is on the specific action of the empirical conduct of the speaker (Widdicombe and Wooffitt, 1995).

What is more, Schegloff (1992) addresses what is pertinent within interaction by introducing the notion of 'relevance' and 'procedural consequentiality'. First, in considering relevance, there are numerous ways in which to describe the event, the self, and the other. Conversation analysts need to demonstrate how the speaker orients to that particular description. Second, procedural consequentiality stresses that it is not sufficient just to demonstrate that the description is relevant to the interaction. Rather, a CA perspective enquires: (1) how does talk, for example, during policy unit debates account for the social action being performed: its shape, content, and character? (2) What are the fundamental design features of an utterance oriented to during the interaction? (3) What is the participants' inferred understanding of, or orientation to, the normative understanding of the specific phenomenon? (Wooffitt, 1991, 2005). Example 2 demonstrate how the speakers attend to these points.

Example 2 – (from Sacks, 1992, vol. 1: 3)

A   this is Mr. Smith, may I help you
B   I can't hear you
A   This is Mr <u>Smith</u>
B   Smith

This extract is from Sacks' classic corpus of recorded telephone calls to the Los Angeles Suicide Prevention Centre. His interest here was in the way the caller (B) seemed to be having some trouble with the agent's name. Initially the agent (A) introduces himself and in the same turn he has performed the action of offering a service with 'may I help you'. The normatively expected next action is an acceptance of the offer, here that is first providing some form of identity then a request for help. In this case the caller (B) replies with a 'I can't hear you'. Instead of treating this utterance as a communication problem, Sacks focused on what the caller tries to achieve. By treating the utterance as the object which participants use to get things done, Sacks raised the possibility that the caller might have been avoiding giving his name. Rather than a specific refusal, the caller initiated a so-called repair sequence by doing not-hearing. Repairs are used to manage some kind of trouble. Sacks did not claim that 'I can't hear you' is always used as avoidance, but in this example it was.

Third, the context of such interaction must be co-constructed, constituted, and accomplished in interaction by each speaker to maintain the intelligibility of talk. The researcher cannot assume that the speakers are within the constraints of the institutional context throughout an interaction, because the external setting is a government department or a school. This must be demonstrated in the course of the context of the talk and reviewed as locally produced from moment to moment.

Moreover, conversation analysts attend to the way a description is treated in the utterance by the speakers and not in truth claims of the formulation. These descriptions are examined for their various performances within the sequential organisation of an interaction. They also assessed for how they are adapted or are challenged over the duration of an interaction, and where a speaker displays their understanding of what has preceded. This is done through a series of turns which cohere and relate the preceding organisational sequences (Schegloff, 2007). The fundamental claim, in comparison, to analysing from a wider critical discursive analytical standpoint, is that there are no ideological assumptions in CA, that precludes displaying what is happening in the interaction by reference to the participants' orientations. Rather, these key assumptions in relation to language use, are micro sites in which specific interpersonal business is accomplished. Schegloff tries to characterise this technical application of CA by explaining:

> the focus of this organisation is not, in general, convergence on some topic being talked about, but the contingent development of courses of action. The coherence which is involved is that which relates the action or actions which get enacted in or by an utterance to the ones which have preceded and the ones which may follow. The very root of the word 'interaction' underscores the centrality of the action to the commerce between people dealing with each other, and this aspect of their conduct is a central preoccupation informing what people do in the turns in which they speak, and informing as well what they heard to be doing. (*ibid.*: 251)

For this study, the conversation analytical approach to data is helpful in explicating the patterns and ways in which the participants in question–answer sequences engaged in various interactional and inferential activities to maintain the normative, contextual expectations and understandings in their discursive work and procedures to construct factual accounts as action orientation productions.

Beside the sequential organisation of talk and their action orientation, there is another aspect of CA, greatly influenced by ethnomethodology, that is relevant to this study. Some view this as a subfield of CA, as opposed to being part of it (Schegloff, 2007). Nevertheless, the way membership categories are constructed is an important analytical device for IR in its quest to understand specific constructions of *the self* and *the other*. In his early work, Sacks (1979 on 'hotrodders', 1972, 1992) paid a great amount of attention to people's common understandings of standardised relationship between *husband–wife*, *parent–child*, and on occupational categories as well as *laypersons*. Others took Sacks initial ideas and examined the way we build our world into different types of collections of things, such as teenage subcultures (Widdicombe and Wooffitt, 1995) or anti-feminist murderers (Eglin and Hester, 1999). These collections of categories and rules of application make up what Sacks coined the Category Membership Device (CMD).

Speakers use CMDs or descriptive category-bound activities and apply specific membership criteria in order to perform some form of social action. Sacks's much-cited example of 'The baby cried; the mommy picked it up' illustrate a category-bound activity from a mother who is expected to pick up a crying baby. Simply mentioning a category invokes a variety of attributes of the specific category such as rights, moral codes, normative expectations, knowledge.

Analysts who insist on examining CMDs and who have developed this notion into 'Membership Category Analysis' (Hester and Eglin, 1997) are on the fringes of CA. However, taking into consideration category memberships could be invaluable for studies that focus on identity formation like this one. Understanding categories such as 'European' is vital not only for EU foreign policy but also for IR. Analytically, these membership categories have to be situated within the sequential organisation of talk (Watson, 1997), but accessing data that would allow such analysis is very difficult in IR. While it is common to collect data through ethnographic means and interviews, none of it is ever recorded.

Discursive psychology: self-making or identity and rhetoric

Although discursive psychology (DP) was specifically developed to counter the rapid expansion of cognition in social psychology studies, its main interest was to examine identity formation as well as to capture the then fresh discussions around poststructuralism.

An important reconceptualisation of the self has been put forward by semiotic and poststructuralist traditions (Barthes, 1974; Derrida, 1978; Foucault, 1980; Der Derian and Shapiro, 1989; Shapiro, 1989; Doty, 1996; Campbell, 1998) as well as linguistic philosophy (Wittgenstein, 1953; Austin, 1962; Heidegger, 1962; Searle, 1995), ethnomethodology (Garfinkel, 1967), and CA (Davies and Harré, 1990; Sacks, 1992; Widdicombe and Wooffitt, 1995). All these approaches deviated from the traditional realist perception of the self, albeit in their own different ways, and focused on the social action and the subject position at a particular juncture during talk or writing (Gergen and Davis, 1985, Potter and Wetherell, 1987; Edwards and Potter, 1992). In order to deter this, Edwards and Potter (1992) advocate not only that we consider the person's psychological make-up such as their personal traits and the humanistic self, but also their sociological make-up or role, thereby creating narrative characters. Put differently, these characters are recognised as separate constructions of state of being which are discursively available to participants for placing in different types of narrative descriptions, or to achieve different types of interactional work. Edwards and Potter also contrast their approach to trait theory. In trait theory, personal traits are treated as character dispositions from which individuals have no separate identities. Consequently, the detailed account of people's descriptions is research for social action, independent of their cognitive actions or abilities. Examining social action this way offers IR a new way to consider the self and the other. By doing so, these descriptions are used to stabilise and make apparently factual accounts of events contribute to the organisation of specific practices. Furthermore, the explication of particular sections of discourse and the accounting of their individual properties as to what they accomplish is also pivotal for discursive psychology (Edwards and Potter, 1992).

Having described the methodological influences on Discursive IR (DIR), I go on to introduce the approach itself.

Discursive IR

Central to DIR is the acceptance of the complex ways in which versions of the world, the self, and the other are mutually linked and dependent. The conceptual model applied in DIR is the Discursive Practice Model (DPM). DPM also shares the same theoretical and philosophical base as the Discursive Practice Approach put forward by Doty (1993) in her seminal article 'Foreign policy as social construction'. Similar to Doty's approach, DPM focuses on intertextuality, the production of subjects, and discursive spaces. But instead of working with the analytical categories, or textual mechanisms, as Doty refers to them, such as presupposition, predication and subject positions, DPM is set out to identify social action, fact/interest formulations, agency, and through them IR practices.[2] The key difference between Doty's approach and DPM is that while Doty relies on a critical genealogy to identify these rhetorical strategies, DPM focuses on discursive strategies employed in mundane, everyday talk and examines their use by practitioners (or speakers in general).[3]

DPM is designed to link different features of speakers' discourse in a systematic manner with particular attention to the speakers' social practices. The model has four parts:

1 Social action: the focus is on identifying the social action, i.e. actor/agents trying to achieve acts such as invitations, refusal, blame, defence.
2 Fact/interest formulations: descriptions are constructed to represents the actor/agent's stake and/or interest in events/phenomena, and also to be factual by a variety of discursive devices (e.g. lists, describe extreme case, drawing comparisons, narrative descriptions).
3 Agency: descriptions address the agency and accountability of the actor/agent.
4 IR practice: through identifying the actor/agent's social action + fact/interest formulations + agency, we can explain foreign policy practices.

The focus of analysis is identifying the action that actors/agents are trying to achieve, and how they achieve this. Actions are predominantly performed and reconceptualised through discursive practices, and observed on both theoretical and operational levels. Theoretically, its concern is the reorientation of the reductive and the individualist inclinations of cognitivism, such as 'what is remembering?', 'what is it for?', and 'what is the nature and the role of attributions and of causal accountability?'. Such attributions, as to how the remembering 'went on' offer: various accounts and formulations, and upshots about the causal relations that are proposed. Furthermore, actions are situated in activity sequences through invitations, refusals, blame, defence and so forth, and are not organised in isolation. What also needs to be considered is their deictic or context specific relevance, rather than the accuracy of the actor/agent's statements (Shapiro, 1988; Edwards and Potter, 1992: 154–8).

Second, fact and interest formulations focus on the representation of a dilemma of interest. Successful management of these dilemmas are rhetorically organised in order to make claims difficult to rebut. Thus, the actor/agent's descriptions are presented as representations of the world-out-there rather than their own individual concerns. A variety of fact/interest formulations are applied: such as lists, extreme-case formulations, contrasts, consensus and corroboration, category entitlements, vivid descriptions, narrative accounts, systematic vagueness, or empiricist accounts (Edwards and Potter, 1992: 158–65). Examples of these will be given in the following analytical chapters.

Third, actors/agents manage their own agency or accountability in their descriptions since they either took part in the described event or have a clear vested interest in them. They do so usually by either offering a report of the event through the testimony of a reliable witness, or by sharing some potentially controversial information from a neutral observer (this is what Goffman (1979) called footing). However, the focus is on the processes and the way they are constituted in discursive acts, even if it may initially appear only to be focused on the individual speaker's practices. Attributions can be constructed on a mixture of individual actors – 'Craig is hungry', sub-agents – 'part of her wants to leave all this behind', or the collective – 'the Kosovars fought for independence for a long time'. For this very reason, it is important to avoid the image of a single individual in sovereign control accounting for the actions of another individual (Edwards and Potter, 1992: 170).

Fourth, through identifying the social actions that actors/agents try to achieve, the specific discursive device or fact/interest formulations actors/agents apply to achieve a specific social action, and the way they mobilise their agency, we can offer a clearer picture of foreign policy practices, and even identify specific patterns more reliably than any other model.

Since all these four points interlink, DPM is to be used as a conceptual scheme, rather than just a model. What is more, it helps to expose normative and moral dilemmas. These are explored next.

Normativity and morality in talk

Many authors have claimed that normativity, morality, and interaction are strongly interrelated (Goffman, 1959; Garfinkel, 1967; Heritage, 1984; Shotter,

1993; Bergmann, 1998; Heritage and Lindstrom, 1998). There are two identified levels at which these notions are entwined. On one level, there is the moral and normative character of the interaction itself. A fundamental ethnomethodological concept, employed by discursive approaches, find that intelligible social action is conditional on speakers' orientation to normative understandings and expectations. Further, these interactions are permeated with obligations and rights, for instance who can speak next and what might be appropriate to say in the context.

On the second level, this entwinement is what Heritage and Lindstrom call 'morality in interaction' (1998). Such moral activities are done either explicitly or implicitly during talk. For example, eliciting information from psychiatric patients during consultations is done on moral grounds, as psychiatry deals with people who are mentally ill and whose behaviour is deemed improper by society (Bergmann, 1992, 1998). Therefore, a clear differentiation between rightful and wrongful conduct is justifiable.[4] There is an abundance of studies that focus in detail on the management of moral concerns, in particular, complaints (Pomerantz, 1984; Drew and Holt, 1988; Drew, 1998), attributions of responsibility and blame (Pomerantz 1978; Watson, 1978; Sneijder and te Molder, 2005; Campbell and Futák-Campbell, forthcoming), accusations (Drew, 1984), and justifications (Pomerantz 1984). There are also other studies that focus more on the way normative issues are managed such as 'doing being ordinary' (Sacks, 1984; Pomerantz, 1984).

Another way of explicitly using morality is during court hearings. Verbatim recital of what the other said by the complainant is the expected way to manage transgressions (Drew, 1998). In his study, Drew also identified that particular prosodic features of these quotes are vital in indicating the unfavourable moral attributes of what was said. For example, a 'deprecating, insulting tone' or a 'mock, innocent tone' assists in displaying these moral concerns. Such recitals are seldom followed up by an evaluation. Therefore, the complainant, without having to even mention the misconduct or transgression, enables the listeners to recognise the prejudiced, misguided, and unjust behaviour of the other.

Attribution of responsibility and blamings are also of great interest to conversation analysts and discursive psychologists. Extreme descriptions are also frequently used when speakers engage in moral activities such as justifying, blaming, and complaining (Pomerantz 1978, 1984). Formulations like *never*, *every time*, *nobody*, or *everyone* elicit the maximal and minimal properties of performed social action (Hutchby and Wooffitt, 1998). They are powerful when making a complaint, as they preclude the committed offence from being dismissed as negligible. Through their use, speakers can reveal an event or action to be common, and thus suggest the rightness of a certain practice. To demonstrate this point, Pomerantz uses the classic data collected by Sacks from the helpline of LA's Suicide Prevention Center. In Example 3, the call-taker has just heard the confirmation that the caller has a loaded gun.

Example 3 – (from Pomerantz, 1984: 225)

Desk   What is it doing there, hh Whose is it.
Caller It's sitting there.
Desk   Is it yours?
(1)
Caller It's Da:ve's
Desk   It's your husband's huh?=
Caller = I know how to shoo it,
(0,4)
Desk   He isn't a police officer:r
Caller No:
Desk   He just ha:s one
Caller Mm hm, It- u- everyone doe:s don't they?

By stating 'everyone doe: s' the caller implies that there is nothing out of the ordinary in having a gun, thus it is a normal and accepted practice of American life to own a firearm. Further, she counts on a commonly shared assumption that what most people do is the right way of conducting oneself.[5] Such formulations have been demonstrated in different data sets. During couples' counselling sessions, participants can show themselves as behaving just like others do, therefore their conduct appears normal (Buttny, 1993). By doing so, they prevent apportioning any blame or responsibility for their own conduct. Others use specific discursive formulations such as a combination of if–then formulations with modal expressions to handle blame and self-responsibility when presenting possible health problems (Sneijder and te Molder, 2005). Combining 'if you do x, then problem y should not arise' with a modal formulation like 'should', rather than a declarative one in the 'then' part of the structure, suggests that problems can be avoided by the person's own actions and the blame for ill health lies with them. Employing such formulations also permits the speaker to appear as a morally responsible actor.

Another frequently used discursive device to validate speakers' morality is comparing their activities to others, preferably individuals with extreme beliefs. McKinlay and Dunnett (1998) examine how members of the National Rifle Association of America infer gun ownership as ordinary by contrasting themselves to criminals and vigilantes, hence making gun ownership typical and approvable for any law-abiding citizen. This type of contrast structures[6] has also been applied to demonstrate how patients' activities are compared to an implied norm of conduct to determine whether they suffer from psychiatric illness (Smith, 1978).

Besides these formulaic attributions to moral activities, the way, for example, blaming is actually done is also important. Pomerantz (1978) argues that moral activity is performed at specific times (or turns) of the interaction while the participants report on an 'unhappy incident'. These reports characteristically do not have an actor/agent; thus, there is no evidence as to what or who is responsible for the incident, and there is no attribution of responsibility. Speakers could use this to avoid attributing blame to another speaker who is implicated in the event.

All these types of attributes are not simply a stable expression of causal thinking, but are made relevant in talk and in specific ways to manage responsibility and personal accountability. At the same time, morality is confirmed as a discursive action. This also means that constructions of morality are likely to be used as a justifiable concern not only by ordinary people, offenders, or patients but also by EU practitioners, diplomats, and politicians. These normative and moral attribution are the focus of Chapter 5 and 6.

Data

All data used in this book emanates from EU practitioners, as follows (1) Council of Ministers officials, both from the policy unit COEST, as well as from the rotating presidency secretariats; (2) European Commission officials from DG Relex and the Commissioner's secretariat; (3) European Parliament (EP) members of AFET Committee. In total, sixty-two semi-structured elite interviews were conducted with practitioners of various rank, from director to geographical desk officers, various nationalities from all twenty-eight member states, and with disproportionately higher numbers of practitioners from the Council and Commission to reflect their institutional lead on EU foreign policy. The practitioners featured in this book represent the large bulk of EU policymakers on Russia, Ukraine, Belarus, and Moldova. It is important to note that a large proportion of the practitioners who participated from the Commission mostly had worked on enlargement before joining the European Neighbourhood Policy (ENP) portfolio. This clearly had an impact on their practice which can be recognised in the extracts and analysis.

It needs to be stressed that the aim was not to compare different institutional takes, different national takes, or the different practitioners' takes depending on their positions, but to identify collections that reflected the collective concerns. Therefore, each collection is built on several practitioners' interactions. This is visible from the numbers each practitioner was given, as displayed in the extract heads. Inevitably, practitioners are individuals, and what they made relevant during research interviews depended on their experience, expertise, values, and understanding of the EU. Hence, there were nuances in their individual takes which do come across in the extracts and in the analysis. However, the four main concepts that all practitioners commonly recognised were concerns about identity, norms, morality and collective EU interests when considering EU foreign policy towards Russia and other eastern neighbours.

31

The data collection took place between 2007 and 2011, and the corpus was digitally recorded and then transcribed verbatim.[7] The recordings were conducted in the working environment of the EU practitioners.[8]

Using elite interviews

Our interest in elites is driven by their being experts in a specific field. Unless the member of the elite group in question has any personal significance, such as being the prime minister while making a decision on war, such interviews are integrated into the study as a representation of a group rather than a single case (Meuser and Nagel, 2002). This is also the case for this study. The contributions of each participant are considered in order to provide an understanding of a collective assumption of EU foreign policy vis-à-vis the East, rather than focusing on a specific person or nationalities.[9]

For expert interviews, a well-structured interview schedule is vital according to Meuser and Nagel (*ibid.*: 77). They argue that such a schedule has two key functions: (1) the researcher does not come across as incompetent; (2) the practitioner keeps to the relevant topic. Although these points are significant where the researcher's main aim is fact-finding, they have far less gravity in the theoretical framework applied here. I used a question schedule, especially during the pilot study and the first interviews, but less so afterwards. There were two reasons for this. First, my questions were deliberately set open and very broad, since the focus was to explore the practitioners' own understandings. Second, I had no trouble remembering the four main topics and the areas of interests within them, nor the prompts to encourage the discussion. Furthermore, I often found that the practitioners initiated some of these areas, thus there was no reason to formally introduce the topic yet again. It could be argued that the researcher might not be taken seriously, as a scientist, without clutching a chart. In contrast, I believe it helped to create a dialogue and more of a discussion, which I was methodologically more interested in. The specific prompts, e.g. reciting EU articles, policies, and political debates sufficed to convince my interviewees of the type of research interview as well as my own competence in the topic.

There are three more important aspects to elite interviewing, according to Meuser and Nagel (2002): the expert proving not to be one, role changing between expert/private, and the 'rhetoric interview'. The first is a specific problem for those who are new in their policy area, and not yet fully aware of the institutions, stakeholders, and other agencies operating in the field. In such eventualities, insider knowledge, or the acquaintance of a so-called gatekeeper is vital. There could still be issues with the expert not being in the position long enough to provide the necessary insight. This however could be eliminated during the recruiting process. Rather than being a potential problem, shifting between the expert and private selves is in fact a methodological interest in this study. It is closely linked with the third element of DPM applied here, or the way practitioners manage their accountability. Finally, 'rhetorical interviews', or the potential for the expert to lecture on but miss the specific topic, is an inherent difficulty in elite interviews. It takes practice, as well as careful choosing of the participants. Further, it could be culturally specific, that is, depending on how accustomed the participant is to being questioned by a researcher. If the latter does not apply, such rhetorical interviews can easily be stopped by prompts. It takes practice to decide what prompts to use at a given time, but we all aware of and wait for silences, changes in intonation, and syntactical organisation, or when it is sequentially possible to intervene in a conversation (Sacks *et al.*, 1974).

Methodological considerations for using interview data in this study

Interview data is a common data collection tool both in political science and in IR, whether it involves elites, specific groups, or parts of society. It is less common to record such data, often due to secrecy, confidentiality, and the perceived limited scope of the available data. The use of verbatim transcripts of such interactions is practically unheard of in either discipline. Nevertheless, in others such as psychology, sociology, medicine, education, or human geography it is rather common to use audio or video transcript data, especially when applying discourse analytical methods. Within these disciplines there is a debate on the value-addedness of research interview data as opposed to other types of data which can be collected without the researcher's direct involvement. This data can be specific forms of institutional talk, for example medical consultations, counselling, news interviews, or mundane conversations (e.g. during family meal times).

Although psychologists favouring discursive psychology initially started off by using interview data, they swiftly adapted conversation analytical norms, displaying a preference for naturally occurring data (Potter, 2002, 2004; Speer, 2002; Potter and Hepburn, 2005). Conversation analysts particularly dislike prearranged, contrived, and orchestrated data as research interviews (ten Have 2002; Speer 2002). This convention derives from their understanding of their own discipline as 'the study of recorded, naturally occurring talk-in-interaction' (Hutchby and Wooffitt, 1998: 14), and their focus on the sequential organisation of everyday talk. Such naturally occurring data is considered preferable for various reasons. First, research interviews are deemed an inadequate substitute for actual interactional practices (Atkinson and Heritage, 1984; Potter, 2004). Second, such data is contaminated and biased by the researcher's own agenda and analytic ideas (ten Have 1999, 2002; Potter 2004), and therefore swamps the interaction with the researcher's own categories and assumptions (Hepburn and Potter, 2003: 183). This is the case, predominantly, because of the pre-planned interview questions. Thus, naturally occurring talk 'has the enormous virtue of starting with what is there rather than theoretically derived assumptions about what should be there, or the researcher wishes was there' as argued by Potter (2004: 212).

Nonetheless, I consider my reliance on research interview data legitimate, and, moreover, valuable for IR, and for the currently developing practice literature. That is so for both pragmatic and more substantive reasons. First, as even Potter (2004) acknowledges, at times, the use of interview data is unavoidable, as it can be difficult to obtain naturalistic recordings. Recording data and using verbatim, conversation analytical transcripts is unknown in IR or in foreign policy. Even those studies that build on elite interviews or interactions rely on notes, or quotes from speeches and documents. Since my study was based on practitioners working in institutional settings, the likelihood of recording spontaneous discussions on EU foreign policy were improbable and difficult to capture. The institutionally established policy unit meetings would have been the only naturally occurring interactions that were available to me. Although I managed to record three such meetings, the data set is too small for analysis.[10]

Second, there is the unavoidable problem of the presence of the researcher, even for collecting naturally occurring data (Atkinson and Heritage, 1984: 2–3). While Potter (2004: 612) maintains that naturalistic data allows the analyst to start with 'what is there', the notion of unbiased, naturalistic direct access to 'what is there' seems unattainable for many reasons, including the inherent selectivity of recordings and transcriptions (Hutchby and Wooffitt, 1998). Besides, this desire to capture unbiased data seems to conflict with conversation analysts, as well as ethnomethodologists' basic interests in the way social actors contribute to the collective production of meaning. Furthermore, Speer (2002) argues that the bias in interview data is theoretically interesting. In addition, the sequential organisation of an interaction makes the influence of the interviewer's turn analysable.

Third, according to Potter (2003) during interviews, participants are encouraged to provide normatively appropriate descriptions of the chosen phenomenon. However, not all participants engage in the specific normative expectations of interviews (Widdicombe and Wooffitt, 1995). Inherently, EU practitioners from the Commission and the Parliament know the research process, as they often contribute to projects; practitioners from the Council far less so. Their reluctance is explained by the traditional secrecy surrounding their work and practices. Further, such institutional participants are likely to base their answers on recitation of specific policy initiatives. While I accepted this, it can still be argued that practitioners' orientations to a particular policy is normatively acceptable, it can also lead to interesting insights in the way they warrant certain practices.

Finally, there is one other key point in this debate. As customary for any ethically sound research project that is based on recorded data, participants are asked to consent prior to their being recorded. The seeking of such approval and the introduction of the researcher immediately proffer a different, to some extent, contrived element to the subsequent recording (ten Have 1999, 2002; Speer, 2002). Equally, research interviews may contain interactionally naturalistic elements, and become less formulaic (Widdicombe and Wooffitt 1995; Speer 2002). Thus, interview data should be treated as ordinary conversation, such as a news interview, unless it is evident that the participants attend to the interaction as being interviewed for research. As I mentioned earlier, this is in line with the specific conversation analytical conventions on procedural consequentiality, whereby contextual features only matter when they are observable through the participants' sequential organisation (Schegloff 1991, 1992). Furthermore, Widdicombe and Wooffitt (1995) argue that research interviews are valuable in order to evoke participants' culturally shared accounting practices, and thus they are a form of social interaction (Wooffitt and Widdicombe, 2006). Therefore, in this book, I adapt their approach to research interviews.

Regardless of the intricate debate on the use of elite interview data, a discursive approach to interviews is very distinct from the standard approaches in the social sciences (Silverman, 1985). For the latter, research participants' assertions are treated as declarations that are categorisable, based on broad similarities of the allocated variables. These categories include sociological (e.g. education or marital status) or psychological representations (e.g. locus of control), and even non-responses to questions (Wooffitt and Widdicombe, 2006).

In this book, research interviews are viewed as a form of social interaction. Thus, the focus is on the interactional element produced and co-constructed by the researcher and the interviewees. Their sequential turns are treated as social actions, and examined for what they achieve with them. Accordingly, silences, in and out breaths, repetitions, false starts, corrections, etc. are all included in the transcripts and extracts used in this book. A list of notations on how these interactional features are captured is provided in the Appendix. Admittedly, they can be a trying read for IR and EU scholars and students who are unfamiliar with the transcript notation conventions applied in CA. However, they are a very important part of the interactions and the analysis, and are therefore a crucial part of the extracts used from the transcripts. As will be shown, interactional features such as silence or laughter play a part in identifying the social action that speakers are trying to achieve during interaction.

In short, research interviews can provide valuable insights into participants' accounts of a specific phenomenon, if they are treated as social interactions. Treating the interviews as social interactions, allowed me to go beyond considering them as mere representations of practices. Even so, I acknowledge the limitations of my findings concerning their generalisability. I attended somewhat to this problem by asking open and broad questions, and by taking into account the questions during analysis.

Notes

1 This is what practice theorists in IR aim to uncover.
2 DPM has further overlap with the analytical model applied in Doty's subsequent book *Imperial Encounters* (1996), through her examination of representational practices by identifying discursive strategies.
3 Just like Edwards and Potter's (1992: 154) Discursive Action Model.
4 This will be further explored in Chapter 5 and how it links to the way that Žižek's (2006) claims that norms are used to separate insiders and outsiders.
5 Again, this will be further explored in Chapter 5, since these types of formulation are in line with following a collective understanding of what counts as proper behaviour, as argued by Buzan (2001).
6 Again, this is consistent with Žižek's claim, examined in Chapter 5.
7 A modified version of the transcript notations developed by Jefferson was applied (Atkinson and Heritage, 1984).
8 All participants were provided with a research participant information sheet and signed the research participant informed consent and confidentiality statement. They also consented and agreed verbally to be recorded before commencing with the interview. The study followed the guidelines and procedures outlined by the University of St Andrews University Teaching and Research Ethics Committee, and it was approved by the committee before data collection commenced.
9 This is so, despite the analytical focus on individual accounts. They serve as one part of the collective.
10 Gaining access to policy unit meetings in the Council was simply not achievable. Without data from the Council any findings on European foreign policy vis-à-vis Russia and other eastern neighbours would be insubstantial and weak.

Part II

Practice

3

Constructing the 'European'

There are only few and varied studies on EU identity and foreign policy,[1] with very different analytical and theoretical focuses. The exceptions are Lucarelli and Manners (2006), an edited volume which starts off by stating in the introduction that identity and foreign policy are interconnected (Lucarelli, 2006: 6) and Manners and Whitman's (2003) article on the international identity of the EU. Moreover, both employ a more interpretivist or reflexive approaches to their analysis. Many other studies, however, choose the EU's capability of developing policy instruments that demonstrate its global actorness (or lack of it) as their focal point (Allen and Smith, 1990; Hill, 1993; Soetendorp, 1994; Whitman, 1997; Bretherton and Vogler, 1999; Laffan et al., 1999: 167–72; Smith, 2000; Damro, 2001). By and large they accept the rationalist assumption, whereby actors are guided by self-interest and material factors; thus, they miss out on the sociological understandings of the social role the EU plays in foreign affairs (Sedelmeier, 2004). Nevertheless, there are other identity-based studies which consider the role of social factors and focus on the social norms that constitute EU identity (Neumann, 1998; Cederman, 2001; Manners, 2002, 2013; Sjursen, 2002; Smith, 2002; Peace, 2004; Tonra and Christiansen, 2004); and some which either use a form of discourse analytical method (Fierke and Wiener, 1999; Larsen, 1997, 2000, 2004; Wodak and Weiss, 2001, 2005; Rumelili, 2007; Carta, 2014) or endorse some form of focus on a discursive framework (Friis, 1998; Sedelmeier, 1998, 2001, 2003; Risse, 2000; Schimmelfennig, 2001; Schmidt, 2007, 2014). Regardless, these studies all agree on the need to examine social norms and their relations to identity formation and they are broadly based within the constructivist theoretical framework.[2] They all, however, support very different forms of constructivism that do not necessarily share the same ontological assumptions. This factor in itself makes it highly problematic to compare them per se; or to suggest that they have the same research agenda. Furthermore, they have very different scopes as to what aspect of EU identify they consider relevant (Sedelmeier, 2003: 6–7), that is, the EU as community of liberal democracies (Schimmelfennig, 2001), as pan-European (Friis, 1998), and as having a vocational identity (Fierke and Wiener, 1999, Sedelmeier, 2002; Sjursen, 2002).

In order to develop a more common constructivist research agenda on EU identity formation through foreign policy, Sedelmeier (2004: 129–30) offers to combine three mechanisms: 'logic of appropriateness' (March and Olsen, 1989: 160, 2004); 'logic of arguing' (Risse, 2000); and 'rhetorical action' (Schimmelfennig, 1997, 2001; Johnston, 2001). As appealing as it might be to assume a single understanding of constructivism, it is highly problematic for the same ontological reasons as before. Despite this research agenda being very fitting for those who agree with the conventional constructivists, there are issues to be considered with such an agenda for all the other constructivists who might contest the cognitive notion of certain rule-led behaviour such as 'appropriateness' for the very reasons that it assumes that the actor/agent is always predisposed to the structure (Sending, 2002). Thus, it presupposes an always biased relational link which is problematic for those constructivists who do not share the conventional constructivist approach. Moreover, such logic takes it for granted that a common-sense notion of what is 'appropriate' is available to all of us and is a culturally accepted norm (March and Olsen, 2004).

Furthermore, the 'logic of arguing' (Risse, 2000: 7), in a simplistic sense, entails that by arguing first, participants always engage in truth seeking in order to achieve reasoned communicative consensus; and second that 'participants are open to being persuaded by the better argument'. Accepting the possibility of a 'truth seeking discourse' assumes that a prior existence of such culturally available notions as 'truth' or 'the true discourse' is again accepted and available to all of us. That might again be the case for those in the conventional constructivist camp but for the others it would be an ontological anomaly.

Finally, on the 'rhetorical action' promoted by Schimmelfennig (1997, 2001), there are two major concerns for those who again are not in the conventional constructivist camp. First, in his approach Schimmelfennig merges two ontologically incompatible positions, except for those in the conventional constructivist camp, that is, rational preferences with constructed identities. Second, he does this by a complex triangulation of various analytical methods including statistical evidence, qualitative data, historical, and comparative recounting of debates. This is again an ontologically challenging task unless one accepts that all the different data sets assume the prior existence of a common ontological position, and furthermore all data sets ask the exact same question, and are therefore comparable.

All of the approaches discussed above promote a cognitive notion of rules, norms, social action, arguing, and rhetoric. In the previous chapter, I made a case for employing a different analytical framework, namely DIR which is underpinned by the conceptual model of DPM to study identity, norms, morality, and interest formation through social action, fact construction, and agency. DPM is based on social constructivist – other than the conventional form know in IR – but also on poststructuralist assumptions. The poststructuralist scholarship of Foucault and Derrida is well accepted and used in both IR and EU studies. Using such an analytical framework to deconstruct commonly accepted narratives has made significant discoveries in both fields. Derrida's work (1992) not only with regard to the theoretical and methodological debates, but also on Europe ones has been significant. His claim that European integration essentially works towards the exploration of the other has been important but had little if any effect on examining identity formation by EU scholars. Derrida's notion is that Europe is not closing itself off to a specific identity but proceeding itself to understand what Europe actually is. His position is similar to that of Kristeva (1991, 2000) who considers European integration acknowledges the stranger or outsider in us, as well as the othering practices of nationalism.

The examination of the 'self' and the 'other' remains central to IR, and also for those IR scholars who work on EU foreign policy. Neumann's (1995, 1998, 2016) focus on the way Russia has been 'othered' throughout history by Europe is crucial to our current understanding of European identity. Such 'othering' is particularly pivotal for a poststructuralist concept of identity, according to which there is no self without an 'other'. Due to the importance of the 'othering' of Europe in the construction of Russian identity, Neumann's genealogy offers key insights into the history of Russian and at the same time European identity formation. Tracing such genealogical lines in accordance with a poststructuralist understanding of the identity has been further advocated by Hansen (2006) in her work on the securitisation of the Bosnian war. Although her focus was not on accounting for the 'European', Hansen's work offers insight and a vital contribution to the methodological dilemmas of investigating the self and the other. Building on Hansen's analytical framework of assessing the hegemony and authority of official discourses, Rumelili (2007: 14–16) puts forward discourse analytical framework to study collective identity formation that combines predicate analysis (Milliken, 1999: 232), mapping of discursive interdependencies (Diez, 2005: 12) of community-building institutions and outside states, and identification of discursive dependencies through counterfactual thought experiments (Tetlock and Belkin, 1996). Through this analytical framework, Rumelili demonstrates that EU identity promotes partly an inclusive and partly an exclusive collective identity depending on whether it is positioning itself vis-à-vis the central and eastern European countries (CEECs) (before enlargement), Morocco or Turkey, thereby the EU resists 'the binary classification of postmodern/modern collectively, and it's uncomfortably (or, alternatively, productively) situated in between' (Rumelili 2007: 17).

Although these conceptualisations are still very valid and will be addressed in the following chapters, in this chapter I examine the category of the 'European'. More precisely, I demonstrate the ways in which EU practitioners both co-construct and deconstruct the concept of the 'European' during research interviews. The analytical framework follows the DPM as put forward in the previous chapter.

41

Two main patterns emerge from the corpus. Practitioners' main concerns while discussing the concept of 'European' identity are to differentiate between European neighbours and the neighbours of Europe, and account for the European credentials of the South Caucasus or Kazakhstan. In addressing differentiation between the neighbours, practitioners draw on geography, culture, history, and economic ties to distinguish between countries which are in Europe, and those which are not. At the same time, practitioners make explicit distinctions between the key EU policies: the ENP and the enlargement policy. They also build up the category of the 'European'. When they offer accounts on the South Caucasus and Kazakhstan, one practitioner relies on a heredity account of the European civilisation, while others seek to justify, in different ways, the Europeanness of the Caucasus and potentially Kazakhstan.

'European' neighbours v. neighbours of Europe

The practitioners interviewed below can be heard differentiating between neighbouring states that belong to Europe and those that do not. These comparisons usually focus on the differences between eastern and southern neighbouring states and/or Turkey. Such distinctions between categories can be crucial in order to identify the self and the other, especially when offering it as a justification for a country's accession to the EU, thus identifying it with the self. Also, this could be particularly significant as Article 49 of the Treaty (TEU) clearly states that: 'Any European State which respects the principles set out in Article 2 may apply to become a member of the Union.'[3] However, the Treaty does not offer a definition of what is 'European'. This lack of clarity has been identified as highly problematic; yet there is no clarification of the issue in the Treaty of Lisbon. Despite this lack of clarity, most EU practitioners made this issue an important part of their account when discussing the eastern neighbours. They often used TEU, Article 49 to justify their support for countries from the region to join.

Furthermore, categorical differentiations of these kinds are highly controversial, especially in the case of a policy like the ENP that initially aimed to treat each and every neighbouring country equally. Even if it is widely accepted that such an aim is improbable, the ENP certainly does not intend to draw on European qualities as a way to describe one neighbour's closeness to the EU, as opposed to that of another. Thus, the construction and justification of the category of the 'European' become crucial, but at the same time controversial in the way that it is made relevant by EU practitioners.

Examples of which countries are in Europe and which are not

Consider the following four extracts that question the importance of the Eastern region for EU external relations. This topic was brought up near the beginning of the research interviews, but it was also raised later on, as the dialogue developed. In extract 3.1, this happens after the practitioner mentions the EU's fundamental goals of external security, internal security, and prosperity as well as the importance of having ties with neighbouring countries in order to achieve these goals.

Extract 3.1 – EUIns.14

66	R	ok (0.1) em and how important in that in that respect that this
67		eastern region is?
68	Inv	not specifically (.) in a sense that it is on the same land
69		mass it is not on the other side of the of the sea so in a way
70		[it is closer]
71	R	[uh huh]
72	Inv	second em (0.2) it is historically [linked] with what is the
73	R	[uh huh]
74	Inv	European Union
75	R	and what do you mean (.) what do you mean by that historical?
76	Inv	(.) well those waters were somewhere else some time ago
77	R	uh huh
78	Inv	(inaudible) interconnections and eh links the societal and
79		political economic
80	R	would you say the same that's the same for Russia?
81	Inv	yeah (0.1) can you imagine European culture without Russian
82		literature?
83	R	no (0.5) .hhh interesting
84	Inv	Russian ballet?
85	R	true un huh
86	Inv	so many of those neighbours east they are undeniably European
87		(0.2) in this common definition or even I would say in the
88		definition of the Treaty of Rome saying every European country
89		[which]
90	R	[uh huh]
91	Inv	culturally historically they are European which you cannot say
92		about Tunisia Egypt Morocco and so forth
93	R	why not?
94	Inv	.hh because I mean Tunisia is not a European country
95	R	uh huh
96	Inv	it is? (0.2) I mean everything but it is not a European country
97		in geographical historical terms

When considering Extract 3.1, a non-discursive analysis would focus on the accurate representation of the participant's description. In contrast, from a discursive–analytical perspective, as outlined by the DPM (see pp. 27–8), the

EU practitioner's account here is viewed as the discursive accomplishment of social identity in interactional terms.

There are four main analytical points I discuss concerning this extract between R (the researcher/interviewer) and Inv (the interviewee/EU practitioner). First, it is intriguing how the category of the 'European' as opposed to the category that is 'not European' is worked up through this account. Justifying these categories is the social action the practitioner is aiming to accomplish. These are managed by drawing upon various discursive devices. These devices will be identified and explained throughout the analysis.

Second, for the researcher's question: 'how important in that in that respect that this eastern region is' which comes after a reference to the fundamental goals of the EU, the practitioner states 'not specifically' (line 68). This could imply that there are elements of insignificance in relation to the 'eastern regions'; thus, the practitioner plays down its importance. It however begs the question that if the 'eastern region' is so insignificant, then why would this EU practitioner devote the time from lines 68 to 97 to build up an account concerning the 'eastern region' being more European in contrast to southern states bordering the EU? To establish such a contrast structure (Edwards, 1997: 237) allows the speaker to situate the production of contrasts and alternatives within the interaction, in order to construct the world as such. This discursive device originates from Smith's (1978) work on psychiatric patients, in which she argues that formulating discursive practices into contrasts is not a mere reliance on established semiotic categories. It is, rather, a rhetorical tool that speakers use flexibly and resourcefully (Edwards, 1997; Smith 1978). In Extract 3.1 the EU practitioner deploys this discursive device to build up the assertion that countries to the East of the EU are more European than those to the South. He does this by implying that the eastern neighbours are not specifically important in achieving the fundamental goals of the EU because they already share similar features to other EU member states. Nevertheless, he builds up a clear distinction between those countries that fit the category of the 'European' as opposed to those neighbouring states that clearly do not.

Third, the practitioner catalogues all the common features that make a country more European: geography (lines 68-9); history (lines 91 and 97); society (line 78); politics and the economy (line 79); culture (lines 81-4 and 91); and finally legal requirements through treaties (lines 85-6). Furthermore, these common attributes are not available to southern states: 'you cannot say about Tunisia, Egypt, Morocco and so forth' (lines 91-2), thus they are in direct contrast to what can be called European.[4] Analytically, the practitioner employs a list construction, a discursive device, to build up the authenticity of the account. Lists are used to construct explanations as complete and standard or representative (Jefferson, 1990). Furthermore, such subtle, systematic, and at the same time highly effective list formulation constructs the practitioner's attributes, as standard and normal, for any country attempting to fit the category of the 'European'.

Fourth, the EU practitioner co-constructs the aforementioned list with the researcher by using corroboration and consensus (Potter and Edwards, 1990). This discursive device is employed to develop factuality, authenticity, and the persuasiveness of the account that is agreed by a reliable witness (here the researcher) or is consented to by a neutral competent, independent observer. In this extract, the practitioner achieves such corroboration by asking the researcher: 'can you imagine European culture without Russian literature' (lines 81–2) or 'Russian ballet' (line 84). These observations are recognised by the researcher as a reasonable assessment, as she makes what may be heard as an agreement at line 85: 'true'. In doing so, the researcher's 'true' is seen as verifying the practitioner's claim.

Such accounting is also crucial as a way of managing and attending to personal accountability. That is, the agency of the speaker (the practitioner) is difficult to challenge on the grounds that the practitioner is merely passing on general knowledge on the topic. This intervention is made more significant, since the interviewee, in essence, challenged the category-driven rights of the interview process by asking the researcher questions. Such provocation also serves as an assertion of personal agency from the interviewee. The way the agency of the speaker is managed in this extract is my final analytical point. Besides the previous point on corroboration, the EU practitioner accomplishes his personal agency through footing shifts (Goffman, 1979). Goffman claimed that footing is when quoting others or presenting oneself as a mere reporter of someone else's views. Through this discursive device the practitioner implies neutral observer status by using the pronoun 'it' or in seeking consensus with the researcher at lines 81–5: 'Inv: can you imagine European culture without Russian literature?' 'R: no (0.5) .hhh interesting' 'Inv: Russian ballet?' 'R: true un huh', and employing the pronoun 'I' only once when making a legal point which makes it difficult to dispute a treaty article: 'I would say in the definition of the Treaty of Rome saying every European country' (lines 87–8). Using the pronoun 'it' is common in political settings that make the footing shift even more important in order to work up the practitioner's account as authentic and factual, and by employing his personal agency.

As emphasised at the beginning of this chapter, the kind of differentiations between ENP countries by this EU practitioner is exactly what the ENP tries to avoid. Nevertheless, it is clearly unavoidable when practitioners discuss potential accession to the EU. The next account from a different EU practitioner offers a further justification of the category of the 'European', by working up an assessment of which countries are in Europe and which are not. This justification is made with specific references to the ENP and to countries participating in the policy.

Extract 3.2 – EUIns.41

430	R	exactly what I wanted to ask you actually then em do you think
431		the ENP kind of defines the borders of Europe?
432	Inv	<u>no</u>
433	R	uh huh?
434	Inv	not at all (1) the ENP is completely distinct from the
435		enlargement [question]
436	R	[ye::ah] sure but(.)ok but either way kind of
437		drawing the [lines?]
438	Inv	[obviously] not because the ENP includes Morocco
439		which is <u>definitely</u> not in Europe.
440	R	right
441	Inv	it includes Ukraine which is <u>definitely</u> in Europe (.) and it
442		includes the South Caucasus about which you can argue where [it
443		is]
444	R	[mmm]
445	Inv	em (.) so no the ENP is definitely not about that (.) it's very
446		clear that a country like Algeria or Tunisia will never join
447		the EU (1) to me it's quite clear that ultimately Ukraine
448		probably will but it's not this format where you discuss that.

What is intriguing in the above extract is the way the practitioner rejects the idea that the ENP and enlargement has anything in common with the question: 'do you think the ENP kind of defines the borders of Europe?' (lines 430–1), which was later repeated in an altered form: '[ye: : ah] sure but(.)ok but either way kind of drawing the lines?' (lines 436–7). The EU practitioner seems to have equated here 'borders' and 'drawing the lines' with EU accession. First, he offers two dispreferred responses[5] to the question at line 432 with 'no' and at line 434 with 'not at all'. Dispreferred responses are replies that can convey several things such as refusal to a request, a disagreement to an assessment, an unexpected answer, or an admission to blame, and they usual contain some delay or hesitation (Levinson, 1983: 333–6). The answer was clearly unexpected, which is confirmed by the question at line 433 plus the researcher's attempt at reformulating the question with a request for clarification. However, the practitioner reaffirms his position (line 438) with 'obviously not' and finally with 'so no the ENP is definitely not about that' (line 445). However, his linking of the question of borders with EU enlargement and offering a clarification that the ENP is not the policy that deals with the question of EU borders is clearly significant. First, despite the researcher's reformulation of the question, the practitioner does not seem to shift from his earlier established position. Second, the practitioner's justification for his position is oriented to the policy that includes, as he lists: Morocco (line 438),[6] Algeria and Tunisia (line 446), which are not in Europe. Nonetheless, he also makes Ukraine (lines 441 and 447) relevant as an example of those states which are in Europe. The importance lies here in the way this assessment is actually achieved, especially concerning personal accountability. It is common for politicians, especially in news interviews (Heritage and Greatbatch, 1991; Edwards and Potter, 1992: 52 'Lawsongate' and 'Watergate') to refer to a policy either directly or by adapting the 'it' pronoun and using the passive voice in order to avoid any alignment or personal responsibility that might come into question concerning the description of events regarding the specific policy in question. In effect, the speaker is attending to personal accountability. In this extract, while the practitioner lists the countries, he does so by stating that 'the ENP includes ...' (line 438), 'it includes ...' (line 441) and repeats the same utterance at the end of the very same line. Such display of neutrality, especially from an EU practitioner in charge of policy shaping, is potentially tendentious. Apparent neutrality has implications on how the listener or the analyst here should view what is going on within the policy (ENP). It reduces the chance of any potentially controversial remarks as being heard as originating from the speaker. Consequently, there is no personal responsibility or accountability at stake for the practitioner.

Through talk, speakers attend to agency and personal accountability routinely. They often do so by employing footing shifts, which is central to accountability. In the above extract the EU practitioner follows this standard pattern except for one footing shift. Footing is generally used to neutralise an account (Goffman, 1979). Thus, the question here is how the appearance of this neutrality is managed. There can however be a breakdown in this standard pattern which can potentially be very revealing. First, Clayman (1992) then Potter (1996: 145) demonstrated the relevance of such footing shifts, between partisan and neutral accounting, when dealing with controversial issues by the former British chancellor of the exchequer Nigel Lawson. What Lawson did during an interview with Brian Redhead on the *Today* programme was to treat the interviewer's account of unemployment as Redhead's own version. Furthermore, he also asserted that Redhead had a stake in making such claims owing to his long-term political affiliation. Accordingly, Lawson ceased to refer to the policy, or using the pronoun 'it', but made personal references to the researcher by using 'you'. News interviews in general, and *Today* in particular, are a very different kind of medium from research interviews. Nevertheless, in Extract 3.2, the change of footing by the EU practitioner (line 442), when he makes relevant the South Caucasus as part of the ENP as a region which 'you could argue where it is' is noteworthy. While listing the different countries, within the policy, the practitioner offers an assessment with respect to which one is European and which is not. This is achieved by continuously referring to what the ENP includes by using the term ENP or the pronoun 'it', as if the assessment offered by the practitioner could be made by any neutral observer. This pronoun shift to 'you' demonstrates the potentially disputable and contentious nature of the question of whether the South Caucasus is European. This implies that the researcher, or any other capable person, could make that assessment, which is not offered by the policy.

Second, the practitioner shifts his footing again: 'to me it's quite clear that ultimately Ukraine probably will' (lines 447–8). This is the only occasion in the extract where he offers his own assessment on which country is most likely to make the accession, and that being Ukraine. Again, this is a highly tendentious reading of the policy and this is made clear with the practitioner's footing shift. After all, Ukraine officially has the same status as Algeria or Tunisia, and does not have candidacy status like Turkey or Croatia. Such footing practices, that present the speaker as both the animator and originator, according to Potter (1996: 148), further increases potential personal agency, and thus the accountability of the speaker.

The next extract follows in a similar vein by attempting to make explicit distinctions between the neighbourhood and the enlargement policy. This EU practitioner has been invited by the researcher to offer an understanding or comparison of the differences between the eastern and southern neighbours' European credentials.

Extract 3.3 – EUIns.7

```
85   R     yeah it's just that I was just thinking about (.) the kind of::
86         you know uhm those countries in the east not just Ukraine even
87         Belarus some people argue that they are closer to Europe than:
88         (.) uhm Morocco
89   Inv   well: let's just take a step back then, the neighbourhood
90         policy isn't about European-ness (.) the neighbourhood policy
91         is about economic integration and political co-operation with
92         the EU. the enlargement question does have a dimension of
93         European-ness in it in that one of the criteria is being
94         defined as a European territory. now there's a whole another
95         debate about how you define that but let's not go there
96         ((laughs)) okay:: it's completely outside my portfolio and
97         outside your subject matter (0.3) anyway:: so Morocco has been
98         told no you are African and Ukraine has not been told- uhm. No
99         on the basis of its European-ness it is for the time being
100        being told that we think the best way of continuing relations
101        is through the neighbourhood, and the reason why Ukraine
102        doesn't like it is the neighbourhood is clearly out of sight so
103        the neighbourhood is not abou- uhmm the neighbourhood is about
104        developing a difference economic integration political
105        cooperation.
```

At the researcher's request, the EU practitioner offers her version on the relevance of the category of the 'European' for the ENP. She begins with a dispreferred response to the researcher's question, first by delaying the response with the 'well:' reaction token which is a common marker of dispreference, then with 'let's just take a step back then' (line 89). After the initial display that a rejection is to come, the practitioner offers a correction of what the ENP is about : 'the neighbourhood policy isn't about European-ness (.) the neighbourhood policy is about economic integration and political co-operation with the EU' (lines 89–92). She clearly rejects that the ENP is anything to do with having an association with the category of the 'European' or the identity of any members of the ENP, but rather to do with more pragmatic issues such as political and economic integration. Thus, ENP counties do not have to fit the European criteria, in contrast to those countries that want to join the EU, as according to her: 'the enlargement question does have a dimension of European-ness' (lines 92–3). Making a clear distinction between neighbourhood and enlargement policy is this practitioner's aim here. However, the category of the 'European' is part of this distinction and it is a contentious one. First, the practitioner attributes the category to geography (line 94), by arguing that such a country has to be 'defined as a European territory'. Then she attempts to avoid more discussion on the subject by stating: 'now there's a whole another debate about how you define that but let's not go there' (lines 94–5) which is further proof of the contentious nature of the question. Following on, she describes the irrelevance of the matter: 'okay:: it's completely outside my portfolio' (line 96). Claiming no expertise on the subject is rather unusual from an expert who is involved with developing the policy itself. This is an interesting turn and it serves the same purpose as her previous utterances to devalue the importance of the category of the 'European' for neighbouring countries. By now the practitioner devotes quite some time (89–97) rejecting any such applicability. However, in the following lines she audibly implies that there is a difference between neighbours as she asserts: 'so Morocco has been told no you are African' (line 98–9). She does not dispute or doubt this claim. Then she offers an explanation on Ukraine that 'Ukraine has not been told-' presumably that it is not European. The cut-off at the end of 'told' and the forthcoming 'uhm' demonstrate the delicate manoeuvring of the topic by the practitioner. Despite her resistance to being drawn into distinguishing between eastern and southern neighbours, she actually offers a distinction (between Morocco and Ukraine). Regardless of her efforts, there is a contrast, which is very relevant for the neighbouring countries.

Extract 3.4 – EUIns.31

85 Inv   I don't like the fact that in the media it's very often
86   pictured as (.) oh the ENP is a bad substitute for membership

87   (0.2) the ENP has nothing to do with membership. that's the
88   problem though it is being perceived (.) also by the Ukrainians
89   who are <u>highly</u> offended. why do you give us the ENP together
90   with [Morocco]?
91 R   [hhmh]
92 Inv what on earth is this? we we're something <u>different.</u> we belong
93   to Europe. which they of course do. (0.3) but we want to do
94   something different: so in a way uhm the ENP is a framework
95   that we have to work with Ukraine.

This extract is a further confirmation of the way another EU practitioner attends to the grievances expressed by Ukraine in response to the offer of similar treatment to the Moroccans. In this extract, the social action that the interviewee can be heard to perform is offering support for Ukraine's plight to be differentiated from other countries within the ENP, like Morocco.

To achieve this action, the practitioner quotes Ukrainians by voicing their concerns 'why do you give us the ENP together with Morocco?', 'what on earth is this?', and 'we we're something different. we belong to Europe' (lines 89–90, 92–3). Such a device, as I indicated before, is to present the views and impressions of others as corroborating, or to display the unexpected nature of what is being described (Wooffitt, 1991, 2005). In the above extract the latter is apparent. It is rather unanticipated that any EU practitioner would draw any differentiation between two ENP countries. Even though the practitioner voices the Ukrainians' viewpoint, her choice of juxtaposing Morocco and Ukraine is significant as both countries historically had clear ambitions to join the EU. Furthermore, her articulation of the Ukrainian belief: 'we're something different. we belong to Europe' (lines 92–3) instigates an immediate personal response from her 'which they of course do' (line 93). Such a response can be heard as the practitioner's acceptance of Ukraine belonging to Europe and consequently being different from Morocco, as it appears not to be classified as such. The practitioner chose not to dispute such differentiation but to state that the ENP is the framework she has to work with in regard to Ukraine. Consequently, she might display an understanding and appreciation of Ukraine's grievances, but the institutional provisions in place restrict her work.

This point links with issues of accountability. Although the EU practitioner's account seems to be offering support for the Ukrainian goal of EU accession, the restrictions placed on her by the ENP limits such support. The display of such moral dimension to the interviewee's practice demonstrates the troubling or problematic treatment of the issue of differentiation between ENP countries, especially when their European credentials are at stake. Despite such expression of support, the practitioner's personal accountability is not compromised.

Nevertheless, such display and troubling treatment has repercussions on European identity formation, and on what is considered European and what is not.

The analytical point I would like to draw attention to in the next five extracts concerns the production of the category of the European by EU practitioners.

Building the category of the 'European'

The subsequent extracts follow a similar pattern of contrasting eastern neighbours, predominantly Ukraine, to southern ones, claiming that the former has far more 'European' qualities, thus it has more chance of accession compared to the latter.

Extract 3.5 – EUIns.15

```
267 Inv   the relationship we have with Ukraine is in a way is a very
268        complete relationship.
269 R      what do you mean by that?
270 Inv   if you look at certain countries (.) a relationship like:: the
271        relationship of the ACP countries is very much assistance
272        driven. Ukraine don't want us to tell them oh you know human
273        rights and so on uhmm but Ukraine is a country that belongs to
274        Europe. wants to be part of our club so the spectrum of the
275        relations we have is really quite amazing.
```

Extract 3.6 – EUIns.6

```
441 R      and what about accession?
442 Inv   in a way the Ukraine would be less controversial. (0.3) there
443        are things that are very controversial in relation to a uhm::
444        Turkey.
445 R      don't you think of course the ENP reaches the limit of the
446        [borders?]
447 Inv   [of course] there's a border with Belarus and then there's
448        Russia. of course you know we're getting towards a very far
449        east but Ukraine is a very European country so and a new
450        generation that needs to develop. so there's absolutely no
451        difference of course the country has still a way to go (0.2) so
452        I mean uhmm we are not ready also for this:: you know:: in
453        taking Ukraine out of the ENP and putting it as a candidate
454        [country]
455 R      [hmm]=
456 Inv   =they're definitely not ready but I mean the direction is
457        pointing to something like [that]
458 R                                [hmm]
```

Extract 3.7 – EUIns.23

```
116 R     so so would you class these countries as European?
117 Inv   I think that umh. (0.2) it's going to be very difficult not to
118       say that the Ukraine or Belarus is or even Moldova is not
119       European(.) and it's going to be very difficult to say that
120       there are parts of the EU countries which are more. they are
121       territorially belong to [uhmm]
122 R                             [it is] an interesting comparison
123       compared to (.) if you can compare these countries to a
124       candidate country like Turkey
125 Inv   yup. they are much more European.
126 R     ((laughs))
127 Inv   ((laughs))
```

All of the above-cited practitioners are heard attending to and working up Ukraine's European credentials, that is, its belonging to Europe. This is the social action that their accounts function to accomplish. There are many interactional points in the extracts that one could draw on, but here let's focus instead on the category of the 'European' and the way practitioners attend to and manage this. Practitioners, like any other members of a social group, attend to the epistemological entitlements of the categories at their disposal (Sacks, 1972). Furthermore, they manage their accountability, as EU practitioners and policymakers, by attending to such entitlements as having the knowledge and the expertise to identify which neighbouring country is European and which is not.

How 'being a member' can be achieved was the focus of Widdicombe and Wooffitt's (1995) study on youth subcultures. This task turned out to be more difficult than anticipated. Despite a membership category being worked up by a particular societal group, others might fail to treat a person as having that certain membership. Such incidents are unavoidable and they appear in this data corpus too. But first, let's focus on one particular point, that all three extracts have in common. All three EU practitioners work up Ukraine as a European country, and as such they attend to the category of the 'European'. The discursive device of category entitlements[7] conveys implicit conventions about knowledge, skills, expertise, or attitudes that are inferred when people apply specific categories to themselves or to others (Sacks, 1992). They also assist speakers to produce factual and authoritative accounts (Potter, 1996).

In Extract 3.5, the practitioner does this by drawing a comparison between African, Caribbean, and Pacific (ACP) countries where the relationship between these countries and the EU 'is very much assistance driven' (lines 271–2). This is an important distinction, since to be accepted to the EU, the relationship has to be mutual. Also, she asserts that Ukraine does not need to be lectured on human rights: 'Ukraine don't want us to tell them oh you know human rights' (lines 272–3). This is again a crucial point as the TFEU states that only those countries can be considered joining the EU, thus fitting the category of the 'European', that respect *inter alia* human rights (Article 2). Furthermore, the practitioner states that 'Ukraine is a country that belongs to Europe' (lines 273–4) and accepts that it 'wants to be part of our club', that is the EU (line 274). Consequently, according to this practitioner, Ukraine has all the category entitlements that a country needs to be part of the EU.

In Extract 3.6 a similar point is made by a different practitioner who relies on geography as a decisive factor in response to the researcher's question on borders. Of course, a question such as 'don't you think of course the ENP reaches the limit of the borders?' (lines 445–6) invokes a response on geography. Nevertheless, one might argue that the respondent could have chosen not to address the question in the way she did. Such a response displays the co-constructive quality of social phenomena by the researcher and the interviewee. Although the practitioner accepts that the EU borders with Russia and Belarus might be too far east: 'of course you know we're getting towards a very far east' (448–9), she also emphasises Ukraine's different nature: 'but Ukraine is a very European country' (line 449), and thus argues that the country belongs to Europe. While the category entitlement of being European for Russia and Belarus could be heard as being debatable, Ukraine's is not in question. According to this practitioner, there is no question as to Ukraine's entitlement to belong to the category of the 'European'.

In addition, this EU practitioner chose to compare Ukraine, which admittedly does not have EU candidacy status, to Turkey, which does. At lines 442 and 444, as a response to the interviewer's question on EU accession, the practitioner raises the Turkish question: 'in a way the Ukraine would be less controversial. (0.3) there are things that are very controversial in relation to a uhm: : Turkey'. Such a claim is highly contentious, owing to Turkey's legal status as an EU candidate currently in negotiation and the conclusion of different chapters of the *acquis communautaire*, whereas Ukraine is not in the same position. In spite of this, Hillion (2007) claims that the details of the New Enhanced Agreement, that was negotiated in 2007 with Ukraine, is legally not far off from the Association Agreements that led the CEECs to eventual EU accession and contains elements of the *acquis*. Consequently, he argues for the possibility of association as opposed to neighbourhood policy. The Association Agreement came into force on 1 September 2017. But to return to the original point and the EU practitioner's assertion that Ukraine's joining the EU would be less controversial than Turkey's is significant. Such a statement displays the troubling nature of Turkey's EU accession and at the same time questions the category entitlement of the 'European'. A candidate country's Europeanness should not come under scrutiny, since it is a prerequisite of being considered and gaining candidacy status. Nonetheless, this EU practitioner clearly implies that Ukraine has more category entitlement to be called European than Turkey. Such comparison will not change Turkey's legal position but it is rather telling that a practitioner, who is directly involved with developing the ENP, would draw on this position. Also, it could further Ukraine's ambition to join the EU, perhaps even before Turkey.

The third extract, Extract 3.7, has a similar pattern. To the researcher's question: 'so so would you class these countries as European?' concerning the eastern neighbouring states, the EU practitioner's response is: 'it's going to be very difficult not to say that the Ukraine or Belarus is or even Moldova is not European' (117–19). He delivers this after some delay 'I think that umh.' and a 0.2 pause. Such hesitation is customary before delivering something potentially contentious. Classifying Ukraine, Belarus, and Moldova as not European is worked up to be problematic. But more importantly here, our main concern is the category entitlement of the 'European'. This EU practitioner, like the one in Extract 3.5, aligns being European with geographical location: 'they are territorially belong to' (line 121). The exchange between the researcher and the practitioner that comes straight after (lines 123–4), when the researcher solicits a controversial analogy: 'compared to (.) if you can compare these countries to a candidate country like Turkey' is important. Significantly, the practitioner does not rebuke such comparison, but rather he offers an affirmative response with: 'yup. they are much more European'. Accepting that any of the eastern neighbouring states have 'much more' European credentials, thus having more of an entitlement to be in the category of the 'European' than Turkey, is noteworthy. This is so for the very same reasons outlined above in the analysis of Extract 3.5. Such a claim that Ukraine, Belarus, and even Moldova have more entitlement to be European than Turkey, a candidate country, is crucial from policymakers and has potential implications on the way policy vis-à-vis the eastern neighbours will develop. The delicate nature of such a claim is analytically further demonstrable with the laughter tokens of both the researcher and the practitioner (lines 126–7). Jefferson (1994) offers different examples of how participants manage to attend to troubles or controversial issues during talk with laughter. She identifies instances where the recipients, sensitive to the trouble within the interaction, respond with laughter. The corpus includes examples when the trouble-teller joins in the laugh or when he or she does not. Interactionally, what is interesting in the Extract 3.7 is that the researcher senses the delicate nature of the practitioner's claim and responds with laughter. While doing so, the practitioner (or trouble-teller) joins in the laughter, whereby he accepts that the nature of his claim is sensitive and potentially problematic.

Additionally, the differentiation that the EU practitioner draws on between the EU's eastern neighbours, that are more 'European' than Turkey, adds to our understanding of the category of the 'European'. It implies that such a category comes with geographical caveats and clear examples of which country can and cannot belong to this category. This also supports what practitioners argued at the beginning of the chapter when they drew on clear examples of which country is in Europe, and which is not. In their accounts, they too use geography as one of the attributes.

A different practitioner offers a similar explanation to justify the category entitlements of the 'European' but through different means.

Extract 3.8 – EUIns.34

561	R	and do you think it will be easier for a country like Ukraine
562		to join than Turkey?
563	Inv	I don't know. (1) I mean that comes down to an argument over
564		you know what is Europe? and who are European? (0.6) I think
565		for some member states it would be easier to accept Ukraine
566		because they feel Ukraine is more European (0.6) I don't myself
567		really think uhm:: (0.4) I'm not very bothered by that idea
568	R	sure
569	Inv	I mean strategically there's more perhaps of an argument for
570		having Turkey in precisely because it is so different and it
571		might be a good think to have Muslim country inside the EU
572	R	uh huh
573	Inv	I'm no expert on Turkey
574	R	no non sure I'm just interested in the debate about who and or
575		which country is more European than another so:: but in your
576		eyes?
577	Inv	w::ell (0.4) Ukraine is definitely a European country so (0.8)
578		but that criteria- (.) it fulfils the Article 49 of the Treaty
579		says that any European country can apply to join. (0.6) Ukraine
580		clearly is a European country so it can apply to join ehmm::
581		(0.6) I don't know whether at some stage people would feel that
582		countries where asking for membership who actually weren't
583		European ehm.

To the researcher's question: 'and do you think it will be easier for a country like Ukraine to join than Turkey?' (lines 561–2), the practitioner produces two questions herself: 'what is Europe? and who are European?' (line 564) after some hesitation of the 'I don't know' and the 1-second gap. Despite the practitioner's claim of insufficient knowledge that usually warrants a refusal of an assessment (Pomerantz, 1984: 58), these questions audibly strike at the very core of the identity concern that the EU is facing and also at the researcher's question. The practitioner herself makes the topic of the 'European' relevant. In responding on behalf of the member states 'it would be easier to accept Ukraine because they feel Ukraine is more European' (lines 565–6), the practitioner disaffiliates from the reported assessment. She further confirms her disassociation with member states' potential assessment: 'I don't myself really think uhm: : (0.4) I'm not very bothered by that idea' (lines 566–7). Nevertheless, her response implies that Ukraine fits the category of the 'European' more than Turkey.

There is further confirmation of Ukraine's European qualities: 'Ukraine is definitely a European country so (0.8) but that criteria- (.) it fulfils the Article 49 of the Treaty says that any European country can apply to join' (lines 577–9). The practitioner offers this assessment after an invitation by the researcher to return to the topic of 'which country is more European than another' (line 575). She cuts off before providing the criteria of being European. Rather, she asserts that Ukraine fulfils such criteria then she resorts to the Treaty article, thus to the legal argument as to why Ukraine is eligible to join the EU. Interestingly, the practitioner is silent on Turkey, or any other country that is less European than Ukraine. Such muteness implies the troubled nature of a comparison between Ukraine and Turkey's European qualities. Her following utterances: 'I don't know whether at some stage people would feel that countries were asking for membership who actually weren't European ehm' (lines 581–3) could also be heard as an assessment. After all, the practitioner does not question Turkey's Europeanness, as Turkey was deemed European when the accession talks began.

Until this point the focus was on practitioner's accounts of comparing eastern neighbours to southern ones or to Turkey to work up the category entitlement of the eastern states as more 'European'. Their descriptions predominantly relied on geographical factors. However, in Extract 3.9 the practitioner can be seen to attribute Turkey's potential problems with accession to having a problem with democracy, minority troubles, and population size.

Extract 3.9 – EUIns.35

```
12  R     and what's your view? because you mentioned that Ukraine and
13        her accession. uhm I mean umh I don't know, do you think as far
14        as you know the EU is suffering from a kind of enlargement
15        fatigue >so< can we talk about further enlargement? quite a lot
16        of people I've spoken to who would describe Ukraine more of a
17        European country than Turkey which is a candidate country do
18        you see Ukraine acceding before Turkey? or at the same time?
19        o:-
20  Inv   you know my quote about that is always- umh I mean I'm always
21        provocative on that point is that I mean I was born in
22        (omitted) but when I am in Istanbul I feel much more at home.
23        and you know I was once for a mission in Galat. you know we
24        dealt with- we were looking at the other side of the Danube
25        with all these planes and I mean to me Turkey is much more home
26        than it is there. so perception varies. and and don't want to
```

```
27        use the argument of the regions. I think because- uhm I think
28        it's not useful. and unless we use it appropriately. NOW
29        whether umh (.) Ukraine can accede before Turkey that's to be
30        seen, but the conditions in Turkey is a problem. also because
31        Turkey has deficits in terms of its democracy and they have
32        problems with bitter minorities and [and::]
33  R                                       [with] population size?
34  Inv  population size
```

In this extract, the practitioner is asked whether he sees Ukraine joining the EU before Turkey: 'do you see Ukraine acceding before Turkey?'. The question was put to him in the context of the initial question of the interview regarding the importance of the eastern region. The topic was also framed by the researcher's assertion that other practitioners she spoke with described Ukraine as more European than Turkey. The latter is attended by the practitioner first.

On this occasion, the practitioner works up Turkey to be more European in contrast to different geographical locations within the EU. He does this by offering a narrative description. Elements of such descriptions are often organised to offer a broader narrative of a general or specific description (Potter, 1996; Edwards, 1997). Pomerantz's (1988/89) study on news reports of President George Bush's involvement in Contras and smuggling aid through laundered drug money. Her claim is that the audience of the reports was primed to be sceptical through the news team. She argues that the news team juxtaposed documentary evidence on a minor CIA associate and a clip of his outright denial of having any CIA association, to demonstrate his being a liar and taking part in covert CIA operations. Creating such narrative contrasts throughout a news report is an important aspect of working up factuality. The points of narratives constructions often include an illustration of the parties involved and usually with particular attention to their moral identities. They are organised to be cumulative to focalise on specific characters through constructing events that are believable and understandable (Potter, 1996: 173).

In Extract 3.9, the EU practitioner offers a similar description. He compares the place he was born in, a town in the EU, to Istanbul where he feels more at home: 'I was born in (omitted) but when I am in Istanbul I feel much more at home' (lines 21–2). Then he launches a further narrative to demonstrate the reasons behind his identifying with Turkey as more homely than the place in which he was on a mission or even the town he was born in: 'and you know I was once for a mission in Galat. you know we dealt with- we were looking at the other side of the Danube with all these planes and I mean to me Turkey is much more home than it is there' (lines 23–6). Incidentally, both places he draws on are current EU territory, whereas Turkey is not yet. What this narrative accomplished here is a demonstration of Turkey's European qualities. It does this by focalising the narrative to the practitioner's own experiences and feelings of homeliness.

Next the practitioner attends to the question of which country is more likely to join the EU first: 'NOW whether umh (.) Ukraine can accede before Turkey that's to be seen, but the conditions in Turkey is a problem' (lines 29–30). Although he does not offer an explicit answer, he implies the difficulties Turkey is facing. He lists these obstacles as democratic deficit, minority issues, and population size. Lists are a common discursive device and used to construct something as normal or standard (Jefferson, 1990). Analytically, what is interesting on this occasion is the collaborative construction of this list with the researcher: 'also because Turkey has deficits in terms of its democracy and they have problems with bitter minorities and [and: :]' (lines 30–4) the researcher in overlap offers: '[with] population size?' which the practitioner accepts by repeating: 'population size'. This co-construction of the problems Turkey is facing with accession between the practitioner and the researcher further demonstrates that Turkey's accession problems are standard knowledge and known to all interested in the topic.

What the practitioner accomplishes in this extract is to work up Turkey's European qualities but at the same time imply the difficulties Turkey faces with regard to EU accession. Interestingly, he does not make any claims as to Ukraine's Europeanness or any insight into its advanced accession to the EU. Even further on in the dialogue, the practitioner does not offer any assessment on Ukraine. This silence is analytically telling. By not offering an account of how Turkey compares with Ukraine, in spite of the researcher's request, the practitioner's claim that Turkey fits the category of the 'European' is not challenged. Therefore, no conclusion can be drawn, as in previous extracts, that Turkey is not eligible for EU accession on account of its lacking European qualities or identity. Consequently, Turkey could be part of a European self. This observable factor however does not stop the practitioner from accepting difficulties with other aspects of Turkey's European ambitions. Consequently, Turkey's problems are not to do with its identity, but by not confirming to European norms in different respects such as democratic deficit, minority rights, and potential power of its population size. Although identity per se is not an issue, otherness is attributed to Turkey through alternative means. Ultimately, such issues could potentially be more compromising to Turkey's EU accession, especially with current developments.

How 'European' is the South Caucasus or Kazakhstan?

In this section, the focus shifts from differentiations between eastern and southern neighbours to the South Caucasus and to a Central Asian country, Kazakhstan. The inclusion of the South Caucasian states of Armenia, Azerbaijan, and Georgia into the ENP took place in 2004. This was partly in response to the region's strategic importance for the EU, owing to its geographic position in relation to Russia, Iran, and Central Asia and also due to the EU's concerns regarding its energy security. Besides the EU's own interests, these inclusions forced the EU to consider some bitterly disputed regional conflicts.[8] These regional disputes are long-standing with no solution in sight. The region's inclusion in the ENP prompted the EU to raise its interest in these frozen conflicts, but it has often been critiqued for not offering any real solutions (Freitag-Wirminghaus, 2008). There are other contentious issues in the region especially with regard to the countries' democratic credentials. Azerbaijan re-elected in 2013 its incumbent Premier Ilham Aliev de facto President for life. The country also signed a memorandum with Gazprom to supply Central Asian gas to Russia at market prices for the long term. Such steps undermined the progress of the Nabucco pipeline, which the EU tried to build in the region, and led to Nabucco being shelved. In Georgia, there were also controversies surrounding the country's former President Mikheil Saakashvili's premiership. Concerning the region's European ambitions, Georgia and Armenia long aspired for EU membership. According to former Armenian President Kocharian, Armenians regard themselves as 'European' and seeking a role and place in the European architecture (Mediamax, 2006). The EU's energy relation with Kazakhstan is predominantly based on the Baku–Tbilisi–Ceyhan oil pipeline that links Azerbaijan and Georgia to the European market. At the same time, it serves Kazakhstan's strategic interests as a bargaining position towards Russia, support from the US and the EU as well as lucrative commercial opportunities especially in hydrocarbons (Kassenova, 2009). Kazakhstan has no formal ambitions to join the EU.

In light of the above, we will examine the South Caucasus and Kazakhstan and whether they fit the category of the 'European'. In the following four extracts, EU practitioners offer various arguments for Georgia, Azerbaijan, and Kazakhstan to be considered as potentially European. In the first extract, a practitioner can be seen establishing a historical link between Georgia and Europe. In the following extracts, the focus will be more on other Caucasian states and the justifications for their European credentials.

The 'very beginning of European civilisation'

This EU practitioner's narrative provides a further explanation of the category of the European by focusing on the origins of European civilisation. In addition, there is another conceptual point that warrants our attention. There is an important relationship here between narratives (or scripts), causal attributions, and identity. The practitioner achieves this by using corroboration and stake inoculation, to support his account and to apportion blame for Georgia not being in line to join the EU. Corroborative evidence is often provided to present a report that is consensual, and thus to transform a merely descriptive observation into a factual account (Potter, 1996). The following extract from the transcript demonstrates evidence of such corroboration through active voicing (Wooffitt, 1991, 2005). Quotations and reports of thoughts are usually presented as the views of others. However, in this case, the EU practitioner aligns himself with the very group who holds the responsibility. Second, stake inoculation, another fact-constructing device, is to assist in boosting the authenticity of the practitioner's account (Potter, 1996). The question here is: what is at stake for the practitioner in terms of both the authenticity of the account and his identity as an EU practitioner formulating EU policy in this region?

Extract 3.10 – EUIns.21

```
737  R    <but to go back to Ukraine (-) it obviously changed again that
738        I mean the democratic process erm
739  Inv  human nature is imperfect but at the end of the day democracy
740        will ensure that (0.2) <there is no Russian intervention
741        (inaudible)= Ukraine will not depart from democracy and human
742        rights media free = I mean Belarus I don't know we are trying
743        to help them but (inaudible)= Georgia [is a fabulous case]
744  R                                          [but then the leadership]
745        is very different there
746  Inv  a moment ago yes sometimes we joke (inaudible) we help the
747        Europeans= and still we are: (0.5) in the woods and it's true
748        Georgia culturally is that's hard to say I mean it's the very
749        beginning of European civilization specifically three thousand
750        years ago they were cultivated people and we were living in the
751        woods (0.2) they started going (inaudible) [Georgia]
752  R                                                [but then-] =
753  Inv  =they're one of the oldest Christian peoples nations of Europe
754        in Britain in Poland we were in the woods and they were
755        Europeans in terms of value and [culture]
756  R                                     [mm hmm]=
757  Inv  =and now we're telling them they're not Europeans .hh they're
758        not ready to join us that's why they (0.1) I mean in four years
759        time they change from a solitary republic to a modern western
760        democracy (0.1) whole country prayed free free spiri
```

Between lines 746 and 755 the practitioner constructs an account as someone whose stake in the talk is contrary to what would be expected from an EU practitioner, who is in full knowledge of Georgia's current situation, as to its future EU accession. In doing so he aligns himself with those who dare to question whether Georgia is European or even has a chance to join the EU. This contradiction is managed by employing the pronoun 'we' when referring to us Europeans, including those who are involved in drawing up policy recommendations vis-à-vis Georgia; and through using vivid description (Smith,

1978; Edwards and Potter, 1992; Potter, 1996). The former point is important, as the use of 'we' at these given points of the interaction (lines 746–7, 750, 754, 757) imply a form of blame that we all have to share, including the practitioner. This point will be further addressed later.

Next, I would like to focus on the highly vivid description of when European civilisation began. Vivid description is another fact construction device and is employed to create an impression of awareness and sensitive re-examination, thus demonstrating particular observational skills that the speaker possesses (Edwards and Potter, 1992). Here the practitioner recalls the origins of European civilisation and claims that it derives from Georgia, while 'in Britain and in Poland we were living in the woods' (lines 754 and 750–1). He unambiguously compares and contrasts cultivated Europeans, that is, the Georgians three thousand years ago to the uncouth Europeans, the ones who call themselves European now: 'still we are: (0.5) in the woods and it's true Georgia culturally is that's hard to say I mean it's the very beginning of European civilization specifically three thousand years ago they were cultivated people and we were living in the woods' (lines 747–51). To create such binary oppositions between the civilised and uncouth Europeans implies that we, Europeans, do not honour our roots. Further, we discredit our current policy and at the same time question our moral responsibility vis-à-vis Georgia. This morality, or doing moral work is managed within the interaction as a result of providing the basis for the right or wrong conduct by the speaker. The right way of conducting oneself would be accepting Georgia as European, thus giving the Georgians' their rightful chance of EU accession. However, 'now we're telling them they're not Europeans' (line 757), which is clearly an immoral way of conducting ourselves. Such attribution is closely linked with responsibility and blame, and consequently with personal agency of the speaker.

To return to the conceptual point regarding the link between narration, causal attribution, and identity; narrative or script formulations can also be accomplished through the speaker's own identity, by attending to his or her own accountability. As pointed out earlier, this EU practitioner aligns himself with the very group who makes the judgement on Georgia's accession but also on whether she is European: 'yes sometimes we joke nostalgically we help the Europeans' (lines 746–7), 'and now we're telling them they're not Europeans they're not ready to join us' (lines 757–68). Bearing in mind the analytical point made earlier on the cultivated v. uncouth Europeans, the practitioner apportions moral responsibility to the group including himself by using the pronoun 'we'. This group comprises the then uncouth Europeans who dishonour our cultural values and heritage of Georgia. In fact, the use of 'we' effectively manages the practitioner's personal accountability. His role is to follow official policy in his capacity of formulating the policy. However, as the above extract demonstrates, the reconceptualisation of the speaker's concern (rather than the analyst's) accomplishes personal stake, thus accountability in the narration.

Consequently, the practitioner manages to produce an account that attends to his interest of proffering Georgia's chances of EU accession.

Justifying other South Caucasian states and Kazakhstan as 'European'

After establishing the European bond with the Caucasus through the practitioner's account of Georgia's heritage (above), as the beginning of the European civilisation, our focus now turns to Azerbaijan and whether it possesses the category entitlements necessary to be 'European'.

The next extract is taken from halfway through a research interview in which the topic of potential future EU enlargement is discussed. The EU practitioner offers an example of a country that in his opinion might be part of a prospective enlargement process. The practitioner's choice of Azerbaijan is an interesting one. This country is in the ENP and of great interest to the EU. However, it is a Caucasian state, thus its 'European' identity is problematic; or perhaps not as much, if one considers this practitioner's account.

Extract 3.11 – EUIns.37

```
518 Inv   ↑now as far as enlargement is concerned (0.4) I will give you
519        one illustration=I was in Azerbaijan last week
520 R      uh huh
521 Inv    eh and very very interesting ↑because:: (.) I had no idea what
522        to expect
523 R      uh huh
524 Inv    I had really none and ↑in fact it is not a sort of exotic
525        Middle Eastern City (.) Baku is quite like a European city em
526        (1) there's an old town which was in fact where I was staying
527        and the old town is (.) <not like (0.5) is not like a European
528        old town but I mean it's not like Jerusalem or Cairo with the
529        souks it's hard to describe it exactly it's more like a
530        European town than (0.4) <oh I'll tell you what it's a bit like
531        em have you ever been to Lisbon?
532 R      yes
```

Here, the practitioner recalls a recent trip, to the country. The social action the practitioner performs is to demonstrate how 'European' Baku really is. He accomplishes this by employing what Wooffitt (1991) coined a 'first I thought then I realised' discursive device. The practitioner does this by evoking 'eh and very very interesting ↑because: : (.) I had no idea what to expect' (lines 521–2). After a brief acknowledgement token from the research 'uh huh' (line 523), the practitioner continues 'I had really none' (line 524) to emphasise the fact that initially he had little or no knowledge of the place. Such an opening heightens the effect of the account being told but also of the implication of what is to follow.

Next the practitioner begins his account of what he found, despite a lack of expectation, which is the second sequence or 'then I realised' part of the discursive device. The practitioner offers a comparison of an exotic Middle Eastern city, which Baku is not, and a European one. It becomes even more explicit when the practitioner draws on more explicit examples of what Baku is unlike: 'I mean it's not like Jerusalem or Cairo with the souks' (528–9); then he goes further by drawing similarities with Lisbon (line 531).

Two more analytical points deserve attention. First, there is the way in which the practitioner builds up an account of Azerbaijan as European, by comparing its capital to European cities. He states that 'Baku is quite like a European city' (line 525), and then he attempts to do the same for the part of town in which he stayed. At first, he admits that this part was 'not like a European old town' (lines 527–8), but it is also unlike non-European old towns such as Jerusalem or Cairo (line 528). He concludes that 'it's more like a European town' (on lines 529–30), finally likening it to Lisbon (lines 530–1). Offering an account of 'what the city is like' as opposed to offering an answer as to whether any South Caucasian state should accede to the EU and how the process will take place, is very significant.

Second, the practitioner uses another discursive device, namely corroboration and consensus (Potter and Edwards, 1992), when he offers a comparison of the European city that has similar features to Baku. He does this by posing a question to the researcher: '<oh I'll tell you what it's a bit like em have you ever been to Lisbon?' (530–1). This question is constructed in such a way that the researcher can understand and identify with the practitioner's description of the town. Furthermore, this way of appealing to factuality makes the practitioner's claim more persuasive, as it implies that anyone would see the Azerbaijani city as being like Lisbon, which is undoubtedly European. Consequently, the likening of Baku to Lisbon is the way this practitioner constructs the 'European', but at the same time works up Azerbaijan's eligibility to be considered for EU accession at some stage. This kind of comparison between Baku and Lisbon is perilous in the context of enlargement.

The following passage from the same research interview draws on further justifications of the European qualities of a Central Asian state this time. After the practitioner's offer of more insight into Azerbaijan's strong European vocation, he turns to Kazakhstan. The following analysis is to focus on the way this practitioner works up Kazakhstan to be 'European'.

Extract 3.12 – EUIns.37

```
581  Inv  Baku was the oil boom town prior to 1914 (1) now the people I
582       talked to were not representative they were young, they were
583       well educated, they had all studied in the west (.) and: they
584       have a very very strong European vocation and basically
```

585		Azerbaijan thinks that you know uhm. it's not going to happen
586		straight away they are very realistic, but they reckon they can
587		get into the European Union (1) <now if you look at EU
588		documents it talks in very vague terms about: the Southern
589		Caucasus (0.4) as being sort of vaguely European (.) just in
590		parenthesis. I was in Kazakhstan the year before last and they
591		said to me (0.4) the extreme Western part of Kazakhstan is
592		<u>Europe</u>
593	R	hmm
594	Inv	and when I was sceptical they said well if you draw a map from
595		the Euro mountains to the South a large part of Kazakhstan
596		[hahh]
597	R	[huh huh]
598	Inv	<they weren't <u>very</u> serious about it
599	R	right ok
600	Inv	because if you look at the map then Almaty is the same
601		longitude as New Delhi
602	R	yup
603	Inv	it's a very very long long way to the East that alters the
604		European chequerboard pattern built by the Russians
605	R	uh huh

This time, in Extract 3.12, the EU practitioner draws on another illustration of a state that has potential to have some 'European' credentials. He begins the example by citing EU documents on the Caucasus '<now if you look at EU documents it talks in very vague terms about: the Southern Caucasus' (lines 587–9). The hesitant description of the Caucasus as 'vaguely European' (lines 588–9) is reflected in the audible pauses that break up the practitioner's speech. Analytically, the 0.4-second pause between the two utterances (line 589) and the micro pause after the word European on the same line are important, as pauses, gaps, and silences are built into interactions for emphasis. Here such delay in speech draws attention to the fact that something controversial is to come. The turn of phrase 'sort of vaguely', further demonstrates the problematic nature of describing the South Caucasus as 'European'. Furthermore, the practitioner begins his example of a South Caucasian state with potential to be called European by employing the phrase 'just in parenthesis' (lines 589–90). First, this phrase is used to introduce what follows as disjunctive and problematic in nature. Yet, it is audibly relevant to the following utterance when the practitioner constructs Kazakhstan as 'European'. Second, 'just' has a specific function here. Lee (1987) offered four different uses of the word *just* during interactions. He argues that it can either be depreciatory, restrictive, specificatory, or emphatic. Here, it is used in its depreciatory capacity.

Its function, along with 'in parenthesis', is to lessen, or even diminish the value of the claim that 'the extreme Western part of Kazakhstan is <u>Europe</u>' (lines 590–2).

There are two more points I want to draw attention to. It is discursively significant that the practitioner did not attribute such an account of the European credentials of Kazakhstan to himself but to the Kazakh people he spoke with. Such footing is helpful to minimise the practitioner's own agency or personal accountability for what is being said. Second, the stress placed on the word 'Europe' (line 592) serves to stress the contention of his claim in exactly the same way as the earlier pauses in his talk.

The remainder of Extract 3.12 follows a similar analytical pattern, that is, the EU practitioner tries to distance himself from being associated with the claims of Kazakhstan's European qualities, but gladly offers the Kazakhs' own explanations. Lines 594–5 provide an example of just that: 'and when I was sceptical they said well if you draw a map from the Euro mountains to the South a large part of Kazakhstan'. By using a direct quote 'they said', which is the active voicing discursive device, the practitioner works up the unexpected nature of the description of where the boundaries of Europe lie. As it turns out, the Kazakhs would argue that it lies at Southern Kazakhstan. Such a quotation or report is often presented as part of the fact construction devices employed by the speaker to strengthen his or her assessment (Potter and Edwards, 1992). Furthermore, the laughter tokens that this statement elicits on line 596 from the practitioner and on line 597 from the researcher is analytically significant. It follows the troubled nature of the practitioner's assertion (Jefferson, 1994). His immediate utterances on the geographical position of the most populated Kazakh city are proof of just that: 'if you look at the map then Almaty is the same longitude as New Delhi' (lines 600–1).

Nevertheless, what is analytically significant is that neither of the statements are claimed as the practitioner's own views. By adapting the third person or the passive voice, the practitioner attends to his personal accountability, here, by not claiming any agency for the statements being made. Such ambiguity does not clarify whether Kazakhstan fits the category of the 'European'. Consequently, it is still unknown whether the EU practitioner believes Kazakhstan's place is in Europe.

So far, we have focused upon the way in which EU practitioners' work up the South Caucasus and Kazakhstan to be European. The next extract follows a different pattern, as this EU practitioner concedes that there is no definition for Europe. This raises a couple of issues; if there is no definition for Europe, how would we know what it entails to be European, and hence, how can we know whether the South Caucasus or Kazakhstan is European after all?

Extract 3.13 – EUIns.44

```
332 R     yeah sure (0.3) I'm just going t- try to refer back to the
333       Treaty Article 49
334 Inv   any European country can join=
335 R     =yeah
336 Inv   nobody wants to define what Europe means. I mean the Kazakhs
337       would say that eh there's more of Kazakhstan in Europe than
338       there is Turkey
339 R     really?
340 Inv   so ehh::
341 R     interesting
342 Inv   it's interesting. (0.8) in my view it's a completely futile
343       argument to try and define the boundaries of the EU .hhh or the
344       boundaries of Europe (0.6) it will always be governed by
345       political (.) political considerations
346 R     uh huh
```

For context, before the researcher made a reference to the Treaty Article 49, the dialogue was progressing on the potential of accession for the bordering states on the east of the EU. Article 49 of the TEU and its applicability is well known to all EU practitioners, as we have seen earlier in this chapter (Extract 3.8, line 578). Once the researcher mentioned Article 49: 'I'm just going t- try to refer back to the Treaty Article 49' (lines 332–3), the practitioner duly obliged her knowledge: 'any European country can join' (line 334). What is more, after the researcher's acknowledgement token 'yeah', the practitioner complains that 'nobody wants to define what Europe means'. She follows this up by raising an argument from the Kazakhs perspective 'I mean the Kazakhs would say that eh there's more of Kazakhstan in Europe than there is Turkey' (line 336–8). Through this footing shift (Potter, 1996; Dickerson, 1997) the practitioner presents herself as mere reporter of the Kazakhs' views. Nonetheless, her utterance serves not only as a complaint of the lack of definition of 'Europe', but also as a critique of when and how the term is applied. The reference to Turkey in the argument above is controversial, as Turkey has EU candidacy status, and if more of Kazakhstan lies in Europe than does Turkey, then Kazakhstan has a stronger claim to EU candidacy on geographical grounds. However, in another footing shift, the practitioner concedes that: 'in my view it's a completely futile argument to try and define the boundaries of the EU .hhh or the boundaries of Europe (0.6) it will always be governed by political (.) political considerations' (lines 342–5). She retreats from the geographical justification as to what defines Europe or the EU, and instead emphasises the importance of 'political considerations'. In this view, it is not the lack of definition of the 'European' that is the problem, as the 'European' cannot be defined (e.g. in terms of 'boundaries of Europe') and hence does not define which country is in the EU. Rather, it is the EU's own political ambitions, or so-called political considerations, which determine a country's candidacy status. If indeed this is the case, then Article 49 and the discussion on the definition of the 'European' becomes more and more irrelevant in the construction of identity.

Conclusion

In this chapter, the main focus was identity and the analytical and theoretical construction of the 'European' by EU practitioners. In accordance with a DPM framework, the analysis of identities, selves, and others requires the development of concepts (such as the 'European') as discursive products, rather than being treated as cognitive entities. In addition to the construction of the 'European', we also analysed the way in which this category was used to assert the European credentials of eastern neighbours in different accounts.

Such accounts included practitioners providing specific examples of which country is in Europe and which is not. These examples mainly revolved around establishing contrast structures between eastern and southern neighbours like in Extract 3.1. The practitioner used this discursive device to develop the assertion that countries to the East of the EU are more European than those to the South. Such a contrast was supported by listing the attributes of what makes a country more European. They included geographical locations, cultural, economic, and historical ties to EU member states and Treaty provisions. Extract 3.2 provides a similar account; and also uses a list format in order to demonstrate such differentiation. Through these examples the practitioners also drew clear distinctions between the EU's neighbourhood and enlargement policies. Another similarity between these two extracts was the way both practitioners attend to their personal agency; both employ changes in footing. By predominantly relying on the third person pronoun 'it', or simply referring to the policy as 'the ENP', they refused any personal accountability for the claims they made. Although Extract 3.3 followed a similar pattern to the previous two, the practitioner initially attempted to avoid differentiating between eastern and southern neighbours, through delays and avoiding the questions posed. Nevertheless, eventually the practitioner implied that Morocco is African and Ukraine is European. In Extract 3.4, another practitioner accomplished the same juxtaposition by voicing what Ukrainians would say. Active voicing, just like footing, relates to concerns of accountability and the agency of the practitioner. Attending to issues of agency and personal accountability, as discursive practices, are routine in interaction. Analytically, it is one of the cornerstones of DPM. Despite a display of support for Ukrainians through active voicing, the practitioner in Extract 3.4 managed not to compromise her personal accountability by referring to the limitations that are placed on her by the ENP. Thus, she is not responsible for Ukraine's failure to achieve its 'European' ambitions.

In the extracts presented in this chapter, the practitioners also attended to the category entitlements of the 'European'. When people, social groups, nations, or (in our case) countries ascribe to a particular category, tacit conventions of this category and of their members can be inferred. These conventions are not just neutral labels; we must consider why that particular selection was made, and why at that particular time. Categorisation of people will have significant consequences for the way the claims of those who do the categorisation and their practices are interpreted (Sacks, 1979, 1992). Here, the practitioners predominantly relied on the geography and territorial attachment, when they argued for Ukraine or Moldova and Belarus belonging to Europe, as opposed to Turkey, in Extracts 3.6 and 3.7. In Extract 3.5, the practitioner managed this by contrasting EU relations with ACP countries to EU relations with Ukraine, to demonstrate the preferential treatment awarded to Ukraine and hence its position as closer to Europe. In Extract 3.8, the practitioner offered two of the basic questions that all scholars of European identity formation are interested in; namely 'what is Europe?' and 'who are Europeans?'. Her reluctance to attend to these questions, or to offer a definition of the criteria she referred to, demonstrated the contentious nature of the subject; as did her unwillingness to compare Ukraine and Turkey in this context. In contrast, for the practitioner in Extract 3.9 there was no doubt over Turkey's European credentials. Thus, Turkey's affiliation to Europe and to a *European self* is incontestable. But he did not stop there. Interestingly he managed to *other* Turkey in other ways; by referring to issues such as the democratic deficit, problems with minorities, and population size. These issues all suggest that Turkey lacks the entitlements to belong to the category of the 'European'.

Subsequently, ascribing these category entitlements to some neighbours but not to others accomplishes a contrast between European neighbours and the neighbours of Europe. These tacit conventions and culturally available category entitlements have great implications for the ENP and the countries participating in the policy. It means that instead of providing explicit agreements on what being European entails through for example the treaties, the category remains to be an implicit, flexible, and indexical one that is only accessible to member states who have an inherent understanding of it, and those countries that the member states deem to be European neighbours. Consequently, to those countries that are just neighbours of Europe, this category is understood to be inaccessible.

The other main pattern that emerged in this chapter was the way practitioners attended to the South Caucasus and Kazakhstan to build up their European qualities. There is no scholarly research that discusses this region in the context of European identity. There are several reasons behind this. For one, the region became more important after the last enlargement, and the Russo-Georgian war in 2008. Also, as EU–Russian relations developed, so did their rivalry for the former Soviet states, which formed the borders between their respective territories. New EU interest in energy supply diversification is another reason for its attention to the region. In spite of all this, what became interesting in this corpus was the ways in which EU practitioners worked up the regions' and Kazakhstan's potential European qualities. In Extract 3.10 the practitioner attributed the origins of European civilisation to Georgia. His vivid description of the civilised Europeans as Georgian, and the uncouth ones as those countries who now call themselves European, was a powerful comparison. Working up such an argument to bring Georgia into the category of the 'European' is significant and effectively questions the moral principles of all Europeans who might question Georgia's European ambitions. Another practitioner in Extracts 3.11 and 3.12 attended to Azerbaijan and Kazakhstan's European credentials. He deployed the discursive device of 'first I thought than I realised' in the case of Azerbaijan by recalling a recent trip to a town near Baku. The contrast of what he initially thought of Baku, that is being a Middle Eastern city, and what he actually found was very telling. Ultimately, he described Baku as a European city, and likened the town in which he stayed to Lisbon, an old European city. Ascribing such entitlement clearly assigns to Azerbaijan the category of the 'European'. The justification for Kazakhstan belonging to this category was managed differently. This time the practitioner relied on the Kazakhs' own expressions of their European credentials as opposed to offering his own assessment. Similarly, in Extract 3.13, a different practitioner managed to ascribe Kazakhstan's European category entitlement in the same way. In addition, this practitioner questioned the relevance of geography and attributed politics as the basis for determining a country's belonging to Europe. This claim is contrary to previous entitlements attributed to the category of the 'European'. However, it is an important one. The following analytical chapters examine such politically motivated alternatives. Next the focus is on the normative role of the EU's interest in the eastern neighbours.

Notes

1 Having said that, research on European identity has mushroomed. Most of these studies explore how the concept fits with other national identities (as in EU member states' national identities) such as the edited volumes of Herrmann *et al.* (2004) and Checkel and Katzenstein (2009), as well Risse (2010); or how it links to Europeanisation such as Harmsen and Wilson (2000), Olsen (2002), Tonra (2001), Knill (2001), Schimmelfennig and Sedelmeier (2005), Graziano and Vink (2006); or to citizenship Habermas (2006a, 2006b); or to Euroscepticism Hooghe and Marks (2007), Szczerbiak and Taggart (2008, 2013).

2 The exception is Rumelili. She locates her work in the poststructuralist tradition of IR theory. Nevertheless she, like all the other scholars, engages with the constructivist literature on identity formation.

3 Article 2 of the Treaty on European Union: the Union is founded on the values of respect for human dignity, freedom, democracy, equality, the rule of law, and respect

for human rights, including the rights of persons belonging to minorities. These values are common to the member states in a society in which pluralism, non-discrimination, tolerance, justice, solidarity, and equality between women and men prevail.

4 This contrast was made already based on geographical grounds (lines 96–7). Other attributions such as accusations, justifications, and complaints are also common when examining moral issues within interactions. All of these, including attributions of blame and responsibility have been discussed extensively within discursive psychology and CA.

5 Responses can be preferred, i.e. in agreement with speaker, or they can be dispreferred, i.e. in disagreement with the speaker.

6 Morocco's application to the EU in 1987 (then the European Economic Community (EEC)) was rejected, based on Morocco not being able to fulfil the Article 49 criteria of being a European country.

7 Or CMD as it's referred to in CA.

8 These conflicts vary from the short war that Georgia and Russia fought over South Ossetian and Abkhaz regions, to the Armenian–Azerbaijani dispute over Nagorno-Karabakh. The cold relations between Turkey and Armenia do not help the region's alliance with the EU.

4

The normative role of the EU in the eastern region

This chapter focuses on norms, and the functions of norms in EU foreign policy. The analysis presented here also offers, along with the next chapter, a form of evaluation of the EU's role as a normative power in the region. It examines what EU practitioners understand as norms and the role of the EU as a normative power in its neighbourhood. It also offers insight into the context in which EU foreign policy is practised through norms which in turn guide the practices of EU practitioners.

Long before references to the normative, the EU was categorised as a civilian power by Duchêne (1972), and later characterised as a soft power (Hill, 1990; Nye, 1990). The development of social constructivism with relations to understanding what kind of actor the EU is, also spurred the introduction of normative theory by EU scholars. Although Christiansen (1997), Weiler (1999), and Laffan (2001) claimed that through treaties, policies, and declarations the EU gradually developed its normative core, it was Manners (2002) who introduced the concept of the EU as a normative power. His description contained the EU shaping, inspiring, and spreading rules and values worldwide, consequently having a 'normalising' effect on international affairs. Moreover, Manners identified five primary norms from the *acquis communautaire* and *acquis politique*, namely peace, liberty, democracy, rule of law, and human rights, and four secondary norms, namely social solidarity, anti-discrimination, sustainable development, and good governance. Such constitutive norms set the EU's polity apart from other states and IR (Manners, 2002: 253).

This independent power of norms to influence other actors' conduct makes the EU a particular type of actor, and thus assigns the EU to a specific analytical category (Diez, 2005: 615). Diez also calls for more empirical investigations into this analytical category. At the same time, he draws attention to studies that validate such analytical category. In these studies, the EU's normative power is more demonstrable in the context of EU membership candidacy where the impact of EU norms is key for joining. Olsen (2002) observes a similar pattern in his study on the different ways that Europeanisation is understood. He identifies five different applications of Europeanisation, two of which are highly relevant for this chapter. One is the effect of rule-following for new member states who are obliged to accept EU policies, institutional requirement, rules, and values (*ibid.*: 927). The other refers to the process of accession that allows the co-development of institutions and institutional norms (*ibid.*: 940). The latter also implies that Europeanisation is based on kinship among EU member states, and on a reflection of their moral duty to reunify Europe.

This EU moral responsibility has also been demonstrated by Sedelmeier (2001) with regard to CEECs. The other variant is the spread of European norms and values beyond European territory. Olsen (2002: 938) argues that traditionally such transfer of European models followed on from 'colonisation, coercion and imposition'. Whereas currently, such norms are emphasised by *inter alia*, the Lisbon process and the Open Method of Coordination (OMC), the development of a distinctly European model of economic efficiency with social justice and responsibility, promoting environment friendly policies (Telo, 2001), as well as through member states using the EU as a common platform on the international stage such as WTO, NATO, and UN (Olsen, 2002). Furthermore, the spread of European models can be attributed to their 'distinctiveness, attractiveness and legitimacy' and the available resources for their diffusion (Olsen, 2002: 940). The concept of rule-following and the acceptance of the same demand from states interested in closer ties with the EU is crucial to Leonard's (2005) thesis as to the way in which the EU diffuses its own model. The EU's own treaty arrangements state that action on the international scene shall be guided by a set of principles which are central to its own existence. The first of these principles is 'democracy' followed by 'the rule of law, the universality and indivisibility of human rights and fundamental freedoms, respect for human dignity, the principles of equality and solidarity, and respect for the principles of the United Nations Charter and international law' (TFEU, Article 21(1)). But whether one could argue for a clear process of Europeanisation, with regard to foreign policy decision, has been questioned by Wong (2007). He maintains, that despite all the convergence of policy decision on the European level, foreign policy is still the *domaine réservé* of the member states, thus of sovereign governments.

Although this understanding is not disputed by Craig and de Búrca (2015: 90), even stating the logical difference between external and EU competencies, they nevertheless draw attention to the limited work of the Court of Justice of the European Union (CJEU) on EU foreign affairs, along with the evolution of Treaty provisions. The CJEU has no jurisdiction over the Common Foreign and Security Policy (CFSP) (TFEU, Article 275) (*ibid.*: 374) although some exceptions apply under Article 40 TEU[1] (Lock, 2015: 87) relating to the boundaries between the CSFP and the rest of EU competencies, and under Article 274 (and 263.4) concerning sanctions being placed on individuals.[2] However, through the implied external competencies and exclusivity, the CJEU has been active, even with great limitations, on foreign matters (Craig and de

Búrca, 2015). These principles have been considered in case law such as *ERTA, Kramer, Inland Waterways, Open Skies, Lugano,* as well the other non-binding secondary legislations, or opinions. Although most of the case law is concerned with trade issues, nevertheless, it is with foreign trade. To the latter point, Article 37 TFEU enabled the Council to agree on international agreements negotiated by the presidency, including CFSP issues, which conferred some legal personality upon the EU. Furthermore, there are expressed external competencies specified in the Treaty which now cover commercial policy, development policy, association agreements, the maintenance of relations between international organisations like the UN or OECD and the Community. In addition, there are two new provisions on CJEU involvement on the CFSP in the Treaty of Lisbon. As mentioned, the CJEU now has jurisdiction, under Article 274(2), to rule on proceedings reviewing the legality of restrictive measures against natural or legal persons. Second, the unified procedure for the conclusion of international agreements as per Article 218 is also under the jurisdiction of the Court through the dissolution of the pillar structure (Eeckhout, 2004: 419) and through the conferral of legal personality upon the Union.

Nonetheless, judicial and parliamentary scrutiny is very limited on CFSP. This is paradoxical in itself for a Union supposedly governed by the rule of law and democracy. These key norms, along with good governance, are what the EU utilises to influence other actors. However, the continual development in this policy area, especially on security and defence, with joint actions and military operations, will be crucial for the EU's evolution as a normative power, together with all other instances where democracy promotion is the expressed aim such as the enlargement and neighbourhood policies or election monitoring.

These developments, and as Manners (2002) claims, the changes in the international system throughout the 1990s and EU leadership in the shaping and promotion of common principles shifted the EU from a civilian to a normative power in world affairs. His argument led to an extensive discussion on the EU's role in the international system beyond its function as a significant economic actor. More recent debates even consider the EU's ethical impact on world politics. The successful utilisation of common European values such as peace, liberty, democracy, the rule of law, and human rights by the EU has been charted over and over, particularly in post-communist central and eastern European states. The EU continues to apply the same principles in its foreign policy, especially in its immediate neighbourhood. The point of departure here is Schimmelfennig's (2001) claim that the EU is a community of liberal democracies. While no one would dispute this, the question is: how does the EU employ these liberal democratic notions in its foreign affairs vis-à-vis the East? Are these norms really transferable? Are the neighbouring countries even interested in accepting these norms?

The most dominant definition of norms in IR links the expected behaviour of specific actors to their appropriate behaviour (March and Olsen, 1989: 51; Katzenstein, 1996: 28). Furthermore, norms can 'either define (or constitute) identities or prescribe (or regulate) behaviour, or they do both' (Katzenstein, 1996: 5). Here Katzenstein draws attention to a key concern for the application (and the attractiveness) of such a sociological approach, as it inherently links norms with morality. He and his collaborators deliberately choose not to focus on 'evaluative norms (stressing questions of morality) or practical norms (focusing on commonly accepted notions of the "best solutions")' (*ibid.*), but rather examine 'regulatory norms' that determine the code of appropriate behaviour and 'constitutive norms' that stipulate identity. This distinction as argued by Wiener (2007) follows a prior sociological distinction made by Morris (1956) between values that are specific and personal, and norms that are prescribed and shared, and thus apply to others. Thereby values can be held by individuals, whereas norms operate within society. In turn, values are subjective and open to bias, but norms are objective and offer a more factual description of society. This analytical differentiation between validity and factuality is widely applied among IR scholars.

For theoretical reasons (and as is made clear in the analysis) such separation between validity and factuality of social practice is not feasible; rather, the two functions merge with each other. However, such separation suits those constructivists who advocate and apply March and Olsen's (1989) 'logic of appropriateness', since this logic deems this distinction structural rather than relational (Wiener, 2007: 50). Wiener also specifies three crucial points that behaviourists and conventional constructivists use to buttress their argument: norms are recognisable and enforceable; legal and social norms do not carry any great distinctions; and types of norms are debates, where contestation of the meaning of a norm between the norm setter and the norm follower are practically unimaginable. While all three rationales are visible in the analytical section of this chapter, the point here is to establish a link between them but also to demonstrate how the lack of contestation between norm setters and norm followers is particularly problematic in the eastern region.

In her article, Wiener (2007) also examines norms as disputed facts through the logic of arguing; another concept that has been mentioned in Chapter 3, p. 40.[3] She argues that problematising normative validity through deliberation does not assume that such validity can be taken for granted. She refers to Risse (2000) and Mueller's (2001, 2004) studies on applying Habermas's theory of communicative action, to demonstrate how such normative validity can be achieved. However, both these authors rely on a shared understanding of truth, moral virtues, and ethical concerns even before applying the notion of deliberation or bargaining, or as per Habermas the logic of arguing. The starting point assumes such shared understandings is problematic for any poststructuralist study. Thus, this chapter examines what norms EU practitioners make relevant, before turning to understanding how those norms are applied and to what result.

There is another theoretical aspect of norm creation that needs to be examined here, and that is constitutionalism. Constitutionalism is the cornerstone of all EU member states' governing systems, as well as the EU's own. There are three key functions that are assigned to modern constitutionalism according to Castiglione (1996: 9–10): it 'constitutes a political entity, establishes its fundamental structure and defines the limits within which power can be exercised politically'. In short, a constitution establishes the fundamental norms of states or state-like structures; while at the same time, it identifies the body of meta-norms or rules that define legal norms and their interpretations (Stone, 1994). Thus, democratic constitutionalism consists of legal limitations or the rule of law, and arbitrary rule or what we know as democracy (Tully, 2002).

Although the EU's constitutional structure has been debated and accepted by many scholars, the EU's IR law stands fragmented. This is because EU foreign policy is dominated by norms arising from at least three different legal orders, including the national, the international, and the overarching EU legal order. Wessel (2006) characterised this as a multilevel-constitution of EU foreign relations. On the contrary, Mendez (2007) has been more critical and described this constitutional picture as 'Byzantine' in nature. Yet the treaties clearly prescribe the norms that the EU is to pursue in foreign policy through Article 21(1) TFEU:

> The Union's action on the international scene shall be guided by the principles which have inspired its own creation, development and enlargement, and which it seeks to advance in the wider world: democracy, the rule of law, the universality and indivisibility of human rights and fundamental freedoms, respect for human dignity, the principles of equality and solidarity, and respect for the principles of the United Nations Charter and international law.

In the following sections the focus is on how practitioners discuss these norms and the role of the EU as a normative power in its neighbourhood. Within the corpus, four main patterns unfold.

The first pattern concerns how norms are constructed, what norms the EU can spread to its neighbours and how practitioners can urge neighbouring states to embrace these norms through the EU's prescribed reform process. In the second pattern, attention shifts to the EU model of norms itself. EU practitioners strive not only to make the specific EU model relevant but also attractive to the neighbours. In addition, they claim to have the necessary expertise to assist these countries to emulate this model. Third, practitioners address two sources of non-compliance: one is non-alignment with the EU model, and the second is the existence of a competing model, the Russian model, that does not quite meet EU standards of norms. Finally, practitioners put forward an all-encompassing EU-centric view that reveals a particular ethnocentric view.

Constructing norms

As stated in the previous section, this book examines the norms and normative practices that EU practitioners draw upon when discussing policy development vis-à-vis the East, rather than taking them for granted. The practitioners refer to specific rules or norms that regulate the EU, which they consider applicable to the neighbouring states. Adapting these constitutional norms is of primary importance for EU practitioners, as will become apparent in the second part of this section.

The norms the EU can spread

Each and every EU practitioner who took part in this study, regardless of their institutional affiliation, could and did list the EU's guiding principles since they are enshrined in the treaties and policies, including the ENP and CFSP. These principles are a reflection of 'European' norms and values. Besides identifying them, the interest of this section is to analyse how they are employed, while constructing policy vis-à-vis the eastern region.

In general, EU practitioners use two different ways to bring EU norms into the conversation during the research interviews. The most obvious one is to answer a specific question on the ideas the EU could export to its eastern neighbouring states, as is the case in Extract 4.1 near the end of the interview. However, most practitioners describe the need for the EU to spread specific norms to its neighbours at different stages of the dialogue without any prompting, as demonstrated in the rest of the extracts in this section. First, however, consider the following practitioner's answer to a direct prompt.

Extract 4.1 – EUIns.22

```
424  R    uh huh (0.2) on that note I've got two more questions to ask
425       you. In a more general view about the EU .hh what do you think
426       is the best idea that the EU could pass on to these neighbours
427       especially in this region?
428  Inv  the principles which are the organising factors of our
429       civilisation.
430  R    and:: they would be?
431  Inv  to have a state of law or a rule of law
432  R    uh huh
433  Inv  ethics as once invented by the Christian world (0.5) prosperity
434       (0.2) peace evolving but based on the freedom of speech (0.1)
435       human rights and and and democratic governance
```

436 R uh huh
437 Inv the philosophical concept of of the human being, one person (.)
438   the dignity of of of mankind.
439 R   <yo:u don't <u>think</u> these already exist in these countries?
440 Inv .hh but it is different
441 R   huh interesting

In lines 425–7 the practitioner is asked directly about the ideas he believes the EU can export to its eastern neighbours. Since the practitioner offers a very broad answer (lines 428–9), referring generally to 'the principles which are the organising factors of our civilisation', there is a further prompt issued in order for her to be more specific (line 430). In her response, the practitioner offers a list of these factors: the state of law or rule of law (line 431), Christian ethics and prosperity (line 433), peace and freedom of speech (line 434), human rights and democratic governance (line 435), and the principles of the individual (lines 437–8), which for her are what constitutes being human. As mentioned previously, listing is a specific discursive device with the aim of constructing descriptions as typical or representative (Jefferson, 1990) in order to develop the authenticity of the account. Furthermore, the components of this very list are not only a catalogue of concepts the EU can export to its eastern neighbours, but they are the norms and guiding principles of 'our civilisation' according to this practitioner. Thus, the practitioner offers a list of what she believes to be the accepted EU norms. What is more, the practitioner's list is not dissimilar to Manners's (2002) inventory of EU norms, as discussed earlier.

The practitioner's initial reply (lines 428–9) 'the principles which are the organising factors of our civilisation' is analytically significant due to the controversial nature of the claim. This reply is the first step in her pursuit to draw a contrast between the EU and its eastern neighbours on the understanding and application of certain norms and standards. In fact, the practitioner appears to imply that we are rooted in different civilisations: usually such contrast structures are built more subtly. Drew (1990: 49) illustrated the delicate operation of counsels in their strategy of juxtaposing testimonies on the non-intimacy of greeting with the intimacy of kissing goodnight during cross-examination. This discursive device can also be found in political speeches (Atkinson, 1984; Heritage and Greatbatch, 1986) or in conflicting accounts between scientists (Mulkay, 1984). After the initial lack of resistance, the researcher orients to the practitioner's use of this contrast structure and issues a direct challenge (line 439), whether these norms are specific to the EU and do not exist in the eastern border states. The practitioner states after an audible in-breath: 'but it is different' (line 440). Her in-breath, instead of an affirmative yes (or no), is analytically important, as it suggests that the practitioner recognises the severity of her position. The practitioner does not question the idea that such norms and principles might be known to the eastern neighbours with her statement 'but it's different', otherwise it would be difficult to argue for further EU cooperation in the region. However, by establishing a contrast she distinguishes between the EU's application of the listed norms as opposed to their application by *others*, such as the eastern neighbours. Thus, a clear distinction can be drawn between EU norms and other norms.[4] Next I consider other less obvious ways of making EU norms relevant.

Extract 4.2 – EUlns.54

```
68 R     you mentioned a little bit earlier but could I ask you to
69       elaborate on why do you think this region is actually important
70       em: for the EU?
71 Inv   emm (0.4) I mean it goes back in a certain sense th- to the
72       creation of the Neighbourhood Policy and in that sense it's
73       (0.4) it's that much applies to Russia as well (.) in other
74       words, the EU sees as one of its major objectives both in
75       security terms but more broadly to create a ring of democratic,
76       prosperous, (0.4) secure a:nd stable neighbours around its
77       borders
78 R     uh uh
```

At the beginning of each research interview, practitioners were asked to reflect on the importance of the eastern neighbourhood. The practitioner in Extract 4.2 considers the main purpose of the EU in the region to be the EU's own security. To achieve this security, the EU needs to 'create a ring of democratic, prosperous, (0.4) secure a:nd stable neighbours' (lines 75–6). Again, the practitioner chooses to rely on the trusted discursive device of listing (Jefferson, 1990) to identify the norms straight out of the policy paper; such as democracy, wealth, security, and stability, which the EU could export to the eastern neighbours to 'create a ring of friends' around the EU who accept the same set of norms. Both Jefferson (1990: 89) and Drew (1990: 54) emphasise the three-part nature of lists. If lists only have two parts, they are seen as incomplete, and subsequently they are completed by a 'generalised list completer' like etcetera. Further, if lists are incomplete, they do not offer the adequate support for an account to be factual. Thus, it is analytically significant that here the practitioner attends to completing the list of norms after a pause of 0.4 seconds on line 76. The stretching on the vowel 'a: nd' adds further hesitation before completing his list with another norm, stability.

Moreover, the admission of the effort to 'create' an eastern neighbourhood that follows EU norms being a key EU objective is important. The practitioner not only links this objective to the establishment of the ENP (line 72), but to Russia (line 73) as an eastern neighbour, despite the fact that Russia is not part of the ENP.

In the next extract, the practitioner reproduces a list of norms that the EU can export to the region (lines 297–8) – just like the other practitioners in previous extracts, but this time it is part of the discussion on the effects of enlargement policy on the CEECs.

Extract 4.3 – EUIns.8

288	Inv	<so:: Neighbourhood Policy replaces in a way:: (0.6)
289	R	aha:
290		enlargement policy (0.6) <u>the strength</u> of the Neighbourhood
291		Policy as foreign policy if the Union was that yo- (0.2)
292		(inaudible) you know French?
293	R	a little
294	Inv	I don't know the English term hmm mm
295	R	that's fine
296	Inv	(0.4) the sun sends light and this is (inaudible) in French
297		(1) so:: the Union was exporting democracy human rights emh
298		market economy (.) eh state of law principles outsi- via
299		enlargement policy (0.4) <now it is starting a:nd as I hope
300		will even <u>more</u> .hh do the same with Neighbourhood [Policy]
301	R	[uh huh]
302	Inv	which itself to go back to what I said before should be an open
303		ended process .hh NOT precluding enlargement
304	R	ok

Besides the list formation, the practitioner applies another two ways to demonstrate the way to accomplish norm distribution. One is the practitioner's alignment of the ENP with the enlargement policy (lines 288 and 291), which is a direct declaration by the practitioner that ENP supersedes the enlargement policy. The second instance is where the practitioner states that '<now it is starting a: nd as I hope will even more .hh do the same with Neighbourhood [Policy] which itself to go back to what I said before should be an open ended process .hh NOT precluding enlargement' (lines 299–303). On both occasions the practitioner makes it abundantly clear that perhaps the initial outcomes of the policy are different but their aim of 'exporting democracy human rights emh market economy (.) eh state of law principles' (lines 297–8) is the same.

Second, the practitioner's social action here is packaged within a description (Edwards and Potter, 1992). This is analytically interesting. In order to apportion responsibility to the EU, and to justify its own attempts to distribute its norms, the practitioner decides to use a French concept that translates as 'the sun sends light' (line 296). Through this term, he likens the EU to the sun. This rather dramatic analogy assigns a very powerful role to the EU, i.e. to spread its norms; the EU is positioned as the sun, with the other countries like planets around it. Collective accountability is linked to this achieved action if such responsibility is expected of the EU.

The final extract in this section considers the essence of the ENP and the kind of neighbours the EU would like to have.

Extract 4.4 – EUIns.13

```
46 Inv   the essence of this policy is the best eh (0.4) I don't know
47        (.) expressing in this: non political, and non legal term .hh
48        ring of friends ring of friends
49 R      right uhm mm
50 Inv    it's the idea of having neighbours who are not that different
51        in terms of thei- kind of conduct friendly who- with whom we
52        have a close economic ties ((simultaneously phone rings
53        interviewee switches off for 32 seconds))
54 R      you said .hh close economic ties
55 Inv    close economic but eh the relationship which is being built it
56        is not there, it is being built gives to the Union a security
57        through stability
58 R      uh huh
59 Inv    and chances of prosperity because of the economic eh links
60 R      ok fair enough eh
61 Inv    so those who are around us help us to achieve our fundamental
62        goals which are external security internal security and
63        prosperity
64    R    ok
```

The practitioner's main concern here is to establish the importance of norms such as peace, security and stability, and prosperity, which are apparent in her references to 'kind of conduct friendly' neighbours (line 51), in addition to the desire for 'close economic ties' (line 52) to increase chances of prosperity (line 59). At the same time, she also emphasises the reciprocal nature of sharing these norms with the neighbours, as they will also mean stability and prosperity for the EU. There are two examples of this reciprocal relationship, first at lines 55–7 where the practitioner states that 'the relationship which is being built it is not there, it is being built gives to the Union a security through stability', and, second, at lines 61–3 where she asserts that 'those who are around us help us to achieve our fundamental goals which are external security internal security and prosperity'. Thus, there is an aim of 'having neighbours who are not that different' (line 50), which is achieved by spreading norms to the neighbouring countries.

Before the practitioner embarks on her description of the 'essence of this policy' (line 46), she begins with a 4-second pause and with 'I don't know'. This assertion can be seen as a disclaimer, similar to the kind Hewitt and Stokes

(1975) coined as 'hedging'. 'Hedging' indicates a minimal commitment to the impending statement and the possibility to receive discrepant information. A classic example of hedging is 'I am not an expert, but [claim]' (*ibid.*). As an EU practitioner who is developing this policy, she cannot quite follow the classical format but by using a disclaimer, she attempts to ward off negative attributions by signalling minimal commitment to her initial explanation (lines 47–8). The 'ring of friends' concept is a reference from the 2003 ENP policy paper but clearly this is not something the practitioner feels fully committed to, preferring instead the norms and the importance of spreading these norms to neighbours (line 50).

Finally, I would like to return to the notion of reciprocity and its theoretical implication. All the above extracts dealt with norms that the EU can export to its neighbours. Nevertheless, these extracts also imply that practitioners are also concerned with reciprocity, or, rather, the EU's own interests in external security and stability; as this practitioner put: 'so those who are around us help us to achieve our fundamental goals which are external security internal security and prosperity' (lines 61–3). Therefore, the EU's own quest to achieve the fundamental norms it set out to attain such as democracy, the rule of law, the universality and indivisibility of human rights and fundamental freedoms, respect for human dignity, the principles of equality and solidarity, respect for the principles of the United Nations Charter, and international law can only be done if other bordering states also adhere to these norms. This demonstrates that norms and interests, security and economic, cannot necessarily be separated. It also leads us to question scholarly arguments that insist on the dissociation of norms and interests. By this, I do not suggest that either norms or interests can be seen as more important than the other, but, rather, that they are always constructed simultaneously and in parallel with each other.

'Please keep on the tab of … reform process'

This section focuses on the importance of monitoring whether the process of EU norm diffusion is continued and implemented. Many EU practitioners raised these topics but I would like to focus on two extracts from one particular practitioner.

Extract 4.5 – EUIns.43

120	R	what do you think the challenges are as far as uhm that region
121		is concerned?
123	Inv	yeah dealing with Ukraine:: umh once (.) one challenge I
124		mentioned to you is: of course this issue of membership
125		perspective.=how do we balance this?=how do we keep on saying
126		to Ukraine yes .hhh <because we're no- (0.2) the first message
127		haven't actually (0.2) .hhh go on and <u>please</u> keep on the tab of

128   European economic and political reform process, .hh of course
129   they had an orange revolution and the work is not <u>done</u> with the
130   orange revol[ution]
131 R   [hmmm]
132 Inv and so much work course they have excellent political will,
133   they can do so many things with that <u>but</u> it doesn't mean tha:t
134   political will is everything and reform process and the
135   membership process takes quite a lot of time.
136 R   hmm
137 Inv and my mother was born in eastern Europe, .hhh in Eastern
138   Germany
139 R   hmm
140   and you can see how long even in Germany it takes .hh for
141   Eastern Germany to so so of course they have to stay on this
142   path of reform for quite a while <and the civility of the
143   country of course is a bit of an issue <so it's definitely not
144   easy how do we keep being attractive? <or keeping Ukraine on
145   this reform path (0.2) without being::: sometimes hijacked by
146   their argumentation saying o::h if you don't give us the
147   membership we will turn our back our back (0.2) and turn back
148   to <u>Russia</u>!

Extract 4.6 – EUIns.43

167 R   a::nd your third point is?
168 Inv a third challenge I would say with Ukraine is is this
169   implementation challenge. they love to make big statements, love
170   to shout out because it's an old soviet way. you shout for one
171   hundred so at least you get forty
172 R   (hmn) okay a:nd how do you deal with that?
173 Inv so:: we concentrate on the membership issue whenever we say oh
174   maybe you should do this and that .hhh and reform that sector
175   yes we've passed a law is a good thing of course <but then you
176   also have to <u>implement</u> it in a way I say what would they do if
178   we <u>gave</u> them the membership (.) .hhh then they now really be
179   looked at o:f course, we are very strict with them and they
180   do a lot homework (0.2) then they would not be able to shout
181   again
182 R   then?
183 Inv they would really have to concentrate on implementation.
(omitted)
192   oh yes you're telling us about the usual pro human rights
193   .hhh respect for human rights standards a:nd for rule of law

```
194      through the pen of the judiciary <but we will never come back
195      like with Russia and say oh: actually not as good as good as
196      you at telling us. who are you preaching to the outside? No
197      Ukrainians will ever say .hh oh yes we have passed law but
198      we're actually doing this because we want to be part of the
199      Union
200 R    right.
```

Both extracts (4.5 and 4.6) focus on the potential of Ukrainian membership through political reforms and 4.6 more with the importance of implementation of the reforms. However, analytically they both attend to the practitioner's own accountability and the way he apportions blame. The action of blaming is packaged in a description (Edwards and Potter, 1992). In Extract 4.5 the practitioner after two abandoned turn construction units (TCUs)[5] ('hhh <because we're no- (0.2) the first message haven't actually (0.2)') implies the difficulty of keeping Ukraine on task to comply with EU norms (lines 125–8): '=how do we keep on saying to Ukraine yes .hhh <because we're no- (0.2) the first message haven't actually (0.2) .hhh go on and please keep on the tab of European economic and political reform process'. The rules of turn-taking determine that a delay through an abandoned TCU, or two in this case, only works up the difficulty of what is to come (Sacks et al., 1974), in this extract: 'go on and please keep on the tab of European economic and political reform process'. As if the practitioner almost has to plead with the Ukrainians to continue to comply with these norms. By lines 132–5, the practitioner brings attention to the fact that reform in itself is not enough. The process of reform has to go hand in hand with political will. In doing so, along with his earlier intervention of abandoning two basic turns (TCUs), the practitioner embeds the action of blaming. According to his argument, the EU is merely attempting to keep a neighbouring state on the path of reform (more precisely compliance with EU norms), but it is Ukraine who is reluctant, or has to be continuously reminded. The direct quotation that the practitioner employs: 'o: : h if you don't give us the membership we will turn our back our back (0.2) and turn back to Russia!' (lines 146–8) works to the same effect. The active voicing device (Wooffitt, 1991, 2005) used here demonstrates an 'unexpected' turn to threaten the EU with Ukraine's veering off to Russia and leaving the reform process and EU norms behind. Thus, the practitioner's own personal accountability, along with the EU's diminishes. Instead Ukraine is to blame if it is not successful in complying with EU norms.

This action of embedded blaming continues in Extract 4.6, but the focus turns on implementation of these reforms. The practitioner continues to switch between direct quotes and description. His use of active voicing clearly demonstrations that if Ukraine fails to comply with EU norms, it is not the practitioner's personal responsibility. Examples of this active voicing can be seen in: 'oh yes you're telling us about the usual pro human rights .hhh respect for human rights standards a: nd for rule of law through the pen of the judiciary' (lines 193–4); 'who are you preaching to the outside?' (line 196); and in '.hh oh yes we have passed law but we're actually doing this because we want to be part of the Union' (lines 197–9). In other words, he is not accountable for the Ukrainians' actions, or more precisely non-action.

The notion of non-compliance with EU norms or the potential of contestation of any norms through non-compliance is practically inconceivable. This practitioner's account further supports Wiener's (2007) claim that there is never room for a norm follower to dispute or debate the meaning or the relevance of a specific norm. Interestingly, the Ukrainians' wavering path of reform and the potential risk of Russian involvement in Ukraine,[6] are still not strong enough threats for policymakers, or norm setters, to engage in any contestation on norms. Rather, they deny any personal responsibility for the situation and blame Ukraine.

The EU as a model

The EU model is considered in this section through the practitioners' accounts, or in other analytical terms, the relevance of the model for the neighbours.[7]

Emulating the EU model

The next three extracts follow on from the question of what the EU can offer its neighbours. In these extracts, the practitioners not only refer to the EU model, but also offer justifications for its attractiveness.

Extract 4.7 – EUIns.26

771	Inv	what we can export is the stability security prosperity that we
772		ha-(.) the model we have built for ourselves
773	R	hmmm
774	Inv	knowing these three are interlinked .hhh and knowing that they
775		are now also interlinked with thei::r you know that this is a
776		mutual [thing so its]
777	R	[uh huh is it?]
778	Inv	not so much an idea but the the concrete reality that makes
779		life better
780	R	uh huh
781	Inv	IF somebody has economic prospects not to make a fortune but if
782		the <u>average</u> person can make a living .hh put a little bit aside
783		for a rainy day (.)
784	R	uh huh
785	Inv	.hh see their children go to school, know they are going to
786		have a better future than <u>them</u>selves .hhh can express their

```
787      views down at the pub, or at the mosque, or >wherever< without
788      the secret police knocking on their door emm (0.8) they are not
789      threatened with becoming refugee
790 R    uh huh
791 Inv  because their local government is fighting with the central
792      government, you know .hh if they could just have a normal,
793      stable, secure, re:latively prosperous life
794 R    uh huh
795 Inv  that's all anybody really wants anywhere
796 R    right
```

Extract 4.8 – EUIns.27

```
526 Inv  these neighbours can imitate this model which is not a perfect
527      one but (.) it's better than the Somali model heh [heh]
528 R                                                      [hehh]
529 Inv  or whatever and and it's something that they're keen in
530      emulating. .hhh some keener than others <particularly those
531      with European aspirations keener than those that don't .hhh and
532      this is what we can offer.
533 R    and and that would be?
534 Inv  I mean (.) we can offer the model we have developed for
535      ourselves which has helped us integrate within the EU. it has
536      been able to overcome deep historic divisions and all kinds of
537      other things
```

Extract 4.9 – EUIns.32

```
14 R     what's the mos- the best idea that the EU can offer to the
15       region?
16 Inv   the best idea?
17 R     yes?
18 Inv   (0.2) I've never thought of that from that point of view. (0.3)
19       I suppose the most important aspect for us towards them is to
20       stil- is to have a good and secure neighbourhood which uhm is
21       developing with no big fault lines where uhm: they will have
22       some kind of EU refined government model.
23 R     okay::
24 Inv   that area I think it's very much a question of our own
25       interests.
```

These three extracts are concerned with the neighbouring states emulating the EU model. The practitioner in Extract 4.7 qualifies this model through a three-part list formation (Jefferson, 1990) of stability, security, and prosperity that makes his description representative and complete. Analytically it is also interesting how he manages to insert the word 'model' into a self-repair sequence (Sacks *et al.*, 1974; Schegloff *et al.*, 1977): 'what we can export is the stability security prosperity that we ha- (.) the model we have built for ourselves' (lines 771–2). By cutting off 'we ha-', which is also a pre-frame of the repair, and the micro pause (.), the practitioner initiates a repair sequence. The repair solution comes with the insertion of the word 'the model' and he continues where he initially left off, or more technically with the post-frame of 'have', and finishes the sentence with 'we have built for ourselves'. The insertion of the words 'the model' is significant here as it defines the nature of 'what we have built for ourselves' and allows the practitioner to work up the 'European' way of living, as a model society.

The other analytically important point in this extract is: '.hh if they could just have a normal, stable, secure, re: latively prosperous life uh huh that's all anybody really wants anywhere' (lines 792–5). As mentioned in Chapter 4, extreme-case formulations are common when the speaker is engaged in moral activities such as justifying (Pomerantz, 1978, 1984). Thus, formulations like 'anybody' and 'anywhere' elicit the social action of justifying the EU model. The practitioner also adds 'normal' to his list of defining adjectives of the EU model, which further implies that this model should be the conventional or mainstream way of life for all to aspire to.

Contrasting the EU model with the Somalian way of life works to a similar effect in Extract 4.8; 'these neighbours can imitate this model which is not a perfect one but (.) it's better than the Somali model heh [heh]' (lines 526–7). Here the practitioner is not only keen to imply a contrast, but to juxtapose two extremes: the European v. the Somali model. Drawing a distinction between the norm and the alternative through such extreme contrast structures (Edwards, 1997: 237) leaves the listener with no real choice, and strengthens the practitioner's argument. However, the difficulty with relying on an argument based on the contrast between extremes is that we all know the choice for the eastern neighbours is not merely between these two models of governance. The overlapping laughter tokens at the end of line 527 '[heh]' and from the researcher '[hehh]' (line 528) are also demonstrative of the troubled nature of the practitioner's claim (Jefferson, 1994). Nevertheless, as the practitioner admits, the model is 'something they're keen in emulating', where 'they' refers to the eastern neighbours (lines 529–30).

Consider next Extract 4.9 where the practitioner again implies that the best idea the EU can offer its eastern neighbours is to emulate 'some kind of EU refined government model' (line 22). What is interesting in her account is that on two occasions she directly links this beneficial model with the EU's own interest. The first example comes in her answer to the initial question (after some delay and hesitation at lines 16 and 18); 'I suppose the most important aspect for us towards them is to stil- is to have a good and secure neighbourhood which uhm is developing with no big fault lines' (lines 19–21). The second example comes when she reiterates 'that area I think it's very much a question of our own interests' (lines 24–5). Such association is both analytically and theoretically interesting, as it suggests that separating the EU's normative intentions from its interests is unattainable. This further supports the argument that these notions are produced in parallel, and that disassociation of the two is ill conceived.

The next extracts follow in a similar vein, after the question of what the EU can offer the EU's neighbours. Each practitioner gives an example of countries that are starting to emulate the EU model.

Extract 4.10 – EUIns.12

75	Inv	I was recently in Morocco and chaired a meeting there and and
76		i- that sector was dealing with at that time em with the
77		question how close the Moroccans have moved to our normal best
78		practices standards etc
79	R	but the main point you would say is the reform that [basically]
80	Inv	[the main]
81		point is the reform which which is a reform where many of our
82		neighbours are willing to model their reform on the European
83		model em (.) to the extent that it can apply to them with you
84		know: .hhh and the main difference between the enlargement
85		process and and the neighbourhood policy is that em you can be
86		confused where it makes sense to align more than align for with
87		everything
88	R	uh huh

Extract 4.11 – EUIns.38

252	Inv	umh .hhh it's clear to me that we're going to get much more
253		cooperation from countries like Ukraine than we are from
254		Russia= why? because::e one the Ukrainians are much more open
255		to Europe, to the European model °than the° Russians are .hh
256		and they don't see Europe as a compe[titor]
257	R	[then] as [what?]
257	Inv	[but] as more of
258		a partner to work with, umh a:nd we started today negotiations
259		with Ukraine on new agreement. .hh it was clear from
260		that meeting tha:t the Ukrainians are willing to go as far as
261		absolutely >as far as is necessary< .hh in developing economic
262		relations with the EU, because they have the overall objective
263		of economic integration, a:nd the Russians don't have that
264		objective of course

While in Extract 4.10 Morocco is used as an example, in Extract 4.11 the contrast between Ukraine and Russia is highlighted to exemplify those neighbours which emulate the EU model. In Extract 4.10 the practitioner refers to a meeting where the question was not whether, if at all, the Moroccans had accepted EU norms, but rather 'how close the Moroccans have moved to our normal best practice standards etc' (lines 77–8). Then between lines 81 and 83 he implies more generally the appeal of the EU model 'many of our neighbours are willing to model their reform on the European model'. Another practitioner in Extract 4.11 follows in a similar vein but evokes a contrast between Ukraine and Russia to illustrate neighbours who are our competitors, i.e. Russia (line 254) or our partners i.e. Ukraine (same line). The contrast structure here is analytically interesting (Edwards, 1997), as well as its co-construction between the practitioner and the researcher. The practitioner links the two competing particles with a conjunction of 'but' to make the comparison explicit, but only after a prompt from the researcher '[then] as [what?]' (line 257) does he provide more information on the contrast: 'one the Ukrainians are much more open to Europe to the European model °than the° Russians are .hh and they don't see Europe as a compe[titor] (lines 254–6), and [but] as more of a partner to work with' (lines 257–8). He continues with giving a concrete illustration of the Ukrainian commitment to the EU model by referring to the recent negotiations of the new treaty with Ukraine (line 258).

'[We] actually know how to transform countries'

Building on the above point the next five extracts each illustrate a different way the EU can assist neighbour states with transforming their system to replicate the 'European' model. Such assistance can involve monitoring, offering advice, information exchange on technical issues, or the application of the classic carrot-and-stick model by the EU. The theoretical implication of these 'supportive' actions only demonstrates the asymmetric nature of the relationship between the EU and its neighbours.

Extract 4.12 – EUIns.49

```
213  Inv   well:: we hav-, we monitor the implementation of the ENP action
214        plans e:m which are action plans that bind both sides (.) I
215        mean we have to do our homework to fulfil the [commitments]
216  R                                                  [sure]=
217  Inv   =there but we monitor that em partly as outcome of the policy
218        dialogue that we have with these countries e:m whe- when we go
219        there, we exchange information with them. we get information
220        from them, what has ha:ppened .hh we discuss it, we see the
221        people, how they act, how the change or whatever (0.2) and then
```

222		of course in all these countries (.) we have not quite all <u>but</u>
223		by next nearly al-, we will have EU delegations, so they will
224		also monitor etcetera etcetera
225	R	okay but how do you monitor o- or check?
226	Inv	as you <u>sa:w</u> we made progress reports which also monitor for the
227		public (.) and public domain where we see progress being made
228		but also what I'd quite like to see over time is (.) .hh there
229		are certain sectors where monitoring should not really be on
230		the administrators' hands
231	R	uhm but?
232	Inv	bureaucrats being bureaucrats where you would need so- sort of
233		civil society stakeholders to take the place of human rights
234	R	uh huh.

This first extract is about monitoring. The practitioner offers an account of how the implementation of the action plan is monitored through the practitioner's team (lines 217–21), through the EU delegations (lines 222–4), and through the country progress reports (line 226). All this official oversight focuses on whether the neighbouring country is complying with the action plans, which contain EU norms. Although the practitioner initially claims that the action plans 'bind both sides', and continues with 'I mean we have to do our homework to fulfil the [commitments]' (line 214), there is no demonstration whether or how the EU's commitments are monitored. This clearly indicates the asymmetric relationship between the EU and its neighbours.

Admittedly the practitioner launches a complaint that certain norms should not be monitored by the EU but their own civil society, in: '.hh there are certain sectors where monitoring should not really be on the administrators hands' (lines 228–30), and again in: 'bureaucrats being bureaucrats where you would need so- sort of civil society stakeholders to take the place of human rights' (lines 232–4). The practitioner's complaint has a wider effect. If the neighbouring states cannot or do not want to monitor their own human rights violations, then the application of such EU norms are a contradiction of the norms themselves. There are two possible understandings of this. First, those practitioners who are following the application of EU norms believe that the development of civil society is intrinsic to the implementation of these reforms, thus the process ought to be organic rather than something that needs specific top-down oversight. Second, those countries that are supposed to absorb these norms go through this process without applying the deeper societal levels of change that such norms presuppose. Either explanation would only further support the theoretical point raised before, that without investigating the process of norm creation, no shared or common-sense notion of 'norms', can be accepted.

Next, I consider how an EU practitioner describes advice as a form of assistance.

Extract 4.13 – EUIns.60 EU

231	R	ar- aren't these action plans jus:t quite protectionist?
232	Inv	I don't think you can say tha- that, it's you know
233		protectionism towards the neighbourhood .hh when what we're
234		doing is actually the opposite. the mos- uhm an awful lot of
235		the action plan is about helping to bring down the non tariff
236		barriers to these countries, gaining <u>access</u> to the general
237		market .hh a:nd as ever there are one or two celebrated cases
238		where there is some resistance, where the cuffs of comparative
239		advantages are applied, o:r whatever <but if you if you were
240		protecting us you wouldn't b- you would <u>not</u> be sending European
241		officials out into these countries to <u>advise</u> them on how to
242		bring their legislation that stands in line with us, <u>if</u> you
243		protectionist. you wouldn't do that.

Consider the practitioner's disagreement that 'what we're doing is actually the opposite' (lines 233–4) of what the researcher suggested, which was to link the ENP action plans to protectionism. The notion of protectionism has clearly stuck a chord with the practitioner, as she returns to it (line 239), offering a further justification as to why the action plans are not protectionist '<but if you if you were protecting us you wouldn't b- you would not be sending European officials out into these countries to <u>advise</u> them on how to bring their legislation that stands in line with us, <u>if</u> you protectionist. you wouldn't do that.' Her justification is based on two points. First of all, practitioners, like herself, offer advice to these states. This advice is presented as crucial, and it is another way, besides monitoring, that the EU is assisting the neighbouring states to emulate the EU model. Second, the advice includes strategies for bringing their legislation in line with EU laws, thus complying with EU norms. But the practitioner's justification is contentious, and her speech illustrates the fact that she is aware of this. From line 234 onwards she offers a description of the action plans. Analytically it is interesting that she abandons 'the mos-', hesitates with the 'uhm', then changes it to 'an awful lot of the action plan' before she talks about their relevance to trade. If the action plans only concerned trade, then her criticism of the researcher's reference to protectionism would be justified. But the practitioner accepts, since she corrected herself, that the actions plans are not just about trade. Such error correction is common and follows the Error Correction Format devised by Jefferson (1974) of [WORD$_1$ + HESITATION + WORD$_2$]. The 'mos-' becomes a recognisable word beginning but through its abandonment it becomes recognisable as an error beginning, especially since it has been the error that has been corrected with the words 'an awful lot'. Thus, the advice is not just about trade arrangements between the EU and its neighbours but rather about norm compliance. Trade issues take up most of the bilateral arrangements but even these are inherently linked with compliance to EU norms.

Another practitioner seems similarly engrossed with issues around compliance.

Extract 4.14 – EUIns.5

```
229 R     and the challenges I was ehh interested in [e-]
230 Inv                                          [exa]mples of them?
231 R     hmm yup
232       (0.5)
233 Inv   you name it and it's it's a challenge! we need a-, more
234       compliance in the neighbourhood, because we have everything
235       they don't
236 R     (hh) okay::=
237 Inv   =and we can share this (0.4) we actually know how to transform
238       countries (0.2) .hh we are not seeking to transform our
239       neighbourhood but we know how to support >whatever< reforms
240       they choose to do.
241 R     right
243 Inv   and we can push them a little bit if we want to
244 R     sure how?
245 Inv   we also know that there is a competitive thing tha- that
246       happens once reforms happen there is spill over within a
247       country to different sectors
248 R     yup [such as?]
249 Inv        [and] maybe also to neighbouring countries. I mean
250       this is a long term policy.
251 R     uh huh
252 Inv   this is not something that's going to produce overnight
253       results, or five year results (0.6) .hh this is something that
254       we will all look back and write books about in fifteen years,
255       twenty years about how some of the countries made progress.
```

This extract focuses on the practitioner's answer to the challenges the EU has in the eastern region: 'you name it and it's it's a challenge! we need a-, more compliance in the neighbourhood, because we have everything they don't' (lines 233–5), continued '=and we can share this (0.4) we actually know how to transform countries' (lines 237–8). The upshot of his statement is that the EU has the know-how, the expertise, and the experience to assist neighbouring states to conform to the EU model, and that this is supposed to be their aspiration. However, the practitioner backs down, and after some hesitation, a 0.2-second pause and an in-breath, he claims that 'we are not seeking to transform our neighbourhood but we know how to support >whatever< reforms they choose to do' (lines 238–40). He spends the rest of the extract developing a more subtle account of the transformative impact that such a reform process might have on a country, arguing that the benefits are likely to spill over into different sectors (line 246), or to different countries (line 249), and will be recorded in historic accounts of these countries progress (lines 254–5).

The imbalance in the relationship between the EU and ENP states is addressed in the following extract.

Extract 4.15 – EUIns.18

402	R	but it's very interesting what you mention be- because I mean
403		the EU obviously often get criticised for having this kind of
404		asymmet[ric?]
405	Inv	[yes]
406	R	relationship and .hhh how are you going to deal with that?
407	Inv	of course I think they are (0.4) they are happy about the kind
408		of information exchange that we (0.4) that we have on technical
409		issues
410	R	of course
411	Inv	to know to really (0.4) to learn from our experience that I
412		think (0.2) in that sense we have <u>influence</u> I think
413	R	uh huh
414	Inv	but when it comes to the more (0.4) bigger political (0.4)
415		things then I think (0.2)eh the incentives are quit-,
416		the incentives are quite important.

This practitioner also focuses more on the practical aspects of EU assistance to neighbouring states who are keen to emulate the EU model. Without showing any denial or strong reaction to the provocative reference to the asymmetric relationship the EU is having with its neighbours, he describes the positive aspect of this imbalance. The practitioner concerns himself with the importance of information exchange on technical issues (lines 407–8). Then he qualifies this, stating that other countries can 'learn from our experience' (line 411). Thus, the asymmetry in this relationship is justifiable, owing to its benefits to the other, here, to the neighbouring states. He also refers to the EU's influence (line 412), but at the same time claims that for larger political issues 'the incentives are quite important' (line 416). Thus, the practitioner audibly accepts that, for the substantive decisions, such technical assistance or information exchange alone will not suffice.

Incentives are further explained by another practitioner in the next extract.

Extract 4.16 – EUIns.21

194	R	so basically migration and and you were saying just illegal
195		immigrations, strengthen the kind of cooperation are th- are
196		the main main ideas?
197	Inv	yeah. I think the main ideas is clearly through the ENP what
198		we're trying to do i- <u>very much</u> like we would try to do anyway
199		in enlargement an- accession do you know as a as a .hh but on a
200		different level is to export <u>our</u> values
201	R	hmm
202	Inv	at least perhaps <u>try</u> to £encourage the reform process and the
203		ENP .hhh as a part of a classic carrot and stick °where if you
204		don't if you're not willing° .hh <if you're <u>willing</u> to reform,
205		to politically, <u>to do</u> more for the rule of law, <u>to</u>: consolidate
206		democracy, a:::h <u>to</u> ensure respect of human rights a::h a::h
207		press freedom °these're king of things°
208	R	hmm
209	Inv	<u>then</u> you will <u>get</u> some mone:<u>y</u> from the ENPI and I from the
210		different assistance programmes, .hh you will get more assistance
211		from the EU so c- technical technical support etcetera a::h and
212		this <u>is</u>=how it works of course.

The final extract in this section on the EU model focuses on how the EU can assist neighbours to comply with EU norms, and makes a reference to the 'classic carrot and stick' method (line 203). This method is characterised by both the offer of reward and the threat of punishment. The answer is triggered by a question concerning the best idea that the EU can offer to its neighbours. The practitioner's response is 'to export our values' (line 200), which is in line with all the previous practitioners. It also provides further evidence to support Wiener's (2007) argument that values and norms are interlinked. Furthermore, the practitioner offers a list of what he believes these values to be, i.e. political reform (lines 204–5), the rule of law (line 205), consolidation of democracy (lines 205–6), respect for human rights (line 206), and press freedom (line 207). The practitioner's use of listing creates the impression that 'our values' (line 200) are normal and standard (Jefferson, 1990).

To return to the initial point of the carrot-and-stick method, the practitioner does offer some insight into what such practice entails. He begins with an attempt to explain the punishment side (lines 203–4) '°where if you don't if you're not willing°' in a quiet voice. Then after a short in-breath he suddenly switches to 'if you are willing' juxtaposing the punishment with reward. Later on (from line 209), he even offers a more precise illustration of this offer, i.e. 'some money', 'technical support etcetera' (line 211) from the European Neighbourhood and Partnership Instrument (ENPI) and other EU assistance programmes. He finally declares 'this is=how it works of course' (line 212), referring to the way in which the carrot-and-stick method enforces compliance in the neighbourhood. The problem for the ENP as a policy tool is that the application of the carrot-and-stick model is inherently challenging, as there is no EU membership on the table for partner states. This model was further developed after the 2011 Review, whereby states who reform more, receive more support. Nevertheless, compliance or the lack of it remains the main concern for practitioners as the following section will reveal.

Issues with (non)compliance

Relations between the EU and the eastern neighbours have never been straight-forward. This issue stems from the geographical position of the region, their proximity, and their historical connection to Russia. This region has been historically contentious between the EU and Russia. Russia applies a different concept to the region, rather than the neighbourhood, they insist on calling it their 'near abroad'. This is a loaded concept. The notion of 'near abroad' conveys a sense of closeness and 'not-quite-abroad-ness' that the current amalgamation of the EU states cannot understand, as they are excluded from this 'Slavonic brotherhood'.[8] The notion of 'neighbourhood' should support some form of community, where the EU and its bordering states belong, but its application to all states on the EU borders dilutes any strong sense of the community notion.

Competing models in the region

The following three extracts are concerned with competing models of governance in the eastern region. The Russian model is referred to as a competing model throughout. Let us begin with Extract 4.17, in which the practitioner offers a clear example of competing governance models and even values.

Extract 4.17 – EUIns.52

```
352 R     are y- are you suggesting that Russian belligerence to Belarus
353       is affecting its relations with the EU? [Could y'exp-]
354 Inv                                        [the Russians are]
355       making a big mistake in the way they deal with their
356       neighbours. umhm but not really much has followed u-, there's
357       not been much followed on the ground there's not been a great
358       deal of change on the ground .hh the
359 R     hmm
360 Inv   THE Ukrainians are very heavily involved in try:ing to
361       encourage the Belarusians to umhm: to be more cooperative, but
362       at the moment we don't really hav->as a result of this
363       situation any real contact within the ENP. there's no action
```

```
364       plan to deal with Belarus and a:nd umh it's difficult to really
365       see how things are going to progress.
366 R     do you mean Belarus needs to shed some some of the long
367       established Russian values?
368 Inv   I mean, we of all have to see how far umhm Lukashenko is
369       willing to open up the country in return for umhm: for (0.4)
370       greater contacts with the EU,
```

The practitioner in this extract complains about the non-compliance of Belarus, or more precisely the Belarusian President, Lukashenko. Belarus is a perfect example of a situation in which EU sanctions are applied for the advancement of pro-democratic reforms, the rule of law, and requirements for free-market liberties. Non-compliance in itself is no news to anyone following events in Belarus. However, what is analytically more significant is the way the practitioner blames Russia for this non-compliance, asserting that 'the Russians are making a big mistake in the way they deal with their neighbours' (lines 354–6). Packaging of social actions in descriptions can vary from being direct to something highly indirect (Edwards and Potter, 1992), but in both instances their effect remains the same. Not only are the Russians making a big mistake, with the emphasis on 'big', but they do not even care about their neighbours as 'not really much has followed u-, there's not been much followed on the ground there's not been a great deal of change on the ground' (lines 356–8), including in Belarus.

Despite the Ukrainians' help with Belarusian adherence to EU norms: 'THE Ukrainians are very heavily involved in try:ing to encourage the Belarusians to umhm: to be more cooperative' (lines 360–1), the practitioner claims that progress is difficult to judge. Also, the way in which the practitioner aligns the Ukrainians with the EU, positioning them as advocates, if not defenders of 'European' norms, is significant. Differentiating between those who encourage EU norm compliance, i.e. the Ukrainians, and those who do not, i.e. the Russians is theoretically important for distinguishing between those who are similar to the self, and those who are the other.

Another practitioner has a different view of the Ukrainian allegiance.

Extract 4.18 – EUIns.9

```
306 R     the challenges for Ukraine? you [mentioned]
307 Inv                           [the challe]nges so that's
308       going to be where the problem is is convincing them of:: the
309       need for a lot of the things in the agreement that they perhaps
310       would like to avoid
311 R     such as?
312 Inv   umm there's going to be big problems including I think anything
313       abo- obviously the Russians. <they say officially they say
```

314   they share our values of course:: BUT they have a different
315   interpretation of certain things so: <u>how far</u> we can actually go
316   in terms of uhmm putting things in the new agreement as clearly
317   as we'd like <u>is</u> remains to be seen

The practitioner employs a contrast structure (Edwards, 1997) between the official and the unofficial Ukrainian discourse during the new agreement's negotiation process. She offers a complaint about the Ukrainians: '<they say officially they say they share our values of course: : BUT they have a different interpretation of certain things so: how far we can actually go in terms of uhmm putting things in the new agreement as clearly as we'd like <u>is</u> remains to be seen' (lines 313–17). The complaint concerns apparent Ukrainian non-compliance with EU norms during formal treaty negotiations. The practitioner begins her complaint earlier in the extract (lines 307–8), where she identifies the challenge of persuading Ukraine to include items in the new agreement 'that they perhaps would like to avoid' (lines 309–10). She also adds to the contrast structure by identifying a problematic influence on Ukraine, which is 'obviously the Russians' (line 313). This influence leads to deliberately misinterpretations of EU norms by Ukraine, despite the fact that '<they say officially they say they share our values of course: :' (lines 313–14).

The next extract concerns Russia more directly, and begins with a question on a specific aspect of the establishment of an EU–Russian deep free-trade area, a policy which is now on hold due to the Russian annexation of Crimea. However, the extract reveals that this policy area has always been laden with 'unresolved issues'.

Extract 4.19 – EUIns.36

328 R   so are you still discussing the setting up of a deep free trade
329   area?
330 Inv yu:p (.) similar to the discussions we are having with Ukraine,
331   <u>but</u> we have very man- a number of unresolved issues hhh
332 R   like?
333 Inv wood exports. .h <u>which</u> is in contradiction >actually< in umh
334   <u>breach</u> of um Russian gas delivery agreements
335 R   mhm
336 Inv <u>but</u> we have a lot of other problems .hh like discriminatory
337   tariffs on railway transport through throu:gh Russia, which
338   increases for example the cost of .hh export for umh any
339   countries who use Russia °for transit purposes° becomes um we
340   have um a lot of other areas you kno:w where the Russians are
341   not willing to engage with us on the political level
342 R   you mean the frozen conflicts?
343 Inv yup! and they never will.

This practitioner begins on a positive note by comparing the negotiation details of a deep free-trade area between the EU and Russia with the one that is negotiated between the EU and Ukraine (line 330) as his answer to the researcher's question. However, the tone changes to a more negative one later in the same turn, and he implies Russian non-compliance: 'but we have very man- a lot of unresolved issues' (line 331). During his utterance, he revises the quantity of the pending issues from 'very many' to 'a number of'. Such downgrading is analytically significant for two reasons. First, it crushes any epistemic priority that might have been implied (Heritage and Raymond, 2005: 18). Second, he reverses this downgrade 'but we have a lot of other problems' (line 336). Just as assessments can be epistemically downgraded, they can also be upgraded (Heritage and Raymond, 2005: 21). In this way, he establishes the number of problems to be far greater than is initially implied in the downgraded statement. This is further confirmed where he complains that 'we have um a lot of other areas you kno: w where the Russians are not willing to engage with us' (lines 339–41).

In addition, on the practitioner substantiates these 'unresolved issues' by listing them. The practitioner begins his list (line 333) with wood exports and links it to 'breach of um Russian gas delivery agreements' (line 334). Then he proceeds with highlighting 'discriminatory tariffs on railway transport through throu: gh Russia' (lines 336–7). We can consider the issue of frozen conflicts as being added to his list, as he offers an agreement token ('yup!') (line 343) in response to the researcher's earlier reference to the political disputes between the EU and Russia.

Furthermore, the practitioner blames the Russians for breaching an existing agreement due to their non-compliance. These embedded blamings (Edwards and Potter, 1992) support the practitioner's initial complaint about not being able to move forward with the negotiation process of the agreement.

When alignment with EU norms is not welcomed

Alignment with the EU and EU norms is not always received well, as is demonstrated in the following two extracts. Furthermore, they confirm the complex nature of the relationship between the EU and Russia concerning their shared neighbourhood.

Extract 4.20 – EUIns.10

```
75 R     and what about the eastern borders?
76 Inv   .hhh we::ll the Russians have said to us u:mh on various levels
77 R     hmm
78 Inv   the fact that (.) many countries of the region, like
79       particularly Ukraine, Moldova, Georgia a:re seeking closer
80       relations with the EU ONLY leads to a worsening of our
```

81   relations with Russia. .hh>almost as though< the fact that they
82   were seeking <u>to a:lign</u> themselves more on the western values as
83   defined by the EU <u>is</u> something that is not competiti- not
84   compatible >I mean< for good relations with Russia..

Extract 4.21 – EUIns.42

322 R   and the Russian? What you make of their involvement in the
323   region?
324 Inv umh I think the problem is that (.) °at least as far as I can
325   see it° the Russians have a: very much a zero sum game towards
326   events particularly in their neighbourhood. Basically, <u>see</u> if a
327   country turns towards the EU .hh it means they're turning
328   against us, ra- rather than recognise that they've got in many
329   respects (0.2) the Ukraine, Moldova, Georgia (.) and and any
330   other countries in the region align themselves with the values
331   of the EU actually makes things better for Russia hh
332 R   how?
334 Inv .hh because it will mean they are much more reliable funds, <u>but</u>
335   (0.2) I think it's a general <u>suspicion</u> as towards the motives
336   of the EU in exporting democracy.
337 R   mhm
338 Inv the Russians have told us, well don't try to export your brand
339   of democracy to the countries of the CIS. it didn't work in the
340   Middle East, it won't work with the CIS .hhh which seems to be
341   a sort of simplification in terms <u>because</u> ba:sically saying you
342   know: we have a different concept of democracy (.) your concept
343   is not necessarily superior (0.2) <u>so::</u> um:: I think that's one
344   of the problems we face with Russia.
345 R   okay

Both of these EU practitioners refer to Russia's hostile response to Ukraine, Moldova, and Georgia's alignment with EU norms. They both rely on quotations, with those in Extract 4.20 being indirect and those in Extract 4.21 being direct. Quoting people or presenting oneself as a reporter of other's views is a discursive device called active voicing (Wooffitt, 1991, 2005). Active voicing is usually involved with concerns of personal accountability. In this case, it is used to suggest that the turn of events or present circumstances are not the practitioners' fault but the Russians, on behalf of whom they are reporting.

In Extract 4.20 the practitioner indirectly quotes what 'the Russians have said to us u: hm on various levels' (line 76), which is 'the fact <u>that</u> (.) many countries of the region, like particularly Ukraine, Moldova, Georgia a: re seeking <u>closer</u> relations with the EU ONLY leads to a worsening of our relations with Russia' (lines 78–81). Besides the active voicing, it is of analytical significance that the practitioner emphasises the word 'closer' (line 79) before 'relations' and uses a relatively louder tone for the word 'only' (line 80). By drawing attention to these words, he establishes the importance of the links between these countries for EU–Russian relations. Furthermore, he implies that Russia sees these alignments as 'not compatible' (lines 83–4) than he qualifies this non-compatibility 'for good relations' (line 84) between the EU and Russia. Thus, the practitioner creates the impression that Russia blames the EU for interfering with countries that used to be part of the Soviet Union and that are currently located in the shared neighbourhood.

The practitioner in Extract 4.21 ups the ante by presenting Russia's view of such alignment as hostile. He offers an explanation of the 'zero sum game' (line 325) that Russia sees in its neighbourhood through a direct quote: 'Basically, see if a country turns towards the EU .hh it means they're turning against us' (lines 326–8). Thus, these previously friendly countries, which used to belong to the Soviet Union, are alienated from Russia by their EU alliance. Analytically, the direct quotation of the Russian view awards a factual status to the practitioner's claim, and prevents any sceptical response (Wooffitt, 1991, 2005). Significantly, he shifts his footing in the rest of the sentence, and delivers the remainder as a mere reporter of another view: 'ra- rather than recognise that they've got in many respects (0.2) the Ukraine, Moldova, Georgia (.) and and any other countries in the region align themselves with the values of the EU actually makes things better for Russia hh' (lines 328–31). Footing shifts are closely related to active voicing in establishing factuality (Wooffitt, 1991).

There is another use of the active voicing device in this practitioner's account that is not only relevant for the theme of this section but also for the chapter as a whole. The practitioner pre-empts his direct quote with 'the Russians have told us' (line 338), then he continues: 'well don't try to export your brand of democracy to the countries of the CIS. it didn't work in the Middle East, it won't work with the CIS' (lines 338–40). In this statement, the practitioner refers to a case in which EU involvement did not work. Drawing on the similarity between the Middle East and the CIS (Commonwealth of Independent States) is analytically important, as embedding blaming in a description is another way to convey a complaint (Edwards and Potter, 1992). This practitioner clearly refers to Russia's hostility towards the EU, as well as Russian 'suspicion as towards the motives of the EU in exporting democracy' (lines 335–6), in short, towards EU norms.

An eternal EU–centric view

In the final extract of this chapter, we consider a highly EU-centric view of the world, through an analogy of the universe. There are many critics of taking an ethnocentric perspective such as this. This extract is part of a prominent practitioner's answer to the question of the best idea that the EU can introduce to the eastern neighbours, which led him to offer the following cosmic explanation.

Extract 4.22 – EUIns.13

```
338 Inv   well (0.4) is it kind of a federo-centric system, you ha:ve
339        big something
340 R      uh huh
341 I      some (inaudible) part of the Union and there are planets
342 R      £I see huh huh
343 Inv    without the law we used to call in concentric circles
344 R      £yeah huh huh
345 Inv    so the centre of th- of the system, solar system is big (0.4)
346        and they are smaller
347 R      £uh huh
348 Inv    £there are big moons and small moons you have Russia and Moldova
349 R      right ok
350 Inv    and the small
351 R      yeah?
352 Inv    with the power of gravity they will join
353 R      huh huh
354 Inv    if they are big they have such a gravity and always turn around
355 R      o- okay so who would that be?
356 Inv    £guess? ((laugh))
357 R      it's your- I'm interested in your views I have mine but I am
358        [here to ((laugh))]
359 Inv    [no it's] much more complex than such a cosmic description
360 R      thankfully
361        ((simultaneous laughter))
```

The practitioner begins his lively narrative description of the centrality of the EU with an account of the current EU model as 'a federo-centric system' (line 338) as opposed to the 'concentric circles' it used to be referred to 'without the law' (line 343) or, put differently, without the introduction of EU norms to the neighbouring states. Such differentiation from a practitioner is crucial, as he implies that through the *acquis*, thus though EU norms, the depth of relationships between these countries and the EU changes. Of course, not all EU practitioners support such a federalist notion of the EU, but this particular description of the EU is analytically intriguing.

The persuasiveness and plausibility of a report can be increased by lodging it in a distinct narrative sequence (Edwards and Potter, 1992); at the same time, narratives can also frame a context of deniability (Bogen and Lynch, 1989). Productions of specific kinds of reality effects have been studied extensively in the literature. There is an increasing number of studies in social psychology, sociology, and politics that explore such narratives, but few of them consider the narrative as a warranting device, as Edwards and Potter do.[9] Establishing a federalist perspective through a 'cosmic description' (line 359) of the EU as being 'the centre of the th- of the system, solar system' (line 345) seems far-fetched. Even if we dismiss such a description as silly, the practitioner clearly put thought into this cosmic analogy, and held the attractiveness of the EU in the region in high regard, as simply through spreading EU norms: 'with the power of gravity they will join' (line 352). Such an analogy from a leading practitioner on EU foreign affairs is significant. It clearly demonstrates his wider understanding of the EU's relevance in the region and within the currently developing power structure between the EU and the neighbouring states.

Conclusion

From constructions of identity, this chapter moved on to examine the accounts of EU practitioners on the EU's normative role in the eastern neighbourhood. Through the practitioners' social practices as outlined by the DPM framework (see pp. 27–8), I demonstrated how they draw upon EU norms and what they achieve with them when discussing EU policy vis-à-vis the East. There were four main discursive patterns in the corpus.

The first pattern concerned the constructions of norms, although there was no specific question asked of the practitioners, either to offer a definition of norms, or to recite them. Significantly, practitioners referred to norms when questioned on the challenges the EU faces in the region, the significance of the region, and on the ideas that the EU can export to the neighbourhood, or often just referred to norms spontaneously. So, despite no prior categorisation, practitioners were willing to list norms such as the rule of law, peace, freedom of speech, human rights, Christian ethics, market economy, stability, security (Extracts 4.1–4.4). These lists were not only compatible with the initial list provided by Manners (2002), but also with the ENP document and naturally the *acquis*. While some of these norms would be known in the region, the practitioner in Extract 4.1 implied a clear distinction between the application of these norms by EU member states' and by *others*, such as the eastern neighbours. Drawing on such a distinction was a discursive strategy also employed in Chapter 3, in which we considered identity formation. Besides its analytically applicability, contrast structures achieved a comparative effect, as in Chapter 3, by distinguishing between the 'Europeans' and their neighbours. The practitioner in Extract 4.3 followed a similar trajectory. After initially aligning the Enlargement Policy with the ENP, he later differentiated between the two based on their different outcomes. Despite their clearly different outcomes, the practitioner still declared that the aims of both policies for the eastern neighbourhood were the same, with regard to exporting EU norms. Furthermore, through his account he attended to the notion of collective accountability as it is expected from the EU, when seeking to align eastern neighbours with EU norms. Another practitioner in Extract 4.4 achieved this by focusing on the kind of neighbours that the EU actually wants. She implied that the importance of reciprocity between exporting norms and meeting the EU's own interest of external security was through having a safe, secure, and prosperous neighbourhood. This was one of the first instances where practitioners' accounts gave equal importance to norms and interest formulations. The coupling of these two notions is significant, especially concerning IR theory when norms and interest are commonly studied separately. References to this significance have been made throughout the chapter and a more in-depth discussion follows in Chapter 5.

Besides norm constructions, I also considered how practitioners attend to the importance of monitoring norms and the implementation process. In Extract 4.5 and 4.6, the analysis focused on one practitioner in particular, as he blamed Ukraine for halting the reform process. His use of active voicing and direct quotes managed his personal accountability, and further supported his action of apportioning blame on the neighbours, but not on himself or the EU.

The second pattern in this analytical chapter focused on the EU model itself. Two discursive practices emerged from Extracts 4.7 to 4.16. First, practitioners described the attractiveness of the EU model by implying that the EU model was the normative model that everyone should aspire to (Extract 4.7), or through employing an extreme-case formulation by contrasting the EU model with the Somalian way of life (Extract 4.8). Similarly, the practitioner in Extract 4.9 claimed that emulating the EU model is beneficial for the neighbours, but at the same time she drew attention to the fact that it was equally important for the EU itself. Thus, yet another practitioner directly linked the EU's norm-forming intentions to serving its own interest. Extract 4.10 and 4.11 offered examples of settings in which emulating the EU model is emerging, i.e. Morocco and Ukraine. Second, practitioners claimed to have expertise in transforming countries, as long as they are prepared to emulate EU norms. Assistance for this transformation can be given through monitoring (Extract 4.12), offering advice (Extract 4.13), support (Extract 4.14), information exchange on technical issues (Extract 4.15), or applying the classic carrot-and-stick method of reward and punishment (Extract 4.16).

The third pattern analysed was the response of practitioners to issues of non-compliance. Belarus is the classic case where alignment with EU norms is rejected, and indeed EU sanctions have been in place since 2004. What is more, the practitioner's account of Belarusian practices in Extract 4.17 blamed Russian influence on Belarus for the non-compliance. Significantly, Ukraine was depicted as an advocate of EU norms. In Extract 4.18, the practitioner complained about the gap between the official and unofficial discourse during EU treaty negotiations with Ukraine. Yet again, Russian influence was blamed for being behind Ukraine's contradictory practices. Not only was Russian influence blamed for the neighbouring states' reluctance and hesitance in aligning with EU norms, but a practitioner in Extract 4.19 complained that there were problems with Russia itself in not abiding by treaty agreements or following the normative model of treaty negotiations. Furthermore, in Extracts 4.20 and 4.21, practitioners offered accounts of the complex nature of EU–Russian relations because of post-Soviet states like Ukraine, Moldova, and Georgia's affiliation with the EU, despite having historically closer ties with Russia. The practitioner even recounted a Russian warning in Extract 4.21 that EU attempts to export democracy to the CIS will end similarly to the current instability of the Middle East.

The final pattern that emerged from this part of the corpus was the common notion of reciting an ethnocentric, or EU-centric, view of the world. Through a striking and highly vivid description, the practitioner in Extract 4.22 compared the role and powers of the EU in the region to the sun in the solar system, stating that the EU's gravity of power came through its insistence on the application of EU norms.

Next I turn to the vocational or moral aspect of the EU's interest in the eastern region.

Notes

1 Now included in Article 275 TFEU.
2 This competence was confirmed in the *Al-Queda Sanctions* case, also known as *Kadi* (case C-402 and 415/05).
3 Scholars applying the same concepts such as the logic of appropriateness and the logic of arguing to assess individually identity, norm, morality, and interest formation only further support the main argument of this book that all these notions are interlinked and practically impossible to separate.
4 These contrast structures will be further explored in the next chapter.
5 Turn construction units (TCUs) are one of the most basic design features of any interactional organisation of social activities that take place during conversation. They are the basis of the interactional rules and procedures that allow the orderly progress of conversations and thus social activities (Sacks *et al.*, 1974; Schegloff, 1997).
6 The data collection took place before the annexation of Crimea. While the proxy conflict in the Donbass region and the annexation of Crimea are leading EU–Russia and EU–Ukraine relations, EU practices have not changed.
7 In their study, Barbé *et al.* (2015: 26–8) focused on how the EU as MODEL (or rule-setter) for global governance was portrayed through statements by commissioners, or more precisely they listed the metaphors employed by the commissioners to achieve that effect.

8 Poland, Slovakia, the Czech Republic, and Bulgaria all have Slavic roots, but they were only satellite states during the communist period, and not actually part of the Soviet Union like Ukraine, Belarus, and Moldova. However, these Slavic roots are felt more strongly in specific Balkan states like Serbia.

9 The analysis of Edwards and Potter (1992: ch. 3) on chancellor Lawson's memory was the first to set the precedent, but few followed.

5

EU foreign policy as a vocation for Europe

The significance of the eastern neighbourhood for the EU has been made clear throughout the previous chapters. This region is important not only for the usual security concerns and the EU's desire to be surrounded by likeminded, stable, and predictable states, but also because of its relevance in shaping European identity, as discussed in Chapter 3. Chapter 4 revealed the importance of EU practitioners' quest for a normative role for the EU in the region. Following closely from the latter chapter's findings, this chapter focuses on the ways practitioners justify a vocational aspect of the EU foreign policy, that is, the necessary course of action that the EU ought to pursue in its eastern neighbourhood. The operationalisation of these moral justifications is closely linked with identity formation. Practitioners apply them in order to differentiate between the European self and the non-European other, as this chapter will reveal. The argument forwarded in this chapter is that if the EU applies the same vocational and moral arguments in the eastern neighbourhood as it did in the post-Cold War context, specifically towards post-Soviet CEECs, but without acting on it, the EU risks being seen as a 'moralising power', rather than offering moral leadership in the region.

While the origins of IR lie in the rejection of idealism and moralism, following the failure of the League of Nations, much of IR theory devotes itself to moral concerns, particularly through questions of intervention, sovereignty, and human rights. But how do we decide what is moral? And what is the relationship between moral concerns and norms? Even classical realist theorists like E. H. Carr and Morgenthau were concerned with morality during the interwar period. According to Carr (1939[1968]: 97), 'Political action must be based on a coordination of morality and power', which supports the argument that morality and political action ought to interlink. In the same vein, Morgenthau ([1948] 1993: 5–6) concluded that the political and cultural context determines the specific interest a state pursues in a particular historical moment. They both inspired subsequent rationalists to investigate the promotion of rights and responsibilities, but only as an instrumental or functional concern to achieve national interests. For some liberals, however, even implying a normative dimension to liberalism, at best, compromises its status as a legitimate IR theory. Furthermore, it derails the main liberal concern of establishing a causal link between the political structure of the state and war/peace (Moravcsik, 1997: 513–53). Nevertheless, many liberals look to Kant's claim of adopting a republican constitutional structure as the key to global order, or 'perpetual peace' ([1795] 1983). In the same way, the English School supports a similar connection between the principles of laws, norms, and moral obligation in order to realise international society. The problem with advocating this position is that it risks vindicating unscrupulous state practices (Hurrell, 2002: 139). Neorealists and neoliberalists, however, consciously moved away from normative and moral questions in the pursuit of establishing IR as a scientific discipline. Only since the arrival of constructivist approaches have IR theorists launched the contestation of the standard IR assumption that material interest, power, and wealth trump the role of norms and moral obligations (Wendt, 1995: 71–81; Katzenstein, 1996). For constructivists, morality is even more nuanced and goes beyond the acceptance or rejection of norms. Conventional constructivist IR theorists insist on separating moral values from norms (Katzenstein, 1996; Ulbert and Risse, 2005: 351–67). However, for critical constructivists or poststructuralists, the image of such a connection between moral values and norms is possible when negotiating foreign policy.

There are three ways of looking at norms and ethics in IR: the role that normative ideas play in the practice of politics; how moral obligations should impact practice; and how they actually impact the practice (Hurrell, 2002: 137). Since these approaches emerged from political theory and its engagement with ethics, Hurrell advocates a departure from Wight's (1966: 17–34) preference for dividing the domestic and the international, as this division imposes different sets of theoretical concerns. These concerns would include the principles and practices of state sovereignty and identity. While issues of identity formation such as the recognition, inclusion, and exclusion of the self and the other have been explored in IR separately of ethical conduct, they are very relevant when examining how norms are put in use.

There are three ways to operationalise norms and ethics in IR. First, actors apply norms that seem to have worked, and thus have obvious consequences. Focusing on successful norms is the most common way to study norm formation, but as Legro (1997: 34) points out, such focus misses all those occasions when norms failed, became obsolete, or just did not emerge. Seizing on these instances can be just as important as studying norms that proved to be effective. Alternatively, actors may choose to follow a collective understanding of proper behaviour that can shape or even curb power without having to abide by political preferences. For Buzan (2001: 477–8), EU integration is an example of just this. Finally, norms could be employed as political instruments by separating the insiders, those within the normative boundaries, and the outsiders, those who violate such norms (Žižek, 2006: 21). This type of norm operationalisation is closely linked with identity formation and thus is crucial for understanding the identity of those who promote the norms, and their concept of the other. It is also often applied by politicians, practitioners, and diplomats to pursue a specific policy, for example justifying humanitarian and economic aid or any type of military intervention.

Implying a vocational element to justify the necessary course of action that the EU ought to pursue in its eastern neighbourhood is not new. Many scholars identified the moral obligations old member states felt for the CEECs when supporting them to join the EU (Fierke and Wiener, 1999: 721–42; Sedelmeier, 2002: 627–49; Sjursen, 2002: 491–513). After enlargement, the EU turned its attention to neighbouring countries. In one of the first books on the ENP, Dannreuther (2004) made a similar link between the EU's intentions towards its immediate eastern neighbours, and the EU's moral dimension that is something more fundamental, existential, and tied to safeguarding peace between battling European nation states. Then Barbé and Johansson-Nogués (2008: 81–96) reviewed the impact of ENP as a 'force for good'. Their finding is that while the EU has achieved some moral stance in its exercise of power within its neighbourhood, all its achievements have been vitiated by certain ambiguous practices such as the lack of ENP–EU policy coordination on visa facilitation or energy policy, and inconsistent principles on political groups like Hamas. As the passion for expansion continues to fade, however, the EU needs a new moral focus for its foreign policy ambitions. Dunne (2008: 15) proposes that the EU should 'both develop and integrate its military capability and to deepen its commitment to cosmopolitan values' in order to occupy a moral middle ground. Although Bailes (2008: 115–30) agrees with Dunne, she calls for clarification on the ethical confusion between 'doing good' and 'being good' before EU military capability is further developed. Calls for consideration of the rhetoric around Europe as an ethical power have also been voiced. By contrasting the rhetoric with action and capabilities, Mayer (2008: 61–79) argues that it would be more realistic to stick to the well-defined concept of 'Europe's global responsibilities', rather than carrying on calling the EU an 'ethical power'. Moreover, Hyde-Price (2008: 29–44) claims that the EU's ethical behaviour is severely constrained by the international system, and hence the EU should act as a 'calculator not a crusader'.

Although no one doubts the increasing efforts the EU is making to exercise its powers, it has been pointed out on numerous occasions that the EU uses its influence 'through what it is, rather than what it does' (Maull, 2005: 778). This focus on the specific character of the EU underpins the argument that the EU has a distinctively normative way of conducting itself as a global actor (Manners, 2002: 240). Even the fiercest critics of the EU's normative impact on the international system would agree that ethics are intrinsic to EU identity. These ethical concerns or moral obligation are the focus of this chapter, or more precisely how they are used by EU practitioners when constructing EU foreign policy in the eastern neighbourhood, and their effect. Morality is an internal part of practitioners' interaction, hence integral to their practice. I demonstrated in Chapter 2 how DIR allows us to reveal how moral concerns are operationalised and the inherent link between language and practice.

The following extracts from EU practitioners demonstrate how they operationalise their specific moral concerns for the eastern neighbourhood. Their norm deployments are consistent with Legro, Buzan, and Žižek's claims of norm use. These extracts also offer a good illustration of some of the specific discursive devices that are used to achieve moral concern through interaction. In addition, these extracts reveal instances when practitioners risk sounding moralising rather than moral. This is highly problematic for two reasons. First, moralising endangers alienating neighbouring states who align themselves with the EU but do not want to receive a lecture from EU practitioners on how they should run their national or foreign affairs. The asymmetric relations between the EU and the countries participating in the ENP already put these countries in an intricate position. Second, moralising is a dangerous strategy for the EU. If the EU cannot deliver on specific promises such as support for democracy or human rights in the region, this will have a long-term impact on the EU's standing in the international system. Many will perceive the EU as a moralising rather than a moral or normative power.

'We have a duty to care'

Concerns of duty, or in other words the EU's moral obligation to care for its eastern neighbours, seem to be a crucial matter for EU practitioners who work in this policy area. Their arguments are often backed by previous successes of state transformation. These claims simply follow norm operationalisation logic, whereby if the norm has worked, it must be effective (Legro, 1997). Spreading norms has been key to EU policy in the neighbourhood. In the following extract, a practitioner attempts to explain the norms that the EU could export to these neighbouring states, while also addressing the EU's duty to these neighbours.

Extract 5.1 – EUIns.61

614	R	what do you think are the most important ideas tha:t the EU
615		could <u>exp</u>ort to these countries?
616	Inv	that's an interesting point!
617	R	mm .hh the most [important?]
618	Inv	[we:ll I gue]ss it would be really really that
619		the fa:ct that the common values (.) shared by the member
620		states are the ones that lead to security, prosperity (0.4)
621		etcetera in the countries that <u>choo</u>se to embrace them.
622	R	umhm

```
623 Inv   one because we will engage much more closely with these
624        countries .hh and the EU does provide an enormous amount of
625        assistance to countries around the world >but particularly< in
626        this immediate neighbourhood .hhh a:nd (.) secondly because
627        countries which are democratically stable a::nd which
628        organise their societies in a wa:y which reflect those common
629        values tend to be much more successful in the end.
630 R      [.hh how?]
631 Inv    [but o:] of course I'm not saying that these countries will
632        become like Switzerland overnight, but we look to see what the
633        EU has managed to achieve in the countries, in central Europe
634 R      umh
635 Inv    mainly because of the pool of the enlargement ((tcht)) it's
636        actually quite amazing countries like hhh umh Slovenia which
637        is the best within the class or look at other countries within
638        the Baltic states (0.6) it's quite amazing what's been achieved
639        in sixteen years.
640 R      sure but but the eastern neighbours is not the CEEC or the
641        Baltic states?
642 Inv    surely not but we still have a duty to them .hh (0.4) as we did
643        with the others.
```

The focus here is on the importance of common EU values (line 619), as the key idea that the EU can export. The practitioner claims that those countries that embrace these values are likely to be more successful (lines 627–9). However, it is significant how the practitioner manages to align the moral concern that the EU has for the eastern neighbours and the duty it previously held for integrating the CEECs. First, he downgrades the effects of adopting EU values by stating '[but o:] of course I'm not saying that these countries will become like Switzerland overnight' (lines 631–2), and thus implies that the eastern neighbours will not transform instantly into established democracies. Then he makes a reference to the EU's achievements in central Europe (lines 632–3): 'but we look to see what the EU has managed to achieve in the countries, in central Europe' and selects two examples: Slovenia (lines 636–7) and the Baltic states (line 638) to illustrate the success. After a long hesitation,[1] from which we can infer the importance of his claim, he declares: 'it's quite amazing what's been achieved in sixteen years' (lines 638–9). This declaration once again demonstrates the EU's successful and positive influence on the region.

Next, the researcher issues a challenge by indicating a difference between the eastern neighbours and the new EU member states 'sure but but the eastern neighbours is not the CEEC or the Baltic states?' (lines 640–1). This provocation leads to an acceptance of the researcher's contrast but at the same time it only unleashes the moral concern that the practitioner implies the EU has vis-à-vis the eastern neighbours: 'surely not <u>but</u> we still have a duty to them' (line 642). Finally, he compares this current moral obligation to the one the EU felt towards the new EU member states (lines 642–3). This implies a sense of collective responsibility the EU has for its eastern neighbourhood, as well as its responsibility to be a moral actor and to do good.

As mentioned before, such a conceptualisation of the immediate neighbourhood is not new. Many scholars made reference to the moral duty the old EU member states felt for the new ones after the fall of the Berlin Wall (Fierke and Wiener, 1999: 721–42, Sedelmeier, 2002: 627–49; Sjursen, 2002), and how member states demonstrated a similar obligation by reverting to similar vocational sentiments when setting up the ENP (Dannreuther, 2004). Thus, finding such accounts from practitioners, who are responsible for this policy area, is not at all surprising. Neither is locating instances of practitioners producing a similar response without having been asked the same question.

In the next extract, a different practitioner displays a different kind of moral obligation.

Extract 5.2 – EUIns.56

```
655  R     can I just press you a little bit o:n (.) do you think any of
656        these countries specifically in the east would ever be able to
657        join the EU?
658  Inv   theoretically the Article 49 promise is there!
659  R     uh huh
660  Inv   the question actually isn't so much can they one day join it's
661        hh (0.6) .hhh are they ready to ask the question?
662  R     right ok a:nd?
663  Inv   and they're not. are we ready to answer the question is the
664        sub part of that (.) and no we're not! but that's irrelevant
665        as long as they are not ready to ask the question.
666  R     sure [but]
667  Inv      [AND] this is not just true of these countries. we spend a
668        lot of time explaining to Macedonia former Republic o- not to
669        ask a question that it wasn't going to want the answer to
670  R     sure
671  Inv   because if a country asks that question this is a serious
672        exercise (.) they send a letter to the presidency then the the
673        presidency puts it on the agenda of council. the council does
674        its first little check list .hh is it European? Tick (.) is it
675        a democracy? hands up yeah good. I think so, is it a market
676        economy? Yes. administrative capacity? what do we know about
677        that? then dump the baby across the street to here and we then
678        spend a yea:r and a bit deeply invasively >not that we don't
```

679   already know something about the country< <u>but</u> really deeply and
680   invasively figuring it all out and then answering honestly
681   <u>beca</u>use we have a duty to the EU!
682 R   sure
683 Inv <u>but</u> (0.2) we also have a duty to not destroy our neighbours!
684 R   uh huh

Here the practitioner attempts to answer a question on the possibility of future enlargement by drawing a distinction between the theoretical, or more precisely the legal argument for future entrants (line 658) and the practical one (from line 671). She claims that 'the Article 49 promise is there!' which only stipulates that the applicant be 'European'. But the practical aspect of joining appears to be a lot more complicated. The practitioner's meticulous explanation of the process of officially being accepted as a candidate country merits its own analysis, and in effect the listing of each and every step serves as part of the justification for the collective moral obligation that she, along with other EU practitioners ('we', line 681), has to the EU 'because we have a duty to the EU!'. However, the focus here is on the duty she implies the practitioners have. This obligation includes a certain level of truthfulness and integrity (line 680). What is equally significant in the practitioner's account, after a short uptake by the researcher with the minimal acknowledgement token of 'sure', is her next assessment (line 683) 'but (0.2) we also have a duty to not destroy our neighbours!'. This assessment of the potential failure of EU policy, and thus a tragic outcome, is the worst imaginable result of the meticulous process of accession put in place to protect both the EU and the future accession state. Furthermore, it has never happened before. Even states like Turkey, which has been a candidate for a long time, have not been destroyed by the process; neither have Moldova or Ukraine, both of which have been negotiating various forms of engagements. Referring to such an exceptional circumstance (or extreme case) is analytically interesting. It accomplishes the justification for the practitioner's moral concern of putting neighbours through the rigorous process of membership negotiations during which states have to absorb EU norms and values when it could have a disastrous effect. Moreover, it positions the EU as a good, fair, and sensible actor in the region that will protect its neighbours even from the EU itself. This also attends to the notion of collective accountability and agency.

Yet another way of attending to moral obligations is by making references to a specific awareness or consciousness one possesses.

Extract 5.3 – EUIns.55

156 Inv I me:an, I think mistakes (0.6) erm: were made, and equally
157   Russia got the <u>wrong</u> impression about the Neighbourhood Policy.
158 R   right okay

159 Inv and and I think that's partly our fault (.) and maybe
160   oversensitivity on the (0.4) on the Russian side
161 R   uh huh
162 Inv in the sense that and I and I think in fact (0.6) erm this
163   applies to a certain extent to the countries within the ENP as
164   well
165 R   uh huh
166 Inv in other words we made a conscious [decision]
167 R   [uh huh]
168 Inv to try .hh and extend the benefits of EU enlargement, to: the
169   countries left outside the 2004 enlargement. (0.4) and our
170   conscious decision was to <u>use</u> the instruments tha:t we
171   applied in the enlargement case to the neighbourhood countries.
172 R   right

Shortly after a question on the role of the practitioner's institution in the ENP the practitioner issues a complaint: 'I think mistakes (0.6) erm: were made, and equally Russia got the <u>wrong</u> impression about the Neighbourhood Policy' (lines 156–7). In his next turn, he offers an assessment of this complaint: 'I think that's partly our fault', which indicates a level of accountability on his, his institution's, or on the EU's side. But at the same time, the practitioner also apportions blame to the Russians: 'and maybe oversensitivity on the (0.4) on the Russian side' (lines 159–60) and also to other ENP countries (lines 162–4). Embedding blamings as part of packaging action in a description is an often used discursive device (Edwards and Potter, 1992). Here these blamings work to justify the practitioner's next turn of describing all the good intentions that the EU had for the neighbourhood policy: 'in other words we made a conscious [decision] to try .hh and extend the benefits of EU enlargement, to: the countries left outside the 2004 enlargement. (0.4) and our conscious decision was to <u>use</u> the instruments tha: t we applied in the enlargement case, to the neighbourhood countries' (lines 166–71). The practitioner not only makes the benefits of enlargement relevant, but more importantly he reiterates twice the 'conscious decision' the EU made to extend those benefits to the ENP countries (line 166 and 170). Such benefits come with the application of highly demanding, challenging, and arduous instruments, all on the EU's terms. Thus, linking this process to a certain level of awareness or 'conscious decision' only accomplishes a justification of moral obligation that the practitioner appears to have for the neighbouring countries, despite his earlier claim of their misinterpretation of the policy (line 159).

Next, a similar claim of moral values is presented, but this time it is already positioned as the entitlement of the neighbouring state, after the EU supported revolution.

Extract 5.4 – EUIns.11

230	R	and:: what if they don't adopt the European model after all?
231	Inv	I think the country will not be able to fall completely back
232		(.) I mean freedom of the media (0.2) once they have certain
233		things in the civil society is much more developed and that's
234		also why they had an orange revolution because there's a
235		certain conscience in the country (.) that certain things
236		cannot happen anymore.
237	R	hmmm

In response to the researcher's challenge that Ukraine might reject the EU model of governance: 'what if they don't adopt the European model after all?' (line 230), the practitioner offers an unequivocal assessment that Ukraine will not return to formerly accepted practices (line 231). That is a reference to conventions that were presumably present before their independence and the EU's subsequent involvement. The practitioner continues his turn to list reasons why such a U-turn is inconceivable. He begins by using freedom of the media as an example (line 232), and links it to development of civil society (line 233), which essentially caused the Orange Revolution in his assessment. Furthermore, media freedoms, the progression of civil society, and thus the Orange Revolution were all possible 'because there's a certain conscience in the country (.) that certain things cannot happen anymore' (lines 234–6). Thus, the practitioner implies that Ukraine's entitlement to this 'conscience', or this sense of right and wrong, was gained through adopting European norms and through EU involvement. This moral standard does not allow the recurrence of previously accepted, potentially undesirable, and amoral practices. Presenting the EU's influence as a guiding moral compass may be seen as part of the moral obligation the EU has vis-à-vis its eastern neighbours, including Ukraine.

According to the following account, having any involvement or alignment with the EU can be seen as a positive endorsement of a country.

Extract 5.5 – EUIns.44

490	Inv	£if you can pose it from from the outside, .hh all the
491		questions were from EU an- and the rest of the world?
492	R	wh- what do you mean?
493	Inv	those who are around us but if you change this perspective you
494		will see that countries want to be neighbours.
495	R	uh huh
496	Inv	which is an answer in itself eh (1) when you talk to
497		Kazakhstan, Armenia, Uzbekistan (inaudible) they want to be

498 considered our neighbours
499 R uh huh
500 Inv which gives you an answer (0.4) .hh the value in in being in
501 touch, or in liaison with European [Union]
502 R [yes?]
503 Inv it gives certain good for geopolitical reasons in relation
504 economic, financial
505 R mo- more than what Russia would give them?
506 Inv definitely!

The practitioner initiated this topic based on the researcher's final invitation to raise any issue that had not yet been covered. He issues a complaint that all the researcher's questions were focusing on the EU and carried an EU-centric view. He attempts to remedy this by speaking on behalf of the neighbouring states, despite being an EU official. This raises issues of accountability, since the practitioner has a clearly vested interest in how EU foreign policy is perceived by other states (as per DPM, see pp. 27–8).

Regardless of the practitioner's initial attempt, he offers an equally Eurocentric view of EU foreign policy. His point is that these countries want to be the EU's neighbours (lines 493–4). He lists the countries who he believes desire to be deemed EU neighbours: 'when you talk to Kazakhstan, Armenia, Uzbekistan (inaudible) they want to be considered our neighbours' (lines 496–8). This list serves to strengthen his justification that not one country is interested in being the EU's neighbour but four. He continues his justification for these countries' desire by offering another list, this time of benefits: 'it gives certain good for geopolitical reasons' (lines 503), 'economic' and 'financial' (line 504). It is also significant that the practitioner highlights the importance of the way in which contact with the EU is perceived favourably. It supports not only the neighbours' quest to be seen as good, but also the EU's own quest to be seen as a good and a principled actor in the region. More importantly, it is crucial for the EU to be perceived as more virtuous than Russia according to this practitioner (line 506). Creating such a contrast does not only serve to accomplish a certain moral perception of the EU, thus attending to the *self*, but at the same time it creates a specific perception of the *other* in the region, that is Russia. It also works to draw normative boundaries between the insiders/outsiders (Žižek, 2006).[2] Although the recent development of both Kazakhstan and Armenia deciding to join the Russian-led Eurasian Customs Union instead of pursuing a European dream challenges the practitioner's account, it still draws a distinction between two different sets of norms present in the region; two norms that states can choose from. The current tension between Ukraine and Russia serves to confirm this.

The next two extracts offer a different account of the EU's responsibility vis-à-vis its neighbours. They represent more direct attempts at constructing

Russia as amoral and the EU as the moral actor with the responsibility of helping those who do not have the same rights and freedoms as EU citizens.

Extract 5.6 – EUIns.39

```
510 Inv   I (.) myself I think, we have a huge machinery working here in
511        Brussels, .hh both scientific and legislative machinery, that
512        is developing new best practices standards (.) legislation for
513        ourselves whe:re we strive ↑you know for reducing carbon levels
514        o::r if it's improving client safety in electrical equipment,
515        o:r if it's whatever e:rm >or ways to< soundly manage macro
516        economic performance (0.2) o:r if it is erm standards that we
517        hold high in terms of media freedom, or if [we,]
518 R                                                  [uhm mm]=
519 Inv                                                         =there is
520        a big system going on erm a so- sort of European model of
521        democratic modern countries. we just need to keep telling them
522        that that it is achievable. we just need to enco[urage them.]
523 R                                                      [yeah: but
524        how?]
525 Inv   [i-] we can help countries that have some stakeholders <not
526        necessarily>always the government (.) sometimes the opposition
527        sometimes the industry. we just find someone who is willing to
528 R     [that's interesting]
529 Inv   [.hhh integrating more] but sometimes unfortunately not many
530        are.
```

Extract 5.7 – EUIns.20

```
692 R     yeah yeah yes I think it has a different meaning to: yeah
693        clarifies the difference between Soviets and Russians
694 Inv   if you are just very cynical and calculated you could say
695        let them be governed by those (0.2) and the pol- let them
696        have this police run state! let the democrats remain in the
697        gulags and prisons.
698 R     uhm mm
699 Inv   it's not that they sell us oil and gas, and allow security
700        for investments there, and gi- and sell us those cheap products
701        even if they're produced by slave labour or by children labour
702        child labour, which you know they're as human as we are they
703        deserve democracy and human dignity! so: we're supposed to
704        to help with the those people (.) those nations who have the
705        same incremental right to be free.
```

Both of these extracts attend to describing the EU as offering the best normative model in the neighbourhood with a conscience to assist those who are
willing, or need to be helped. What is analytically striking, when considering
the two extracts together, is the way practitioners can juxtapose description
when attending to the EU's moral credentials.

In Extract 5.6 the practitioner begins with working up a justification of the
'huge machinery working here in Brussels .hh both scientific and legislative
machinery, that is developing new best practices standards' (lines 510–12), or
as he later refers to it 'a so- sort of European model' (line 520), through listing
the EU's specific legislative achievements of this 'machinery': 'we strive ↑you
know for reducing carbon levels' (line 513) 'o: : r if it's improving client safety
in electrical equipment' (line 514), 'o: r if it's whatever e: rm >or ways to<
soundly manage macro economic performance' (lines 515–16), and '(0.2) o:
r if it is erm standards that we hold high in terms of media freedom' (lines
516–17). The practitioner offers a rather comprehensive list in five parts that
is difficult to argue with, owing to its inclusiveness and detail (Jefferson, 1990).
In the same turn, the practitioner makes relevant the notion that such living
standards and the replication of the EU model 'is achievable' (line 522) for
others, as long as the EU motivates them (line 522). Next, the practitioner
offers a response to the researcher's request for clarification on how this could
be achieved (lines 523–4). He describes the EU as an organisation who would
work with anyone willing, in order to assist eastern neighbours to adopt the
EU model: '[i-] we can help countries that have some stakeholders <not
necessarily>always the government (.) sometimes the opposition sometimes
the industry. we just find someone who is willing to' (lines 525–7). Such openness
to work not only with the government, but also with opposition and private
companies, implies the EU's impartiality, objectivity, and open-mindedness
in order to support an amenable country. Expressions of this moral duty are
very similar to those in the first extract (Extract 5.1).

Turning now to Extract 5.7, the practitioner issues a disclaimer (line 694):
'if you are just very cynical and calculated you could say', in order to distance
himself from the provocative statement he is about to make: 'let them be
governed by those (0.2) and the pol- let them have this police run state! let
the democrats remain in the gulags and prisons' (lines 695–7). For any decent
person, it would be impossible to agree with, let alone allow such acts to take
place. The practitioner's assertion works to that effect. Without any contestation,
the researcher responds with a weak acknowledgement token of 'uhm mm'
(line 698), and allows the practitioner to carry on. According to him the
problem is not that they sell the EU energy, allow the security for investment
flows, or let their cheap products enter the EU market (lines 699–700), but
what they actually do to their own people (lines 701–2). This further confirms
the practitioner's initial assertion about Russia being an undemocratic and
amoral country. He then offers an alignment between the people of Russia

and us – the people of Europe – who are both human beings, and implies that these Russian people deserve the same rights and values that we enjoy (lines 701–3). This works to separate the Russian people from the Russian state and hence accomplishes the contrast between the EU and the Russian state. Furthermore, the practitioner issues a plea that the EU has to do what is morally right and help the Russian people to stand up against their own government (lines 703–5).

The next account offers a concrete example of a narrative in which the influence of EU norms and values is undeniable and evidently transferred.

Extract 5.8 – EUIns.29

```
503 R      and how do you see the EU's influence on Ukraine?
504 Inv    with a big neighbour like Ukraine I think we have a certa-, we
505        have this attractiveness because we're so close .hh and also
506        because they lead the east. now in the interest of having money
507        investing (0.3) and you know it's quite telling, we had a case
508        the other day when an Austrian bank was to be sold. it was sold
509        and there was an eastern Ukrainian consortium who put in
510        an offer which was actually lower than the one who in the end
511        got it. uhm:: higher than the one who in the end got it.
512        sorry >so< the Ukraine has complained bitterly about it and in
513        the end uhm: since the competition is open to an enquiry
514        because they're upset that things were not done correctly and
515        that shows that the Ukraine has start-, that the trend is now
516        also going towards general- (.) the other direction .hh so I
517        think the interests that the economic part have free trade and
518        now giving access to our market is a very strong one. and there
519        that means that in the relationship (inaudible) so I think
520        there the influence is certainly strong and .hh and that gives
521        us also political influence.
```

The practitioner offers a simple narrative account of the selling and buying of an Austrian bank in this extract. Plausibility of a report can increase by embedding it in a specific narrative sequence (Edwards and Potter, 1992). Here the practitioner sets the sequence up by an anticipatory announcement: 'and you know it's quite telling, we had a case the other day when an Austrian bank was to be sold' (lines 507–8) which makes the listener expect a compelling story. The practitioner delivers, and the Ukrainian consortium with the lowest bid loses out on the open competition to buy this Austrian bank. The upshot of her account is to work up the good influence the EU had on Ukraine. Her narrative accomplishes this by claiming that 'Ukraine has complained bitterly about it and in the end uhm: since the competition is open to an enquiry' (lines 512–13). So, Ukraine did not only feel resentful, but clearly challenged the decision, through the official roots, by instigating an enquiry into the decision. Such an act demonstrates not only that Ukraine is able to apply and comply with EU legislative norms, but is willing to do so. Besides knowing how to contest a potentially unjust decision, the practitioner describes the Ukrainian officials as 'upset': 'because they're upset that things were not done correctly' (line 514). References to emotions (or emotional treasures as they are technically called) like being upset or angry intensify the criticism of the EU's actions (Edwards, 1999). Nevertheless, this discursive device is used along with other criticisms to work up the positive influence that the EU had on Ukraine by not only accepting but also using norms that are available in the EU.

The final extract in this section provides an account of the duties that different EU institutions have in the policy, following the question of the practitioner's specific role in the negotiations. The practitioner embarked on a lengthy account, but his portrayal of the EP as the 'bad cop' and the European Council as the 'good cop' is analytically interesting.

Extract 5.9 – EUIns.15

```
466  Inv   if a parliamentary delegation meets you'll have a few people
467        who'll say a few nice things (.) a:nd you'll have a few
468        delegates, .hh few members, a few that is parliamentarians
469        who'll say really horrible things about these countries
470        beca:use they think that these countries should not join (.) or
471        those countries the parliament (they're) talking to is corrupt.
472  R     okay?
473  Inv   and they will say things in very very harsh terms, and I think
474        to a certain extent it's also good as a part of discourse and
475        so on: >to learn< to be a bit sa:y more critical approach
476        (0.6) as far as sometimes fro- just the more diplomatic tones
477        that we we're more used to with the Council
478  R     there you are you have really important role in the
479        negotiations ((laughs))
480  Inv   £important but an informal role
481  R     right
```

This account is a clear example of the interinstitutional cooperation between the Council and the EP. Furthermore, it demonstrates not only their need for each other, but also the way they use each other's competencies during treaty negotiations. First, I would like to focus on the portrayal of the parliamentarians as the 'bad cops' versus the Council officials as the 'good cops'. The practitioner offers an assessment of his meeting with Members of the European Parliament (MEPs), which usually begins with a few positive remarks (lines 466–7), but he implies that parliamentarians can be ruthless: 'a: nd you'll have a few delegates, .hh few members, a few that is parliamentarians who'll say really horrible things about these countries beca: use they think that these countries should not join (.) or those countries the parliament (they're) talking to is corrupt' (lines 467–71). He describes the practices of parliamentarians as ranging from saying 'horrible things' to voicing allegations of corruption. The practitioner continues his assessment of the MEPs as being severe on the neighbours: 'and they will say things in very very harsh terms' (line 473). Working up this harsh image is interesting, especially as next he praises the MEPs' approach: 'and I think to a certain extent it's also good as a part of discourse and so on: >to learn< to be a bit sa: y more critical approach' (lines 473–5), and then contrasts it with the more diplomatic tone of the Council or the 'good cop': '(0.6) as far as sometimes fro- just the more diplomatic tones that we we're more used to with the Council' (lines 476–7). Contrasting the two institutional approaches is significant for many reasons. The EP can be more severe and critical in scrutinising neighbouring states, especially if they have ambitions to accede, as its competencies are limited in foreign policy. Nevertheless, the EP is the only democratically elected institution; its voice represents and reflects popular values. Thus, parliamentarians can act as the moral compass to other EU institutions that are more concerned with staying on good terms, rather than being more principled with the neighbouring states. This separation of duties reflects perfectly the democratic values of the EU, since the elected body applies the scrutiny, that is, the moral code.

The importance of getting the message right

As we have previously discovered, there is always potential for a country to get the wrong idea about the ENP (Extract 5.3, line 157). The following two extracts demonstrate practitioners' concerns in making sure that the right message is put across to the neighbouring states. While it could be argued that the practitioners follow Buzan's logic of norm operationalisation, since they reflect on the EU's collective understanding of appropriate behaviour vis-à-vis the neighbouring states, I argue that at the same time they also follow Žižek's logic of drawing attention to those who stay within the boundaries of what is normative (France and Germany) and those who are not yet there (Armenia and Azerbaijan). Furthermore, these can be seen as specific instances where practitioners risk sounding moralising to those neighbours who just cannot quite conform to EU norms.

Extract 5.10 – EUIns.33

```
185  Inv   a:nd in terms of enlargement and the Neighbourhood Policy there
186        is <perhaps? a a tendency to say this is the way you have to
187        do things! this is the way you have to reform in this area, and
188        that area, .hhh a:nd also obviously the idea is that you accept
```

189   the *acquis.* what we are trying to do is <u>bring</u> the neighbourhood
190   countries closer to the EU system.
191 R   hmm mm °sure° [bu-]
192 Inv   [for] all of those reasons that is the wrong
193   (0.3) message to send to Russia which is a ↑proud country with
194   a: lo:ng ↑<u>history</u> (.) which regards itself increasingly under
195   Putin as a world player which has to be respected.
196 R   uh huh
197 Inv   SO: to try and say to Russia ↑look we know all about how to
198   reform your society in political and economic area what you
199   have to do is this and [that]
200 R   [£uh huh]
201 Inv   [and] obviously the closer you get
202   to adopting our rules the better for you!
203 R   uh huh right
204 Inv   that kind of language does not go down well with with Russia
205 R   I'd expect [so]
206 Inv   [cle]arly they wanted to distance themselves in
207   what they regarded a:s this patronising approach
209 R   uh huh
210 Inv   ↑how could you put Russia in the same category as Tunisia?
211   Moldova? and the Palestinian West Bank? (1) so strategic
212   partner to be treated on an equal basis, or or all of that
213   required us to deal with Russia in a different way and hence
214   hence the common spaces and the common space road maps
215 R   sure

Extract 5.11 – EUIns.59

966 Inv   things are better >than they were< in the days of the Soviet
967   Union
968 R   mm
969 Inv   then they are going to be less receptive. So: [maybe]
970 R   [hmm mm]
971 Inv   that's the solution! it would be nice if they all grew up and
972   <u>actually</u> ↓came to ma<u>tu</u>re adult solution b- before that ↑bu:t
973   maybe it is (.) that we simply have to wait out (0.4) for ↑for
974   reform processes.
975 R   uh huh and I'd guess that's one that you could ↑explain?
976 Inv   yeah and also the thing (that) we will have Armenians and
977   Azerbaijanis ↓who: <u>wouldn't</u> normally speak to each other .hh
978   >but< we'll have them on the same training course about
979   Intellectual Property Rights a:nd >over the coffee break< you

```
980        never know (.) they might (.) accidentally pass the sugar, or
981        say excuse me (0.2) o:r >this is what we have done< in the
982        Balkans, as well as (.) this is what ↑we did in the EU. This
983        is how we made the EU (.) we tied our coal and steel committees
984        together
985  R     sure >°(I) understand°<
986  Inv   SO: again it's a proven model. we don't stand up there and say
987        to Armenia and Azerbaijan we we will tie you together in the
988        same way as we tied France and Germany. NO ↑because you can't
989        just do that to someone else (.) you can do it to yourselves
990        but it's a model
991  R     sure
992  Inv   it's out there, it just takes a lot of vi- (.) historical vision
993        and patience and nothing else going on.
```

The practitioner in Extract 5.10 discusses on several occasions the problem of the EU's condescending manner to the ENP states, which stem from: 'a tendency to say this is the way you have to do things!' (lines 186–7). He admits that this tone is most problematic with Russia as: '[for] all of those reasons that is the wrong (0.3) message to send to Russia' (lines 192–3). After his admission, the practitioner offers further justification for the Russian position such as being a proud country (line 193), having a long history (line 194), and their increasing ambition to become a geopolitical actor (lines 194–5). His next turns are in support of this admission. First, the practitioner uses the active voicing device: 'SO: to try and say to Russia ↑look we know all about how to reform your society in political and economic area what you have to do is this and [that] [and] obviously the closer you get to adopting our rules the better for you!' (lines 197–202). Direct quotation, as employed in Extract 5.10 (lines 186–7) and by the practitioner (lines 197–202), is used to show the vivid and unexpected nature of what is described (Wooffitt, 1991, 2005). This is supported by the practitioner's next turn: 'that kind of language does not go down well with with Russia' (line 204) and then again when he issues another admission of 'this patronising approach' (lines 206–7). Next, the practitioner shifts his footing and presents himself as a mere reporter of a set of rhetorical questions: '↑how could you put Russia in the same category as Tunisia? Moldova? and the Palestinian West Bank?' (lines 210–11), as if even he does not understand the condescending manner of typecasting Russia a 'strategic partner' (lines 211–12). However, all of this is used to work up the EU as a good and considerate actor, who knows its role, and who can judge its own neighbours, as the final assessment is issued: 'all of that required us to deal with Russia in a different way and hence hence the common spaces and the common space road maps' (lines 212–14).

Extract 5.11 offers a different example of the importance of getting the message right. Before the practitioner makes relevant the hardship of the Soviet Union (lines 966–7), she complains about Georgia not having a functioning state,[3] and the problems that this is causing between Russia and the EU. This part has been omitted, as the focus here is on how the practitioner used that to set the scene for a more attainable conflict resolution narrative sequence (Edwards and Potter, 1992) between Armenia and Azerbaijan, that the EU can indeed facilitate[4]. But consider first the way the practitioner accomplished the topic shift. The practitioner raises the new topic of a reform process: 'it would be nice if they all grew up and <u>actually</u> ↓came to ma<u>tu</u>re adult solution b- before that ↑bu: t maybe it is (.) that we simply have to wait out (0.4) for ↑for reform processes' (lines 971–4). She accomplishes this by complaining about the childlike behaviour of states. 'Actually tagged' turns typically perform three main acts: informing, self-repair, and topic shift (Clift, 2001). On this occasion, there is an element of a hearable anecdote launch, thus the word *actually* is used as a continuer (Schegloff, 1982) to draw additional information on the topic (or a different set of 'mentiona-bles') (Maynard, 1980). At the same time, it advances (or, to use the technical term: upgrades) her initial complaint of immaturity and lack of receptiveness 'things are better >than they were< in the days of the Soviet Union' (lines 966–7).

Following this topic shift and the researcher's request for further clarifications (line 975), the practitioner presses on with the narrative sequence of the EU acting as a potential catalyst during training courses such as 'Intellectual Property Rights' (line 979) where Armenian and Azeri officials coincidentally engage with each other. She offers four speculative scenarios (lines 980–2): 'they might (.) accidentally pass the sugar, or say excuse me (0.2) o: r >this is what we have done< in the Balkans, as well as (.) this is what we did in the EU'. All these hypothetical situations are used to advocate the EU model (lines 983–4 and 986), and to imply that the EU performs valuable and morally admirable work as a mediator between hostile countries. However, the practitioner accepts that: 'we don't stand up there and say to Armenia and Azerbaijan we we will tie you together in the same way as we tied France and Germany' (lines 986–8). This illustrates the EU's awareness of the sensitivity of its role as a facilitator, grounded in a conception of right and wrong and a knowledge of what the EU can and cannot do morally, that is 'you can't just do that to someone else (.) you can do it to yourselves' (lines 988–9). Thus, the message from the EU has to be carefully crafted, even in situations where practitioners perhaps feel obliged to help. However, if the justification of being involved in the eastern neighbourhood of the EU is a moral one, it is not possible only to focus on getting the message the right, otherwise the EU risks being seen as moralising rather being moral.

Neighbours who have different moral values

According to EU practitioners, some EU neighbours have different moral standards and are reluctant to change, despite all efforts by the EU. Their complaints are directly aimed at Russia. This type of norm operationalisation is similar to the applications seen in Extract 5.5 and functions to draw a distinction between those who follow norms and those who violate them as put forward by Žižek (2006).

Extract 5.12 – EUIns.48

```
31 R    .hhh wha- what about our relations with Russia?
32 Inv  we have a big interest in developing our relations with Russia.
33      on a political level there are a lot of frozen conflicts in the
34      region (.) erm which the EU would like to see resolved. it's
35      clear that they will not be resolved without the Russians.
36      secondly (.)
37 R    uhmm
38      Russia as a permanent member of the UN Security Council plays a
39      very important role in a lot
40      uhmm
41      areas of foreign policy where the EU has a direct interest.
42      heh ((smirk)) unfortunately Russia doesn't always follow the
43      way we would like to see things done.
44 R    ahh could you give an example?
45 Inv  .hhh Russia's been causing us a lot of problems over Kosovo
46      and continue to cause us problems.
```

Russian non-compliance with EU norms, i.e. 'the way we would like to see things done' (line 43), is implied by this practitioner despite his own admittance that the EU has a big interest in having good relations with Russia. According to him, a primary area of common concern is the resolution of numerous frozen conflicts (line 33), for which the EU would require Russian support. Then the practitioner continues with a complaint that 'heh ((smirk)) unfortunately Russia doesn't always follow the way we would like to see things done' (lines 42–3). He begins with laughter which already implies the troubled nature of what is to come (Jefferson, 2004: 117–33). He knows that Russian non-compliance is unsurprising, especially in regions where they also have direct interests. The example of Kosovo, which he offers at the researcher's request, is illustrative of just that. The repetition of the practitioner's initial complaint of Russia causing problems (line 46) only adds to the presentation of Russia as an unhelpful, reluctant, and difficult partner in the region for finding resolutions to unresolved problems. In short, the Europeans are presented as the ones seeking a resolution, whereas the Russians are holding the EU's effort back. Again, this contrast works to separate the actors who follow norms from those who do not, just as put forward by Žižek (2006).

Demonstrating the different moral values held by Russia and the EU in domestic and foreign policy is examined next.

Extract 5.13 – EUIns.45

51	R	what are the challenges for the EU with with:: [Russia?]
52	Inv	[it's clear] the
53		Russians I think at the moment (.) are going through a period
54		where they tried to mark that they're kind of important
55		country trying to come back to the world stage in terms of (.)
56		but politics (0.4) and that it will (.) Russia will maintain or
57		try and restore our policy it is quite quite normal of course
58		but we have an interest to try to bring Russia more into into
59		our way of seeing things.
60	R	what do you actually mean by that?
61	Inv	we also have a big interest of course in making sure that
62		Russia addresses some of its domestic political developments
63		be:: it freedom of [press]
64	R	[um right]
65	Inv	[to] operate freely um:: a whol- (.)
66		just a general concept of democracy and democratic development
67		who would rule? being the judiciary? where we have quite
68		considerable differences of opinion with Russians. the big
69		problem that I see is .hh that Russians are very suspicious of
70		the motives of the EU. and certainly also interestingly member
71		states when it comes to pronouncing democracy
72	R	uhmm
73	Inv	I think the view towards the EU is a little bit more nuanced
74		than towards the United States
75	R	why would that [be i-?]
76	Inv	[the Uni]ted States is much more umm: a sort of
77		conflictual approach
78	R	aha:
79	Inv	whereas in Europe I think in EU it's not so much more
80		conflictual but more of a:: competitive approach
81	R	right
82	Inv	the Russians recognise:: that probably we have a greater RIGHT
83		to be concerned what's happening there because it's a
84		neighbour.
85	R	mhm
86	Inv	the Americans are a different category (0.2) we are

87   also only a soft power and don't have any military powers and
88   they are much more worried about NATO than worried about the EU
89   I think

The practitioner's assessment of Russia's quest to reassert itself as a global power is unsurprising (line 55), and recent events in Crimea, Syria, and the Iran sanction deal are all proof of this. Even more important here is the practitioner's justification for bringing Russia into line with European norms. Instead of presenting foreign policy differences like the previous practitioner, he decides to raise concerns over domestic issues. He lists 'freedom of [the press]' (line 63), 'general concept of democracy' (line 66), and freedom of the judiciary (line 67), as the political problems that EU would like Russia to address. It is one thing to draw direct comparison between the different positions that actors take on foreign policy matters, but it is another to critique a state's domestic political choices. The issue here is not the legitimacy of the practitioner's concern but that he raises his concerns in a direct comparison between EU and Russian norms, thereby implying that Russia has very different moral values that determine how they run their own state.

Next, the practitioner draws a distinction between US and EU relations with Russia. He qualifies the US–Russia relationship as 'conflictual' (line 77) and the EU–Russia relationship as 'competitive' (line 80). This is an important difference, as competitiveness implies an acceptance of the other's intention and of having to take these intentions seriously, whereas a conflictual relationship implies struggle, disharmony, and incompatibility. He resumes his justifications of this difference (lines 86–9) by grounding it in the lack of military capability the EU has which makes Russians far less fearful of the EU than they are of the US and NATO.

Embedded within the comparison between US and EU relations with Russia is the practitioner's claim that: 'the Russians recognise: : that probably we have a greater <u>RIGHT</u> to be concerned what's happening there <u>because</u> it's a neighbour' (lines 82–4). With this he reinforces the entitlement that the EU has to be involved in Russian affairs and/or to criticise its handling of its own domestic affairs based on the geographical location of the country. Furthermore, his assessment infers yet again a moral obligation the EU feels to assist Russia in aligning itself with the EU norms which the practitioner listed previously (lines 63–7). This entitlement also results from the collective responsibility or accountability the EU feels for its neighbours. At the same time, it could also be perceived, especially by Russia, as patronising, and thus having a moralising effect rather than offering moral authority in the region.

Extract 5.14 – EUIns.15

209 Inv   so far is that: (.) some countries have been less willing to
210   conform than others. some have taken the offer >others< have

211   done ↓less (0.2) the big example °of course° is .hh ↑<u>Bel</u>arus
212 R uhm::
213 Inv <u>but</u> (.) ↑our aim <u>really</u> is t- to try and encourage Belarus
214   to take on >our values<, our <democratic> values and then of
215   course you've got the whole question of economic development
216   (and) integration that but they don't seem to care
217 R umh:: [°why wo-°]
218 Inv   [because] we will at le:ast try to strengthen the ENP
219   (.) to be at least ENP partners greater access to the EU market
220   so better living standards (.) the I- <u>least</u> we can do.
221 R okay.

Besides stressing the non-compliance of Belarus, as has been examined in Extract 5.13, here the practitioner complains that Belarus does not care about its own people's living standards, but the EU does. This account is developed through reference to the fact that Belarus seems not to care about cooperation with the EU (line 216), despite the EU's genuine concern about improving living standards (line 220). Thus, by implying to care about the transformation of the Belarusian economy, the practitioner is not only attending to the concerns of the Belarusian living standards, but also the EU's moral obligation to support their transition to a market economy, which also links to the EU norms he identified before.

When is it morally wrong for the EU to be involved?

There are also occasions when it is necessary for the EU to take a more principled stance against neighbouring states and declare that it is morally wrong for the EU to be involved with them.

Extract 5.15 – EUIns.28

326 Inv once they meet the criteria (0.4) but we are with Poland,
327   probably one of the most vocal supporters of the Ukraine
328   (0.2) with Belarus we have (0.2) ermm an embassy there and the
329   situation is difficult (.) you know the regime is pretty
330   horrible
331 R clearly
332 Inv (0.2) we don't see any signs of (0.2) of progress at the moment
333   em (1) our ambassador in Belarus was sceptical of the benefits
334   of having a special advisor come over <u>because</u> he thought
335   there was a risk that it would just get used against us
336 R right

Extract 5.16 – EUIns.51

```
148  Inv   with Belarus (0.5) the e:m (0.5) adviser to the head
149        of the policy [unit]
150  R                [↑yeah]
151  Inv   is in Belarus at the moment a:nd e:m (1) we (0.6) there were
152        sort of mixed views within the EU as to how (0.5) we:ll
153        how sensible that visit is because it is important to us
154        that president Lukashenko can't use that .hh to his own
155        advantage, and say oh you that that the EU is doing business
156        with me! (0.5) they like me now! .hh and so on
```

In both extracts the practitioners are implying concern over the EU involvement in Belarus. In his response to a question on future enlargement, the practitioner in Extract 5.15 decides to specify Ukraine and Belarus. But he decides to focus on Belarus and lists several issues from difficult circumstances (line 329), to having a horrible regime (lines 329–30), and no sign of progress (line 332) to support his grievances with the country. All these problems work to justify minimal levels of EU involvement, as does his claim about the ambassador's own scepticism over having an EU adviser for Belarus (lines 333–4). Furthermore, the ambassador is not only unconvinced, but he also believes that it would be dangerous for the EU to build further relations since this could undermine the EU's own role and moral authority in the region.

A similar complaint is put forward in Extract 5.16. The practitioner references his head of unit's visit to Belarus, and the mixed reviews his visits received from other member states. By making relevant the others' opinions, the practitioner begins to distribute accountability for questioning the rationale behind this visit, since it is not only his personal view. Further, he declares that 'it is important to us that President Lukashenko can't use that .hh to his own advantage, and say oh you that that the EU is doing business with me! (0.5) they like me now! .hh and so on' (lines 153–6). There are two analytical points to consider here. First, the practitioner offers a direct quote from Lukashenko and by using this discursive device (also known as active voicing) he constructs his account to be more vivid and believable (Wooffitt, 1991: 267–88). Second, through the application of this device, he attends to his initial complaint, which he reissues (lines 154–5), that the only person to profit from this visit is the Belarusian president. Being seen as helping the last dictator of Europe is not beneficial for the EU. For that very reason, the practitioner is questioning EU involvement in Belarus which again only serves to jeopardise the EU's moral authority in the region and the EU's reputation as a moral actor.

Conclusion

This chapter focused on the ways that EU practitioners managed moral concerns when discussing EU policy vis-à-vis the eastern neighbours. While doing so, I demonstrated the close connection between the identified moral concerns and the previous chapter's subject of EU norms and the normative role of the EU in the eastern neighbourhood. As the analysis unfolded, the evidence demonstrated how practitioners embed moral concerns in their practice. This further supports the theoretical point of linking normative and moral concerns. Four key patterns emerged from the corpus concerning the EU's moral obligations to the neighbours.

To begin with, in both Extract 5.1 and 5.2 practitioners accounted for the duty of care they EU had for the neighbours. They likened the success of the new member states and the potentially similar outcome for the eastern neighbours, with the EU's moral obligation to help them both, which is very similar to Dannreuther's (2004) claim. Furthermore, both practitioners made relevant EU norms and values and the importance of alignment with these norms as part of the EU's moral obligation to its neighbours. Extract 5.3 follows a similar trajectory, but it drew attention to the possibility of such alignment leading to failure and destruction, which would affect the EU's duty not only to the specific state in question, but also to itself. Such assertion of moral duty is closely bound up with issues of collective and personal accountability, both of which is analytically relevant when examining the practitioner's account, but also theoretically when claims of responsibility are attended to.

Another way of attending to moral concerns is through invoking awareness or consciousness as we saw in Extracts 5.4 and 5.5. Practitioners justified their moral obligations through 'conscious decisions' of extending the benefits beyond the CEECs, or as an entitlement after having received EU support, respectively. Being associated with the EU brings a certain credibility, which is *good* for geopolitical reasons, according to the practitioner in Extract 5.6. Furthermore, he employed a now familiar contrast between the Russian and the EU model that the eastern neighbours could choose from. Drawing on this contrast the following two accounts further demonstrate this gap. While the practitioner in Extract 5.6 worked up the EU and its good practices and openness to work with practically any organisation or body from the neighbouring states, the practitioner in Extract 5.7 constructed Russia as immoral, and he implied obligation on behalf of the EU to help those who are not granted the same conditions as EU citizens.

Practitioners also employed different discursive resources to manage moral obligations. In Extract 5.8 the practitioner offered a specific narrative sequence on the selling/buying of an Austrian bank to give plausibility (Edwards and Potter, 1992) to her working up the EU's moral obligation based on what the EU has already taught them. This narrative was also accompanied with a specific discursive device that attends to emotions (Edwards, 1999). Descriptions of Ukraine being upset supported the building up of Ukraine's criticism of the EU, but at the same time demonstrated how well the EU educated it for good moral principles and for its own norms and values. The final extract, Extract 5.9, in this section attended to the role different EU institutions play in treaty negotiations, and how the EP as the 'bad cop' and the Council as the 'good cop' ultimately both attend to moral concern they have for the neighbours.

The second pattern that emerged from the corpus was practitioners' concerns over communicating the right message on the ENP to the neighbours. Issues of states getting the wrong idea about the policy were mentioned before (in Extract 5.4), but in Extracts 5.10 the practitioner is concerned with building up accounts of the EU as a good and considerate actor, after accepting that the patronising tone did not work with Russia, thus the message has to be adjusted. Another practitioner, in Extract 5.11 employed a narrative sequence to work up the persuasiveness of her account Edwards and Potter, 1992), while attending to the EU's conflict resolution work between Armenia and Azerbaijan. Simultaneously, she accepted that the EU could not force states to apply the EU model in order to achieve peace, even if there are compelling arguments for it and would fall beneath the EU's moral concerns.

The third pattern related to accounts of practitioners attending to complaints about Russia and Belarus, who have different moral standards to the EU and who are reluctant to change, despite all efforts. While working up the Europeans' eagerness to find resolutions for political problems in the regions in Extract 5.12, the practitioner implied that Russia has no such concerns. He used Kosovo to illustrate this point. In Extract 5.13 the practitioner attended to the issues of Russia's own domestic politics and the EU's obligation and 'right' as a neighbour to support a reform process. He also contrasted Russia's relations with the US, as 'conflictual' to those it had with the EU, as 'competitive'. Despite accepting the competitive nature of the relationship, the practitioner still argued for EU involvement in Russian domestic politics. Extract (5.14) complained of Belarus's neglect of its own people's welfare and worked up the EU's moral obligation to support Belarus in achieving a market economy.

The fourth pattern in this chapter related to practitioners' accounts of instances when it is actually morally wrong for the EU to be involved in a neighbour's affairs. Belarus is the classic example. In both extracts practitioners worked up justifications for minimising relations from citing Lukashenko's authoritarian regime. Moreover, in Extract 5.15, the practitioner invoked concerns raised by the EU ambassador over the EU, to build further relations which would only compromise the EU's own moral position in the region. A similar complaint was proposed in Extract 5.16, where a practitioner apportioned blame among all member states, thus he distributed accountability, while questioning the rationale behind the visit of his head of unit to Belarus. He was concerned that Belarus's aim is to use the EU's reputation to improve its own.

Besides identity, normativity, and morality, EU practitioners are equally concerned with the collective interests. Accounts of interests in energy, energy security, and energy supply are the themes of the next and final analytical chapter.

Notes

1 A silence of 0.6 seconds is considered long in conversation.
2 Further examples of this type of operationalisation of norms are explored in the next section.
3 The practitioner begins her complaint with 'even if Georgia functioned properly' which is followed by a 'then' clause (line 969). The use of the if-and-then device will be examined in the next chapter. The inclusion of the omitted part would only offer a digression from the analytical point, but it offers an understanding of a 'receptive' claim.
4 This is a reference to the conflict in the Nagorno–Karabakh enclave of south-west Azerbaijan where the majority population is ethnic Armenians. The Armenian separatist movement began in 1988 and escalated into full warfare until 1994 (Melander, 2001). There is a ceasefire but several attempts to broker a peace deal have failed and active fighting still breaks out sporadically.

6

Justifying the EU's interests in the region: energy security

Building on the findings of the three previous chapters on collective 'European' identity, norms, and moral concerns, this chapter turns to collective EU interest formulations. There are numerous collective interests such as terrorism, hybrid threats, economic volatility, climate change, and energy security that have been identified as the EU Global Strategy (EU HR/VP, 2016). These interests not only bind EU member states to act together, but also signifies to other, non-EU states, what the EU is focusing on. The practitioners who participated in the study also identified migration, the environment, organised crime, and transport as collective EU interests. Unsurprisingly, they identified energy security as the most pressing common security interest that unites EU member states' interest into a collective interest, in the eastern neighbourhood.

Notions of interest and material capability have always been a pivotal part of IR theory and EU foreign policy analysis. There are many studies that examine the EU's capabilities, and policy developments that measure its potential role as a global actor (Allen and Smith, 1990; Hill, 1993; Soetendorp, 1994; Whitman, 1997; Bretherton and Vogler, 1999; Laffan et al., 1999: 167–72; Smith, 2000; Damro, 2001). These studies demonstrate the fact that power and interests are important factors for EU foreign policy. My main concern in this chapter is how to differentiate collective European interests from traditional state interests. Neorealist assumptions do not account for the composition of international actors and the complexity of the EU, as they argue that actors, including international organisations, are solely interested in maximising their material capabilities (Wendt, 1995). For neoliberalist institutionalists regard actors' identities and interests as pre-existent and predetermined (Kowert and Legro, 1996), although these interests can be more varied than solely maximising material capability.

The constructivist turn in IR and EU integration studies, influenced by poststructuralist philosophy and the rise of new interest in social interaction, allowed scholars the intellectual space to consider interests and material capabilities together with normative and moral concerns. Their focus on institutions meant that the development of shared interests, normative and moral values were taken into account (Katzenstein, 1997). Thus, there is an acceptance that a political community cannot only be defined by material factors (size, wealth, geography, social structure) but also by normative factors (identity, culture, norms, and moral values) (Hoffmann, 1995). The inferences of this analytical chapter are further proof of this.

Three main patterns emerged from the corpus. First, practitioners' constructions of energy interest are examined. These constructions are also linked to issues of the shared eastern neighbourhood. The second pattern reveals practitioners' accounts of future plans to manage the collective EU concern over energy supplies. Besides offering justifications for this common concern, they also offer accounts of introducing an early warning mechanism and energy diversification. In the third and final pattern, practitioners offer justifications of EU interest in the eastern region, beyond the collective interests in energy supplies, and again through invoking moral concerns and the vocation attributes the EU has for the eastern neighbours. This is analytically significant, and supports the claim this book makes that identity, norms, and moral concern cannot be separated from interest.

EU energy interests in the shared neighbourhood

Practitioners are heard referring to the collective EU energy interests, while attending to the concerns of the shared neighbourhood. In Extract 6.1 the collective interest that unites not only member states but also the neighbourhood are identified. We will then proceed to accounts from EU practitioners concerning the potential problems of sharing a neighbourhood with Russia (Extracts 6.2 and 6.3).

Extract 6.1 – EUIns.46

```
408 R    it's it's just as you were saying ↑that there is quite often
409      the EU has been criticised for its asymmetric relationship
410      with these countries
411 Inv  hmm
412 R    ↑but quite often, the EU br- brings up its interest in energy
413      resources and >pipelines< and that's kind o::f demonstrate
414      interdependence? DEspite the ↑very asymmetric attitude.
415 Inv  yes this is true. ↑but as we discover we: >you know< the
416      Ukraine and Russia are interested in energy. we have a shared
417      interest there.
418 R    yeah sure
```

In Extract 6.1 the researcher makes a provocative claim relating to the general disapproval of the asymmetric nature of EU relations with the eastern neighbours while the EU depends heavily on their energy resources and transport routes (lines 408–14). The practitioner's response to this claim is somewhat two-sided;

partially agreeing with the researcher but with some significant alterations. First, he offers a preferred response through two agreements: 'yes' and 'this is true' (line 415). Both assessments would imply that the practitioner accepts the offered claim, but he continues with a 'but' clause: '↑but as we discover we: >you know< the Ukraine and Russia are interested in energy. we have a shared interest there' (lines 415–17). By resuming his turn with 'but', the practitioner actually offers a dispreferred response for the researcher's claim. His argument is that there is a 'shared interest' (lines 416–17) between the EU, the Ukraine, and Russia, which goes against the researcher's claim that the basis of the EU relations with its neighbours is one-sided, as after all energy is not exclusively an EU interest. Thereby, claims that the EU would just take advantage of the neighbours are unfounded, which leaves the EU's reputation intact.

The next two extracts both attend to the potential issues that the shared neighbourhood might cause between the EU and Russia concerning energy supply and security.

Extract 6.2 – EUIns.17

```
187 Inv  w- we need Russia's help wi:th (0.6) >all sorts of security
188       issues (0.5) Iran (0.4) Kosovo .hhh all sorts of things bu:t
189       we >°just°< need=to=be in a better position with Russian f- for
190       energy security .hh as >of course< probably what most people in
191       the EU would call number one is the EU Russia relationship
192       concerning our energy
193 R    uh huh you mean sup[ply?]
194 Inv                     [yeah]
195 R    okay bu:t what about the transit routes?
196 Inv  we:ll yeah .hh that's another of our security issue w- we just
197       need their help. but the issue of transit countries is ((tcht))
198       tricky.
```

Extract 6.3 – EUIns.53

```
69 R    IN your (opinion) How does Russia sees these neighbouring
70      countries?
71 Inv  I hold Russia's [opinion]
72 R                    [uhmmm]
73 Inv  Russia still doesn't take them fully seriously! .hh a:nd I
74      think that Russia still sees these countries AS be:longing to
75      their sphere influence >as I mean< Russia still is a
76      country which is big on geopolitical °assumptions° in itself
77      which is regrettable <bu::t
78 R    uhmmm
```

```
79  Inv    (0.8) ↑but I think that we do have to change. >I mean< we've
80         been looking at this the problems in terms of our own gas and
81         oil supplies, .hh a:nd I think you have to accept to a certain
82         extent that you have Russia expressing his own frustration.
83         at the same time you have a Russia which um I think >more=or=
84         less< ↑ACCepts or at least acknowledges that she has los::t
85         (0.8) these countries that these countries are no longer
86         reigned by ermm a sort of sphere of influence.
87  R      uhmm
```

In Extract 6.2 the practitioner states that: 'w- we need Russia's help wi: th (0.6) >all sorts of security issues', and begins his list with Iran and Kosovo (lines 187–8). The pauses in between demonstrate the careful consideration his response involves. As we know from Jefferson's (1990) study, lists need at least three parts to sound complete, representative, and rhetorically effective. Here the practitioner finishes his list with a non-specific component of '.hhh all sort of things' (line 188). This is similar to 'etcetera', which Jefferson (1990) notes is often used as a 'generalised list completer'. Even though the practitioner's list sounds complete, he returns to add another element to it, after being prompted (line 195): 'okay bu: t what about the transit routes?'. First, he offers a preferred response: 'we: ll yeah' (line 196). Then he invokes the subject of the transit routes as: '.hh that's another of our security issue w- we just need their help' (lines 196–7). Besides itemising the different security issues, the practitioner also demonstrates the joint interest of these problems between the EU and Russia, by identifying them as areas where the EU requires Russia's help.

There is another important point here. The practitioner's decision to refer to the subject of energy and security as 'our energy' (line 192) and 'our security' (line 196) is analytically significant. By choosing the pronoun 'our', he implies the collective nature of the energy and security issues that the EU is facing.

The same point is raised in Extract 6.3, but in this case it is embedded in a complaint about Russia. The practitioner identifies the problems in the shared neighbourhood as 'our own gas and oil supplies' (lines 80–1). Again, the pronoun 'our' works to the same effect and implies that energy security is a collective EU interest in the eastern region. Adding the adjective 'own' to the possessive pronoun works to amplify the sense of belonging.

The issue of the shared neighbourhood is invoked through the practitioner's complaint about Russia. In response to the researcher's question: 'IN your (opinion) How does Russia sees these neighbouring countries?' (lines 69–70), the practitioner issues the first part of his complaint: 'Russia still doesn't take them fully seriously!' (line 73). Then he upgrades his complaint (lines 73–5) after an in-breath: '.hh a: nd I think that Russia still sees these countries AS be: longing to their sphere influence'. Claiming that Russia does not regard

134

the eastern countries as worthy of attention is problematic, but implying that Russia is playing the controlling card further complicates EU–Russian relations in the shared neighbourhood. The notion of Russia identifying the eastern regions as its own sphere of influence is not new. It is part of Russia's foreign policy as mentioned in Chapter 4. Next the practitioner accepts that the EU will have to adjust its perspective owing to its own collective energy issue and reliance on the eastern neighbours: '↑but I think that we do have to change. >I mean< we've been looking at this the problems in terms of our own gas and oil supplies' (lines 79–81). But instead of attending to the adjustments the EU will have to make, the practitioner reissues his complaints about Russia's assertions of the eastern neighbours as her sphere of influence: 'at the same time you have a Russia which um I think >more=or=less< ↑ACCepts or at least acknowledges that she has los:: t (0.8) these countries that these countries are no longer reigned by ermm a sort of sphere of influence' (lines 83–6). According to this practitioner, it would seem that energy concerns and the historic ties between Russia and other eastern states that lie between Russia and the EU have created a stalemate. Despite his attempts to dispel the notion of Russian control in the region, the practitioner accepts the complexity of the shared neighbourhood. He does so by downgrading Russia's acceptance of having lost the region to an acknowledgement (line 84) of Russia's weakened position.

In the final extract in this section, a practitioner draws on a comparison between Ukraine and Moldova, while attending to concerns in the shared neighbourhood.

Extract 6.4 – EUIns.43

97	R	mm hmm and how important do you think Ukraine is for th the EU
98		compare to Moldova?
99	Inv	you don't .hh you <u>never</u> want to compare countries like these
100		↑because <I me::an> they're all important in their own right,
101	R	okay
102	Inv	and our relationship with them <u>is</u> in their own right.=<u>A</u>nd of
103		course it's a huge erm w-we share a <u>long</u> border with them <u>s</u>o:
104		there are issues of mi::gration, it's also a >transit country<
105	R	hmm mm
106	Inv	the European union's energy market is big.=<u>A</u>nd we transit from
107		<u>Russia</u>, .hh from Central Asia, transited via Ukraine <<u>but</u> of
108		course energy has become quite topical <I me:an> polit[ical.]
109	R	[umhh]
110	Inv	political attention <u>that's</u> that's given to Ukraine <u>compared</u> to
111		Moldova. Moldova is different, <u>because</u> it has lots of problems.
112		<just lot's!

First, consider the practitioner's dispreferred response to the researcher's request to compare Ukraine and Moldova: 'you don't .hh you <u>never</u> want to compare countries like these ↑because <I me: : an> they're all important in their own right' (lines 99–100). The upgrade from 'don't' to an audibly louder '<u>never</u>' adds further emphasis to the practitioner's negative assessment of this suggested comparison. From line 102 he attends to an explanation of the similarities of these countries based on their geographical position. He begins his list with a reference to shared borders (line 103), issues of migrations (line 104) and the fact that 'it's also a >transit country<' (line 104). Lists, as it has been pointed out before, are vital for rhetorical effectiveness (Jefferson, 1990). However, in the final component of his three-part list, the practitioner changes from making general claims of shared EU interests in these countries to specifying one of them as 'a >transit country<'. This shift is not accidental. The practitioner continues to work up the significance of this transit country, based on the collective EU interest in energy: 'the European union's energy market is big.=<u>A</u>nd we transit from <u>Russia</u>, .hh from Central Asia, transited via Ukraine' (lines 106–7). He identifies the transit country to be Ukraine. Furthermore, the practitioner offers a point of contrast between Ukraine and Moldova and notes their relevance for the EU: '<but of course energy has become quite topical <I me: an> polit[ical.] political attention <u>that's</u> that's given to Ukraine <u>compared</u> to Moldova' (lines 107–11). Evidently Moldova is not a transit country. As a result of the political importance of the collective EU energy interest, Ukraine gets more attention. The contrast structure is also established by the practitioner's claim that: 'Moldova is different, <u>be</u>cause it has lots of problems. <just lot's!' (lines 111–12). This discursive device is designed to show what in attribution terms would be distinct information (Edwards and Potter, 1992). Thereby, Ukraine and Moldova are treated differently by the EU based on their capacity to transit its energy supplies. At the same time this distinction attends to the collective EU interest of energy supply and the relevance of the eastern region.

Future plans to manage the concern about the energy supplies

The EU not only has to manage its collective energy interest in the eastern region but also the problems with interruptions to its supplies, as a result of various disputes between Russia and the other eastern states. These rows endanger the security of the EU's energy supply and question Russia's reliability as a trustworthy supplier. The next three accounts attend to two different ways of managing concerns over interruptions to the EU's energy supplies. In Extract 6.5 the notion of the early warning mechanism is introduced, while Extracts 6.6 and 6.7 raise diversification and the new pipelines as potential solutions.

Extract 6.5 – EUIns.24

486	R	↑so how about energy? (0.2) ↑cause obviously these countries
487		are transit countries?
488	Inv	erm (1) >as you know< the EU is developing (0.3) its energy
489		policy <u>both</u> <u>internally</u> a:nd <u>externally</u> .hh a:nd what we <u>want</u>
490		externally <u>is</u> (.) to build a <u>series</u> of partnerships (.) <u>both</u>
491		with producer countries such as (0.2) .hh such as Russia,
492		Algeria, and elsewhere (0.4) <u>as</u> well <u>as</u> with <u>transit</u> <u>countries</u>
493	R	okay
494	Inv	and that primarily means Russia and central Asia as producers
495		as well of course erm ((cough)) but <u>also</u> Ukraine a:nd eh (0.3)
496		a:nd Belarus. .hh <u>And</u> I think what we are trying to do:
497		<u>specifically</u> in the short term is try to erm (0.2)
498		encourage Russia=Belarus=Ukraine to <u>est</u>ablish some kind of
499		early warning mechanisms.
500	R	<u>right</u>
501	Inv	.hh where we'd consult in advance <u>so</u> that we are not faced
502		with the problems of Ukraine <u>last</u> <u>year</u> a:nd Belarus this year
503	R	uh huh

In Extract 6.5, the researcher makes reference to energy policy and the transit countries (lines 486–7). The practitioner initially offers an explanation of the collective EU energy interest and policy. He begins his account with some hesitation 'erm', and a second-long pause (line 488), before stating that: '>as you know< the EU is developing (0.3) its energy policy <u>both</u> <u>internally</u> a: nd <u>externally</u>' (lines 488–9). Through his claim of the researcher's familiarity with the topic ('>as you know<'), the practitioner implies consensus and corroboration (Smith, 1978; Potter and Edwards, 1990). This discursive device is used to standardise an account, making it appear as something that everyone would agree with. It also attends to issues of accountability as if the claim that is raised is commonly accepted, which then diminishes the practitioner's own personal accountability (Potter, 1996). After drawing a distinction between the producers Russia and the Central Asian countries (line 494) and the transit counties Ukraine (line 495) and Belarus (line 496), the practitioner invokes the notion of the early warning mechanism as a short-term solution: '.hh And I think what we are trying to do: <u>specifically</u> in the short term is try to erm (0.2) encourage Russia=Belarus=Ukraine to <u>est</u>ablish some kind of early warning mechanisms' (lines 497–9). Then he presents the reason for having to call for the introduction of this early warning mechanism: '.hh where we'd consult in advance <u>so</u> that we are not faced with the problems of Ukraine <u>last</u> <u>year</u> a: nd Belarus this year' (lines 501–2). This warning system is clearly to support the member states and to prepare them for any future interruption in the energy flow in case there are future instances of supply stoppage; however, it is not a solution.

In the following two extracts, practitioners raise the possibility of diversification, including alternative pipelines, as a management strategy for future interruptions of energy supplies.

Extract 6.6 – EUIns.50

883	Inv	there is also (.) <I mean> <u>our</u> member states <u>DO</u>n't=<u>Even</u>=think
884		as a unit, sometimes vis-à-vis Russia.
885	R	why is [that?]
886	Inv	[there] is this great fear (.)↑you kno:w Russia has us
887		over a barrel about oil, <u>because</u> <u>I</u>t <u>C</u>ontrols <u>T</u>he <u>S</u>ource. <the
888		oil is <u>no</u> use if Russia does not have power to do with energy.
889		↑if it doesn't have a market.
890	R	hmmm
891	Inv	<u>SO:</u> if if we find <u>alternative</u>=sources that <u>reduces</u> Russia's
892		↑influence .hh (.) of course the reality of the world, it is
893		now selling to (.) India and China as well so its erm it will
894		lose that influence b- but erm that's talking in the long
895		term! And hopefully the various alternative pipelines come good
896		too. <u>right</u> <u>now</u> the situation is <u>as</u> it is.
897	R	.hh whe:ll yes

Extract 6.7 – EUIns.30

623	R	I wanted to just ask yo:u a little bit more on energy and and
624		energy issues with Russia? .hh the sticking points?
625	Inv	I think <u>it's</u> an issue, wh:ich is <u>part</u>icularly important now,
626		and I have been doing a lot of work on energy (0.4) and the
627		recent actions against the Ukraine and Belarus have <u>natur</u>ally:
628		alarmed the EU. We should have listened to t- the analyst. they
629		saw it- saw it coming.
630	R	right.
631	Inv	↑it gives the impression that our energy security from Russia
632		is in doubt (0.6) erm: so (.) yeah I think we are considering
633		alternatives .hh like <u>s</u>olar and wind energy.
634	R	long term ↑you mean?
635	Inv	£ye:ah (.) first we are negotiating with Russia because it is
636		important for us, tha:t w- <<u>you</u> know that we feel that
637		our investment in Russia <u>is</u> <u>safe</u> (.) and <u>that</u> the security of
638		our supplies are secure (.) <u>that</u> we are going to get <u>what</u> we
639		sign up for! a:nd that Russia <u>isn't</u> going t- to turn off the
640		taps <the way it did to Ukraine.

Consider the practitioner's initial complaint concerning member states not acting in a unified way towards Russia (Extract 6.6, lines 883–4). In her reply to the researcher's 'why is [that?]', she spells out the root of the trouble in a rhythmic fashion: '[there] is this great fear (.)↑you kno: w Russia has us over a barrel about oil, <u>because</u> <u>I</u>t <u>C</u>ontrols <u>Th</u>e <u>S</u>ource' (lines 886–7). She offers two more assessments of this situation, first: '<the oil is <u>no</u> use if Russia does not have power to do with energy' (lines 887–8), and then: '↑if it doesn't have a market' (line 889). Controlling the source and the market is crucial for Russia. Nevertheless, it needs a market. Next the practitioner offers a solution to reduce Russia's power, over EU energy, through diversification: '<u>SO</u>: if if we find <u>alter</u>native=sources that <u>reduces</u> Russia's ↑influence'. She also mentions Russia's new markets, India and China (line 893), which she implies will curtail Russia's impact on the EU's security supplies. However, the EU's strategy of finding alternative energy sources and the changes that will result from Russia's new markets are long-term concerns (lines 894–5); as is the development of new pipelines and transit routes (lines 895–6). After discussing these issue of energy supplies and the potential solutions to these worries, the practitioner's final assessment is striking: '<u>right</u> <u>now</u> the situation is <u>as</u> it is' (line 896), thus she implies acceptance of having to live with the worries over energy supplies, for now at least.

In Extract 6.7 the practitioner raises the same collective EU concerns over energy supplies as all other practitioners before. He also makes references to specific disruptions of Russian energy supplies to Ukraine and Belarus (line 627), and the anxiety that caused for the EU member states that rely on that energy flow. After the researcher's short uptake through issuing an acknowledge-ment token: 'right' (line 630), the practitioner reissues his complaint: '↑it gives the impression that our energy security from Russia is in doubt' (lines 631–2). He continues, following some hesitation, by presenting a solution: '(0.6) erm: so (.) yeah I think we are considering alternatives .hh like <u>s</u>olar and wind energy' (line 633). He does not only imply that there are alternative resources but he gives two specific examples being solar and wind. Nevertheless, his assessment, just like that of the practitioner in Extract 6.6, is that diversification is a long-term solution. The practitioner issues this assessment in collaboration with the researcher: '↑long term you mean?' (line 634) and: '£ye: ah' (line 635). He seeks further consensus with '>you know<' (line 636) while working up the importance of working with Russia before seeking alternative resources. The use of 'you know' as a corroboration device is not new. The practitioner in Extract 6.5 employed it (line 488) '>as you know<', and so did the practitioner in Extract 6.6 (line 886): '(.) ↑you kno: w', in order to standardise their accounts so others would agree with and confirm (Smith, 1978; Potter and Edwards, 1990). As before, this consensus seeking attends to issues of accountability, and reduces the personal responsibility of the practitioner for his or her account (Potter, 1996).

'[It] isn't philanthropy' but we still care

The final section of this chapter considers how practitioners manage moral concerns, while attending to collective energy security in the eastern neighbourhood. The next four extracts demonstrate how these two issues are combined in order to leave the EU's reputation as a conscious, virtuous, moral actor in the region intact.

Extract 6.8 – EUIns.16

```
338 R    <and one more thing that I would like to press you on (.) how
339      do y- how do you .hh cause, I me:an these countries sometimes
340      criticise the asymmetry in the relation[ship,]
341 Inv                                          [yeap]
342 R    a:nd the EU has quite a lot of interest in these countries'
343      natural resources
344 Inv  yeap
345 R    and pipe- pipelines, So: how do you see this criticism in terms
346      of [th-,]
347 Inv     [°ummm°]
348 R    the evenness of EU interest in these countries, beca:use they
349      have most of the natural resources that the EU requires!
350 Inv  that's I think's quite normal (.) of course [we:]
351 R                                                 [uhm mm]
352 Inv  to be honest we are just interested in our energy security, we-
353      we have to.
354 R    uhmm
355 Inv  And we do want predictable neighbours and so on that's normal
356      but:: e:rm:: IF >sort of< our policy ends there and that
357      we erm:: stop ↑being interested in their well be:ing and so on
358      then we have a ↑problem.
359 R    okay
360 Inv  but, if- our if we have these elements as part of our policy
361      (inaudible) and that >°of course°< is °another way of looking
362      at it°
363      (2)
364 Inv  ↑cos .hh I mean <of course> the oil crisis=the gas crisis with
365      Ukraine (.) what we were interested was the predictability of
366      O:UR e:nergy supplies AT the same time. SInce we see it is in
367      our interest that these countries don't become chaotic and
368      build a more stable Ukraine (inaudible) we will be as
369      interested in their energy security.
```

Extract 6.8 begins with the researcher referring to the criticism of an asymmetric relationship between the EU and its eastern neighbours (line 340), the EU's interests in their natural resources (lines 342–3 and 349), and their transit routes (lines 345). Throughout the researcher's several turns, the practitioner issued brief acknowledgement tokens of 'yeah' and 'uhm', before beginning his full assessment: 'that's I think quite normal (.) of course we have to say that' (line 350). The practitioner clearly takes no issues with this. He continues his dispreferred response with the phrase 'to be honest' (line 352). Edward and Fasulo (2006)[1] examined such constructions as part of complement structures within the classical sequential environment of dispreferred responses to questions (Atkinson and Heritage, 1984). Their observation is applicable to the EU practitioner's use of this phrase, to preface his account, that it is indeed acceptable to forge relations with a region where strategic EU energy interests are: 'to be honest we are just interested in our energy security, we- we have to', thus lines 352–3 are part of the 'to be honest' + complement structure. It is also a dispreferred response, as agreement with the researcher's list of criticisms would be the preferred response. Another important feature of the 'to be honest' account is that it retains a considerable amount of semantics in presenting honesty as the basis of the utterance. Given this, such structures not only attend to the objectivity or factuality of the utterance but also its subjectivity, or to the speaker's knowledge and motivation (Edwards 2000, 2005, 2007). Here it implies that the practitioner's action is being done out of honesty rather than any other kind of motive. It also implies the EU is a moral actor, which is frank and open rather than deceitful.

There is another key analytical point in the extract. After the practitioner's attempt to present the EU's skewed interest in the region as 'normal' (line 350 and 355), he begins to work up the EU's moral obligation for the region through the introduction of the 'if–then' discursive formulation: 'but: : e: rm: : IF >sort of< our policy ends there and that we erm: : stop ↑being interested in their wellbe: ing and so on then we have a ↑problem' (lines 356–8). As mentioned in Chapters 3 and 6, such discursive formulations follow a pattern of 'if you do x, then problem y should not arise' (Sneijder and te Molder, 2005). Here, the script follows a slightly alternating form by 'if you do not do x, then problem y remains'. In either form, the application of this discursive formula enables the speaker to appear as a morally responsible actor who can make a decision as to what is best. The wider effect of this is that the EU appears to care for its neighbours. This is further confirmed by the practitioner's account where he states that: 'what we were interested was the predictability of O: UR e: nergy supplies AT the same time. SInce we see it is in our interest that these countries don't become chaotic and build a more stable Ukraine (inaudible) we will be as interested in their energy security' (365–9). Thereby, collective

EU energy interests are interlinked with creating a stable, secure, and predictable neighbourhood.

The next extracts follow a similar trajectory.

Extract 6.9 – EUIns.4

564	R	↑that's what I was try:ing to get to. tha- the EU's interest is
565		o̲ften criticised (.)↑because of the energy resources in these
566		countries rather than others idea th- that you YOURself have
567		mentioned them too: human rights, [and]
568	Inv	[A̲re] you trying to say, that
569		that our sentiment towards those countries should be pure̲ly̲
570		pla̲t̲onic? ↑And only lo̲ve and N̲O̲ interest? (.) £Whell:
571	R	I- I ↓know
572	Inv	I̲T's more complicated. >A:nd if we have balance between the two
573		that is fine! the r- rea̲l̲ problems come when you close your
574		your eyes on those various human rights violations beca̲:u̲se you
575		want to buy oil and gas!
576	R	and do you think that's happening?
577	Inv	.hh might be
578	R	hmm

In Extract 6.9, the researcher offers a criticism of the EU for the practitioner to assess: 'tha- the EU's interest is o̲ften criticised (.) because of the energy resources in these countries rather than others idea th- that you YOURself have mentioned them too: human rights, [and]' (lines 564–7). This request also includes a reference to a prior turn: 'you YOURself have mentioned them too', and thus, would expect a positive assessment. In this prior turn, the practitioner also brings up human rights which is one of the fundamental norms that the EU aims to transfer to the neighbours. The practitioner begins in overlap with the researcher and delivers a rhetorical question as his assessment: '[A̲re] you trying to say, that that our sentiment towards those countries should be pure̲ly̲ plat̲onic? And only lo̲ve and N̲O̲ interest? (.) £Whell:' (lines 568–70). Interestingly, 'well' is usually used at the beginning of a dispreferred response to delay the action that is being performed. Here, it also acts to emphasise the rhetorical questions. Furthermore, it forces the researcher to back down from her initial assessment and deliver an agreement (or preferred response): 'I- I ↓know' (line 571). The researcher's response is met with acceptance from the practitioner, who then offers further assessment of the complex nature of the EU's relations with the eastern neighbours. He implies that a balance between interest and compassion for these countries is what is expected: '>A: nd if we have balance between the two that is fine!' (lines 572–3), but 'the r- rea̲l̲ problems come when you close your your eyes on those various human rights violations beca̲: u̲se you want to buy oil and gas!' (lines 574–5). Thus, he finally deliveries the preferred answer to the researcher's initial request (lines 564–7). This positive assessment initiates the researchers next request: 'and do you think that's happening?' (line 576). His in-breath and the choice of the modular verb: '.hh might be' (line 577) delays the action being performed and produces a weakly stated component of this action. Hedging or systematic vagueness is a standard feature of the official's institutional talk, especially after delivering a hugely contentious statement (Drew and Holt, 1988; Edwards and Potter, 1992). It indicates that while rich detail can be warranted, it can also be denied. Here the practitioner can be seen as purposefully vague about a contentious issue that potentially endangers the EU's credibility as an ethical, honest, and decent actor, or as it is argued before a moral actor in the region.

Extract 6.10 – EUIns.47

```
170  Inv   ONE way of ↑answering that question is to say that clearly
171        one of the objectives of the ne:ighbourhood policy is .hh a:
172        policy tha:t
173  R     hmm
174  Inv   >SEeks to support political a:nd economic reforms (.) .hh a:nd
175        we=have=a=number=of=countries=in=transition=with=that=programme
176        erm:↑where we have A:: particular opportu:nity to support
177        >political and economic reforms<
178  R     uhmm
179  Inv   in THEIR inTeRest and in OURs a:nd (.) tha::t's an important
180        dimension of the ENP! it's in >their interests=that isn't
181        philanthropy=>it's=in=our=interests=<too SO that's number one
182  R     okay
183  Inv   >supporting=political=and=economic=reforms< .hh SUpporting is
184        An: important word in that sentence ↑because ↑you can't buy
185        reform.=↑you=can't=bribe=people=into=reform. ↑if you want
186        reform to be sustainable there has to be some bot[tom up]
187  R                                                     [ummh]
188  Inv   Push And Raw >appetite< for reform. ON the=other=hand ↑you can
189        help=it=along=↑you=can=remove=Obstacles=later ↑If you want to
190  R     umhm
191  Inv   so ↑that is one objective. NOW ↑clearly ↑there ↑are ↑other=
192        =objectives dependent on: (0.2) ↑how=you=look=at=the=thing.
193        >↑and=lets=take=one=example< the EU is no:w very=focused=on=
194        =>energy=security<
195  R     oka::y
196  Inv   a::nd the >countries=that=worth=talking=about< have one
197        producer .hh ↑that's Russia. °but=they=are=very=important=
198        =transit=routes° (or transit opportunities) (.) LOOK. ↑it would
```

```
199        be: invalid i:f you:: try: to depict the eastern neighbourhood
200        AS be:ing=>guided=by=that=interest=in=energy< .hh a:nd it's
201        certainly TRue ↑that Energy IS >one of the things< tha:t's: on
202        our mind these days but the concept of the eastern
203        neighbourhood was developed before the emh >the first of
204        January 2006<
205 R      uhmm
```

Many interactional as well as policy-relevant inferences could be drawn from Extract 6.10. However, I will focus on the way the practitioner justifies collective EU energy interests, while attending to the moral obligation that the EU has vis-à-vis the eastern neighbours. The practitioner begins by presenting the objectives of the ENP as being supportive of political and economic reform (lines 174–7). Then she devotes a long period of time to establish the fact that this support is: 'in THEIR inTeRest and in OURs a: nd (.) tha: : t's an important dimension of the ENP! it's in >their interests=that isn't philanthropy=>it's=in =our=interests=<too' (lines 179–81). She continues until line 189 with only small interruptions of continual tokens from the researcher to demonstrate listening (lines 178, 182, 187).

Then the practitioner raises the second objective of the ENP without prompt from the researcher: 'NOW ↑clearly ↑there ↑are ↑other=objectives dependent on: (0.2) ↑how=you=look=at=the=thing. > and=lets=take=one=example< the EU is no: w very=focused=on=>energy=security<' (lines 191–4). In this way the practitioner returns to the issue of collective EU energy security, and she does so without giving an opportunity for the researcher to intervene. This is clearly marked by the equal signs throughout her turn. Again, the researcher just delivers an acknowledgement token (line 195) to signal to the practitioner to continue. In her next turn the practitioner describes 'the >countries=that =worth=talking=about<' (line 196), namely Russia (line 197) and the transit countries (line 198). There is still no uptake from the researcher. The practitioner then issues a warning: 'LOOK. it would be: invalid i: f you: : try: to depict the eastern neighbourhood AS be: ing=>guided=by=that=interest=in=energy<' (lines 198–200). This warning is directly issued to the researcher. By issuing this warning the practitioner attends to her personal accountability. She implies that it is the researcher's responsibility if she chooses to depict the ENP as a policy guided purely by EU energy interests. Furthermore, the practitioner claimed this to be wrong and invalid, so it is not representative of her own understanding of the policy. The result here is that the practitioner's careful management of combining the collective energy interest and moral concern, with the eastern neighbours, is presented as unbiased. The rest of her turn offers further confirmation of this: '.hh a: nd it's certainly TRue ↑that Energy IS >one of the things< tha: t's: on our mind these days but the concept of the eastern neighbourhood was developed before the emh >the first of January

2006<' (lines 200–4). She not only refers to energy as relevant but also the date of the first energy dispute between Ukraine and Russia (first of January 2006), which was also the first tangible threat to EU energy supplies from Russia. However, the practitioner claims that the policy towards the eastern neighbours was developed before, thus the EU cared about the eastern neighbours before the start of the crisis.

Importantly the practitioner also aligns EU interests with the neighbours' own interests (lines 180–1) which supposed to further support the EU's moral position on not just taking advantage of these countries or only focusing on the asymmetric relations. What is striking in her turn is the practitioner's inference in between raising the issues of interests, that the ENP and EU relations with these countries is not being 'philanthropy'. If it is not, that implies that the relationship is based on pure interests-driven objectives, rather than any moral obligation.

The next and final extract concerns the Caucasus. The researcher posed a question to the practitioner on the possibility of the Caucasian states joining the EU one day.

Extract 6.11 – EUIns.25

```
569 R     as members?
570 Inv   not as members. NO, but with closer relations >I mean< we have
571       the ENP we can build the ENP with additional agreements a:nd
572       particularly we're interested in these countries and wh- what
573       route they take.
574 R     okay
575 Inv   countries like Turkmenistan which where we might be: it is
576       CERTAINLY=NOT=THE=CASE. let me say quite so: quite clearly
577       because some people- human rights activists, Amnesty
578       International said that the E:U: is is trying to umh (0.2) IS
579       WILLING to put Energy before human rights concerns which is
580       which is which is garbage.
581 R     hmm
582 Inv   ↑because that is actually quite the exact opposite of the
583       EU but the central right- >Asia strategy which we're >currently
584       working on< ↑but it still doesn't me:an we aren't interested
585       £in heh £ene£rgy £resources but of course we are also looking
586       to encourage=Turkmenistan >and=other=countries=to=open=up
587       °>particularly=Turkmenistan°< and if you give them enough
588       carrots we hope that °they will do soon°
589 R     .hhh sure
```

The practitioner attends to the collective EU interest in the Caucasus in Extract 6.11. He offers a negative assessment of these states' chances of joining the EU, but at the same time he implies the need for closer ties with them (lines 570–3). He presents Turkmenistan as an example of one such country: 'countries like Turkmenistan which where we might be:' (on line 575). The practitioner syntactically has not finished his turn (line 575), as the infinitive is missing, but he stretches the word 'be:' to signal that he has not finished so there is no transitionally relevant space where the researcher could come in. However, the practitioner himself realises the contentious nature of his suggestion of closer relations with Turkmenistan, so he starts a new turn to refute any doubt of that, with a sudden change to a much louder tone: 'it is CERTAINLY=NOT=THE=CASE. let me say quite so: quite clearly because some people- human rights activists, Amnesty International said that the E: U: is is trying to umh (0.2) IS WILLING to put Energy before human rights concerns which is which is which is garbage' (lines 575–80). Additionally, the practitioner uses active voicing (Wooffitt, 1991, 2005) to report the views and impressions of the human rights activists and Amnesty International, in order to distance himself from the claims so that he can deride them. In fact, he implies the idea that 'the E: U: is is trying to umh (0.2) IS WILLING to put Energy before human rights concerns' is absurd by referring to it as 'garbage' in a loud tone. He devotes his next turns to work up the nonsensical nature of the allegation and describes the EU policy in Central Asia as the 'exact opposite' of that at line 582. The practitioner soon delivers another assertion on the importance of collective EU's energy interests: 'but it still doesn't me:an we aren't interested £in heh £ene£rgy £resources' (lines 584–5). The smile voice (indicated by the pound signs) and laughter tokens of 'heh' demonstrate the troubled nature of the practitioner's claim, considering that he was refuting the human rights activists' allegations. He issues a further justification for the EU's interest in a country like Turkmenistan through invoking moral concern: 'but of course we are also looking to encourage=Turkmenistan >and=other=countries=to=open=up °>particularly=Turkmenistan°< and if you give them enough carrots we hope that °they will do soon°' (lines 585–8). The practitioner implies that while the EU tackles its collective energy security interests through a country like Turkmenistan, it also assists these undeveloped countries to connect to the rest of the world through EU involvement. The practitioner's line of argument implies that no moral actor should disapprove of this project, as it is mutually beneficial to both countries. Thus the practitioner is doing being moral, while looking after collective EU interests.

Conclusion

This final analytical chapter focused on the ways in which EU practitioners managed the collective EU interest and specifically energy security. Most practitioners identified that to be the most significant security concern, as the supplier and transit countries are all located in the eastern neighbourhood. It also considered how practitioners connected interest formulations with moral concerns when discussing EU policy vis-à-vis the East. These findings closely link with constructivist understandings of complex international organisations, as discussed before. They also demonstrate the possibility of identifying collective EU interests that unite member states, and energy security is evidently one of them. Three patterns emerged from the corpus to illustrate this.

The first pattern was concerned with constructions of energy interests. In Extract 6.1 the practitioner identified energy security as the collective EU interest in the eastern neighbourhood. Besides making reference to the same interest, Extracts 6.2 and 6.3 also attended to issues around the shared neighbourhood. In Extract 6.2 the practitioner implied that the problem with the transit routes was a security concern between the EU and Russia. While in Extract 6.3, the practitioner complained about Russia's treatment of the shared neighbourhood, despite accepting these states to be in Russia's sphere of influence, not only owing to their historic link, but also to Russia's current foreign policy in the region. Although the eastern neighbours appeared important for the EU, some mattered more than others. In Extract 6.4 the practitioner demonstrated this through contrasting Ukraine and Moldova. Ukraine was evidently more important for the EU, as it transits the EU's energy supplies from Russia, but the EU's stake in Moldova was different since no transit pipelines ran through it and it struggled with various other problems. The practitioner implied these other problems to include poverty. Nevertheless, drawing a distinction between these two neighbours attended to the collective EU interest of energy security and the relevance of the eastern region, but at the same time it implied a hierarchy of relationship.

The second pattern that emerged from the corpus was concerned with the solutions that practitioners offered to manage the security concern over interruptions or suspension of energy supplies. In Extract 6.5 the practitioner discussed the introduction of an early warning mechanism, whereby EU member states would be forewarned if there were disruptions to the flow of energy through the transit states. In Extract 6.6, the practitioner raised the notion of diversifying EU energy needs through finding alternative resources. While in Extract 6.7, the practitioner even identified two possible alternative energy sources: solar and wind energy. Despite claims of diversification, they all agreed that resolving issues with Russia was paramount for EU energy security. Interestingly, all three practitioners employed the phrase 'you know' in their accounts in order to seek consensus and imply the researcher's familiarity with their claims. The 'you know' phrases also worked to standardise their accounts to something that everyone would agree on (Potter and Edwards, 1990; Smith, 1978). By doing so, the practitioners also attended to issues of accountability. Claims that are commonly accepted diminish the speaker's personal accountability (Potter, 1996), as it did for these practitioners.

The final pattern in this chapter revealed the way practitioners managed moral concerns while attending to the collective energy security interest in the eastern neighbourhood. In Extract 6.8 the practitioner first normalised the EU's energy interest in the eastern region, and to support his account he used the 'to be honest' + complement structure as part of his dispreferred response. Besides its interactional significance, the semantic feature of honesty carries an objective or factual aspect, as well as a subjective element or the knowledge and motivation of the speaker to be truthful (Edwards, 2000, 2005, 2007). Then the practitioner attended to working up the EU as a moral actor in the region, through the 'if-and-then' discursive formulation. The application of this formulation enables the speaker to appear as a morally responsible actor (Sneijder and te Molder, 2005). Extract 6.9 followed a similar trajectory. The practitioner complained about the complexity of the relationship between the EU and the eastern neighbours, but hedged (was vague) when asked to confirm his claim that the EU would deliberately ignore human rights violations just to secure its own energy supplies.

In Extract 6.10, the practitioner identified two objectives of the ENP as supporting political and economic reforms and managing the EU's energy interests; in addition, she issued a warning that it would be invalid to portray the policy as just attending to the EU's interests but rather that it merges the two objectives. In the final account, Extract 6.11, the practitioner made reference to the EU's interest in Turkmenistan. After recognising the contentious nature of his claim, which implied closer relations with a country that has an authoritarian regime but a vast undeveloped energy resource, the practitioner worked up the moral and vocational ambitions of the EU with a country like Turkmenistan, to encourage them to open up to the world, and their energy resources to the EU.

In short, this chapter demonstrated how collective foreign policy interests are identified even in an organisation such as the EU, and how practitioners merge such interests with normative and moral ambitions in order to manage concerns over the collective EU interest.

Note

1 Edward and Faulo's study also examines 'to be honest' or 'honestly' constructions in another classic sequential setting of assessments, as well as in a different interactional environment of police interrogation on answers to questions.

Conclusion

This book sought to gain insight into how EU practitioners consider the policy for which they have direct responsibility. By first summarising its findings, I reflect on the theoretical, methodological, and practical implications of this study and studying EU practitioners in general.

I examined data drawn from research interviews with EU practitioners who work on EU foreign policy vis-à-vis Russia, Ukraine, Belarus, and Moldova. Following a poststructuralist theoretical and methodology position within the practice turn, and having an open research question, allowed me to focus on the data and the topics that EU practitioners raised. I analysed these interactions through the application of DPM. DPM enabled me to draw attention to the discursive patterns that practitioners employ when they discuss EU foreign policy in the eastern neighbourhood, what they accomplish with them, how they manage their personal accountability or agency through them, and what implications these formulations have for the practitioners' practices. This led to a focus on the ways that practitioners manage identity, normative, moral, and collective interest concerns. These four concepts are crucial for IR theory, and also for understanding EU foreign policy. Although each concept was addressed in a separate chapter, I demonstrated points of interdependency throughout the analysis. Their parallel existence is key for this study and for poststructuralist practice theory. It builds on previous constructive works that linked identity and interests, but expanded it to normative and even moral concerns faced by practitioners when developing a specific foreign policy. Drawing this inference was only possible owing to the openness and refusal to take anything for granted advocated by poststructuralists; thus, the focus lies on the topics made relevant by practitioners, and how their accounts build up specific constructions of our world, rather testing for specific categories or for the truth value of their account.

First, in Chapter 3, I introduced the different understandings of the category of the 'European' and the way that practitioners attended to the category entitlement of the 'European'. It became apparent from the corpus that practitioners differentiated between 'European' neighbours (i.e. Ukraine and Russia) and neighbours of Europe (i.e. Tunisia, Egypt, and Morocco). The problematic nature of building the category of the 'European' emerged in Extracts 3.6–3.8, when practitioners favoured Ukraine's 'European' credentials in comparison to Turkey's. Invoking such a contrast is controversial on many levels. Despite their reservations, practitioners must be mindful of the different legal status Turkey holds as candidate state, compared to the Ukraine. A similar contrast was also made in Extract 3.13, but this time it was drawn between Turkey and Kazakhstan, claiming that more of Kazakhstan is in Europe than Turkey.

Practitioners also discussed the European credentials of the South Caucasus. Besides working up these states' category entitlements to be part of the 'European', in Extract 3.10 a practitioner argued for the EU's moral and vocational obligation to support Georgia's quest to join the EU. EU's interest in to the Caucasus was also addressed in Chapter 6, where accounts of the collective EU energy security are discussed.

Second, I considered the ways that EU practitioners accounted for the normative role and power of the EU in the eastern region. I began by focusing on the practitioners' listings of these norms and their similarity to the norms specified within EU treaties and also by scholars like Manners (2002, 2013). Interestingly, in Extract 4.1 the practitioner drew a distinction between the EU's application of these norms, as opposed to norms promoted by other actors. This contrast was further highlighted in practitioners' discussions of the different countries that attempted to emulate the EU model. Although in Extract 4.10 Morocco's attempt to take on EU's best practices was portrayed, the contrast between Russia and Ukraine's closeness to the EU model in Extract 4.11 was analytically more significant. This distinction is also important for building up the category of the 'European', and added to Ukraine's credentials of being more 'European'. Following on from this, examples of states that failed to comply with EU norms such as Belarus in Extract 4.17 were used. Crucially, Ukraine was identified in this account as being more supportive of the EU's intentions in Belarus, whereas in Extract 4.18 the EU was portrayed as having a potentially stronger allegiance to Russia. This ill-defined categorisation of Ukraine clearly problematizes EU policy and implies reservations about Ukraine's category to be fully 'European'. Furthermore, I identified instances when alignment with EU norms was unwelcome. These accounts demonstrated the complexity of EU–Russian relations in their shared neighbourhood. This intricate relationship was also addressed in Chapter 6, in which the collective EU interest of energy security, concerning transit states, was examined.

Third, I examined the way that practitioners justify the EU's vocational interest in the region through claims of moral duty, similar to the ones that the EU expressed for the CEECs before their accession. Besides attending to the moral duties of the EU, notably in Extract 5.5, the practitioner also implied a change to Ukraine's consciousness after EU support for the Orange Revolution, which effectively halted any chance of Ukraine's return to previously accepted governance practices. The anecdotal account of purchasing an Austrian bank by a Ukrainian consortium in Extract 5.9 served a similar effect. Practitioners seemed very conscientious about ensuring that the EU gave the right message to its neighbours. More interestingly, practitioners identified Russia and Belarus as neighbours who have different morals. In Extracts 5.13 and 5.14 practitioners complained of Russia's reluctance to resolve the frozen conflicts in the shared neighbourhood, despite the EU's strong urge to do so. Although in Extract 5.15 Belarus was exemplified as another state having different moral concerns, the practitioner implied a sense of duty that the EU felt for the Byelorussians. Not all practitioners agreed with this sense of morality. In the final section, practitioners claimed that in fact it was morally wrong for the EU to be involved with Belarus.

Fourth, I considered the way that practitioners identified a collective EU interest: energy security, and the way they attended to concerns regarding the shared neighbourhood, especially to those countries that carry transit pipelines in Extracts 6.2 and 6.3. Although these concerns were similar to those raised in Chapter 6, they also invoked the practitioners' awareness of the Russian concept of 'near abroad' and the significance of the shared neighbourhood. The comparison of Ukraine and Moldova in Extract 6.4 was important on two counts. The fact that Moldova is not a transit country was raised to demonstrate its reduced importance. In contrast, Ukraine's transit route status further supported its entitlement to the category of the 'European'. In addition, practitioners demonstrated ways to manage their concern over EU energy supplies that also dealt with Russia as a potentially unreliable energy supplier. The final section revealed practitioners' justifications of EU interest in the eastern region through moral concerns and the vocational attributes similar to those expressed in Chapter 5.

In sum, the analytical chapters demonstrated the significance of identity, normative, moral, and interest concerns for EU practitioners when they consider EU foreign policy in the east, and at the same time these four concepts are completely interconnected during policy development. But the reach of the findings of this book goes beyond this.

Theoretical contributions to the development of the practice turn

This book also contributes to the practice turn in IR and EU studies, and more specifically to the poststructuralist IR practice theory. It does so through its keen focus on what the practitioners made relevant in their talk about EU foreign policy rather than constrained by specific preconceived concepts of the policy, or testing the truth value of the practitioners' concerns. Therefore, it fulfils Kratochwil's (2011: 47) call that theorising practices ought to be based on the actual 'actions' of the practitioner. This does not mean that during the research interviews the researcher's participation in the (co)(de)construction of the topic was overlooked.[1] This is again in line with Kratochwil's (*ibid.*: 47; 50) argument for accepting the researcher as a constitutive part of the research process rather than being a 'neutral observer'. The focus on practitioners and how they discuss their own practices also enable us to consider their utterances as the basis of patterns of actions that are socially meaningful, as advocated by Adler and Pouliot (2011: 6). The patterns presented in the chapters are built on the social actions that the practitioners' utterances achieved.

For poststructuralist IR practice theory, identifying social action is a key aspect of theorising. In the following section I discuss how the DPM helped to identify practitioners' social action. Before that I return to the significance of practitioners' connecting identity, normative, moral, and collective interest formulations for IR practice theory.

It is commonly accepted that identities are often built through contrast structures of the self and the *other*, as claimed by Connolly (2002), or Neumann (1995, 2016) and Makarychev (2008) on EU–Russia relations. In my analysis, I also pointed to instances when such differentiation became more complicated. There were ample examples when Ukraine's category entitlement to the 'European' were discussed (Extracts 3.6–3.8, 4.11, 4.17, 5.5, 5.9, 6.4), with the exception of one account in Extract 4.18.[2] These findings not only demonstrate the intricate nature of the EU's relations with Ukraine, but also practitioners' seemingly greater approval of Ukraine's identity being 'European' than for instance, Turkey's (despite its candidate status) or Moldova's. Turkey appeared to be a point of high contention as one practitioner even apportioned more 'European' entitlement to Kazakhstan than Turkey (Extract 3.13). This further signifies the complexity and ill-defined nature of the category of the 'European', and also the potential for EU practitioners' ambiguity over the self and the *other* when considering the eastern neighbours. For these reasons, in the EU context, Ukraine serves as a perfect example of being in-between the 'European' self and the *other*. Thus, my conceptualisation of the self and the *other* is not like other poststructuralists such as Campbell's (1998) radical depiction of the *other*, but more nuanced, whereby the *other* is varied, inconsistent, or erratic depending on the specific time, context, and contingency in which the *other* is participating in, along with the particular function or social action that the *other* is aiming to achieve. In short, the *other* is occasioned, fleeting, and indexical and cannot be taken for granted. To some extent this definition is more similar to Hansen's (2006) positions, yet, it allows for contingency and is less concerned with predictability. It helps us to appreciate why Ukraine is seen closer to the (EU/European) *self*, but not part of it. Even though very many IR scholars (not poststructuralists) are concerned with predictability, I would argue that this is the quality of states' behaviour that is least possible to calculate. Therefore, doing so seems a rather futile exercise; whereas focusing on their practice during specific events or periods would offer a better understanding of states' behaviour.

Furthermore, my conceptualisation of 'European' identity also includes notions of normative and moral attributes beside collective interests. I advocate, as demonstrated through the analysis, an interdependence between all four concepts when analysing EU foreign policy vis-à-vis the east. This theoretical framework offers a better understanding of foreign policy practices, as opposed to necessarily incomplete attempts to separate interest from identity, norm, and moral concerns, or even considering them individually for EU foreign policy as some of the EU studies literature does (see normative power Europe, ethical power Europe). Finally, the identification of collective EU interests is significant. In this book, I focused on energy security, but there were other shared interests that were made relevant by practitioners such as migration, terrorism, organised crime, transport, and the environment. However, none of these seemed as important in the region as energy security. The practitioners' identification of collective EU interests also confirms Wendt (1995) and Katzenstein's (1997) claim that international institutions facilitate the emergence of shared interest, norms, values, but most of all a sense of community, a common identity but at least a community of practice. To capture these practices, the analytical framework was key.

Methodological contributions to practice turn

This study raises several methodological points for IR practice theory, but most specifically it introduces a new conceptual model to examine foreign policy practices. It also advocates the use of a new data form. DPM attends to Duvall and Chowdbudy (2011), Kratochwil (2011) and Bially Mattern's (2011) call for the application of more linguistic approaches in IR practice theory. This is necessary to balance the more prevalent focus on behaviour or conduct. I would argue that this preoccupation with *habitus* is not necessarily always a theoretical or a methodological choice, but rather a pragmatic one. Attaining data beyond policy documents and speeches by politicians to conduct a discursive enquiry into IR is difficult, if not impossible. Practitioners rarely ever want to go on record. Therefore, the best practice theory articles combine interview notes, anecdotes, or previous work experience with official documents to demonstrate the behaviour or practice of the state/institutional/actor.

DPM combines IR practice theory with a discursive framework that focuses specifically on identifying social action, fact and interest formulations, and agency. It has been influenced by the wider social practice theory (Schatzki *et al.*, 2001), ethnomethodology, CA, discursive psychology, and poststructuralist IR theory. It also builds on discourse analytical methods applied in IR especially Doty's (1993, 1996) Discursive Practice Approach. Although DPM follows a similar poststructuralist format to Doty's approach, it is nevertheless different and novel to IR. It offers a new way to identify social action through its focus on the micro levels of interactions. The implications of focusing on the social actions achieved by speakers in their turns (during their interaction); their use of specific fact and interest formulations, or discursive devices, and their wary of managing their own accountability or agency are significant for our understanding of EU practitioners' understandings of foreign policy, or their own practice. The discursive devices that practitioners used in this study have previously been observed in various conversation analytical and discursive psychology studies in mundane as well as institutional settings (Smith, 1978; Atkinson, 1984; Heritage and Greathbatch, 1986; Drew and Holt, 1988; Potter and Edwards, 1990; Jefferson, 1990, 1994; Wooffitt, 1991, 2005; Edwards and Potter, 1992; Sacks, 1992; Edwards, 2000, 2005, 2007; Clift, 2001; Edwards and Fasulo, 2006), thus their general applicability to any IR topic is clear and demonstrable. Furthermore, the application of DPM offers a methodologically more coherent, sophisticated, and orderly analytical method as DPM is replicable.

DPM's other contribution to the methodological development of IR practice theory is the adoption of a new data source. By gaining access to EU practitioners in different EU institutions and by conducting digitally recorded research interviews with them, I introduced data that had never been used before in IR, or in EU foreign policy analysis. The verbatim transcripts of these institutional interactions allowed me to focus on the practitioners' interactions, their turns, sequence organisation of their talk, their orientations, and discursive practices. This was only possible because the data was recorded. Through the application of DPM, I advocated looking beyond policy documents or other available documentary evidence; and, rather, to obtain a digitally recorded corpus that offers a new and original perspective on practitioners' practices.

Practical implications of this study

There are also several practical implications of this study for EU practitioners. First, practitioners are very aware of the complex relationship between the EU and Russia. The change in their attitude since the collapse of the Soviet Union is evident as they do not simply assume that Russia will want to join the EU. However, practitioners do assume that countries in the neighbourhood would be better off having closer ties, although not necessarily membership, with the EU. Practitioners should take Russia's ambitions and historical ties with the region into account, as this would put them in a better position to understand how Russia uses the shared neighbourhood to challenge the EU's ambition regionally and internationally, and how it uses the EU's energy dependency to prevent member states from developing a more comprehensive, concrete, and collective policy in the region.

Second, despite not having well-defined guidelines on what the category of the 'European' entails, practitioners seem to have a clear understanding of the criteria. They are not only able to list them but also give clear examples of the countries that fit these criteria, and those that do not. The difficulty arises when countries with candidate status that have passed the European test and are legally declared a membership candidate (i.e. Turkey) are deemed less qualified to fit the criteria than those who have not even applied (such as Ukraine or Kazakhstan). Invoking such contrasts can have repercussions, as it is argued in Chapters 4 and 5.

The current crises in Ukraine are not helping to clarify this situation. In fact, the crises are directly linked to the ongoing EU–Russian turf war in the region. The most recent crisis was started by the former President, Viktor Yanukovych's refusal to sign the Association Agreement with the EU in November 2013, which led to widespread demonstrations and eventually Yanukovych having to flee the country. Russian involvement in the crises escalated the situation to the annexation of Crimea and to two eastern Ukrainian regions (Donetsk and Luhansk) officially declaring themselves autonomous from Ukraine, but not yet part of Russia. Although Ukraine signed an Association Agreement with the EU in May 2014, the country's situation is still precarious; or at least within its currently recognised borders. These events and the new dimension of EU–Russia relations only cast further ambiguity over the category of the 'European', rather than clarifying it. Furthermore, the two breakaway regions seem to have taken up a similar position as other regions with frozen conflicts such as Transnistria, Nagorno–Karabakh, and Azdjaria, or the more recent ones in South Ossetia and Abkhazia. These regions run like a state within the state. They are involved in organised crime, human trafficking, and arms trafficking (Shelley, 2004). They do not follow EU norms and principles such as democracy, rule of law, market economy, respect for human rights. Therefore, these regions only hinder their countries ambitions to become an EU member state. Not abiding by EU norms allows EU practitioners to isolate the countries where these frozen conflicts are located.

While drawing on such contrasts is necessary to point out the problems these regions and countries are facing, practitioners ought to be careful in how they do so, as there could be repercussions for the EU itself, especially if it wants to be seen applying principled pragmatism. Practitioners' tendencies to evoke the EU's moral obligation to the eastern regions complicates the policy. As argued in Chapter 4 and 5, these tendencies are transferred from the previous enlargement despite the clear acceptance by practitioners that further enlargement is simply not on the table. However, implying that the EU has a moral obligation in its eastern neighbourhood not only contradicts EU policy, but also makes the EU seem like a moralising power, rather than having moral authority in the region, or a multifaceted power. This effect would only be amplified if the EU is seen to care more about its energy security (Chapter 6) than all the other important work it does in the region, such as opening up these countries and engaging them in a different model of governance.

Practitioners have control over this. They are the ones who develop policy and put it into practice. Therefore, they ought to be aware of the fact that the way in which they practise foreign policy is just as important as the policy itself. Due to practitioners' central role in foreign policy, scholars of IR need to study them and their functions. They need to do so through new and innovative means either through new data or new methods, both of which have been put forward in this book. They need to do so not only to support the practitioners in their jobs but also to take the discipline of IR to new heights.

Notes

1 My role was explained extensively in Chapter 2 and the impact it had on the data. It is also clear throughout the analytical chapters within the extracts as well as the analysis.
2 Having exceptions or variants to patterns is normal. In effect, they demonstrate variability in the accounts, and hence they are consistent with the validity and reliability criteria applied in the study.

Appendix: transcript notation

Modified version of the transcript notations developed by Gail Jefferson as proposed by Atkinson and Heritage (1984).

Aspects of the relative timing of utterances

[ ]	square brackets	overlapping talk
=	equals sign	no discernible interval between turns; also used to show the same person continues speaking across an intervening line displaying overlapping talk
<	'less than' sign	'jump started' talk with loud onset
(0.5)	time in parentheses	intervals within or between talk (measured in one-tenth of a second)
(.)	period in parentheses	discernible pause or gap, too short to measure

Characteristics of speech delivery

.	period	closing intonation
,	comma	slightly upward 'continuing' intonation
?	question mark	rising intonation question
!	exclamation mark	animated tone
-	hyphen	abrupt cut-off of sound
:	colon	extension of preceding sound – the more colons, the greater the extension
↑↓	up/down arrows	marked rise or fall in intonation, immediately following the arrow
you	underlining	emphasised, relative to surrounding talk
YOU	upper-case	louder, relative to surrounding talk
°you°	degree symbols	softer, relative to surrounding talk
>you<		speeded up or compressed, relative to surrounding talk

\<you\>		slower or elongated, relative to surrounding talk
£	pound sign	smiley voice
hhh		audible out-breath – the number of 'h's indicates length
.hhh		audible in-breath – the number of 'h's indicates length
(h)		audible aspirations in speech (e.g. laughter particles)
hah/heh/hih/ hoh/huh		all variants of laughter particles
( )	empty single parentheses	transcriber unable to hear the word
(you)	word(s) in single parentheses	transcriber uncertain of hearing
((coughs))	word(s) in double parentheses	transcriber's comments on, or description of sounds, other audible sounds are presented as closely as possible to orthography e.g. 'tcht' for tongue click, 'auhm' for thought clearing

References

All URLs and websites valid as at June–July 2016

Adler, E. and Pouliot, V. (2011) *International Practices*, Cambridge, Cambridge University Press

Adler-Nissen, R. (2016) 'Towards a practice turn in EU studies: The everyday of European integration', *Journal of Common Market Studies*, 54(1): 87–103

Allen, D. J. and Smith, M. H. (1990) 'Western Europe's presence in the contemporary international arena', *Review of International Studies*, 16: 19–37

Ashley, R. K. and Walker, R. B. J. (1990) 'Reading dissidence/writing the discipline: Crisis and the question of sovereignty in international studies', *International Studies Quarterly*, 32(4): 367–416

Atkinson, J. M. (1984) *Our Masters' Voices: The Language and Body Language of Politics*, London, Methuen

Atkinson, J. M. and Heritage, J. (1984) *Structures of Social Action: Studies in Conversation Analysis*, Cambridge, Cambridge University Press

Austin, J. L. (1962) *How to Do Things with Words*, Oxford, Clarendon Press

Bailes, A. (2008) 'The EU and a "better world": What role for the European security and defence policy?', *International Affairs*, 84(1): 115–30

Barbé, E. and Johansson-Nogués, E. (2008) 'The EU as a modest "force for good": The European Neighbourhood Policy', *International Affairs* 84(1): 81–96

Barbé, E., Herranz-Surrallés, A., and Natorski, M (2015) 'Contending metaphors of the European Union as a global actor: Norms and power in the European discourse on multilateralism', *Journal of Language & Politics*, 14(1): 18–40

Barthes, R. (1974) *S/Z*, London, Jonathan Cape

Bergmann, J. R. (1992) 'Veiled morality: Notes on discretion in psychiatry', in P. Drew and J. Heritage (eds), *Talk at Work*, Cambridge, Cambridge University Press

Bergmann, J. R. (1998) 'Introduction: Morality', *Discourse Research on Language and Social Interaction*, 31(3–4): 279–94

Bially Mattern, J. (2011) 'Emotional practices in world politics', in E. Adler and V. Pouliot (eds), *The Practice Turn in International Relations*, Cambridge, Cambridge University Press

Biedenkopf, K., Geremek, B., and Michalski, K. (2004) 'The spiritual and cultural dimension of Europe', Reflection Group, Concluding Remarks, initiated by the President of the European Commission and coordinated by the Institute for Human Services, Vienna/Brussels, p. 12, https://ec.europa.eu/research/social-sciences/pdf/other_pubs/michalski_091104_report_annexes_en.pdf

Bogen, D. and Lynch, M. (1989) 'Taking account of the hostile native: Plausible deniability and the production of conventional history in the Iran–Contra hearings', *Social Problems*, 36(3): 197–224

Bourdieu, P. (1977) *Outline of a Theory of Practice*, Cambridge, Cambridge University Press

Bretherton, C. and Vogler, J. (1999) *The European Union as a Global Actor*, London, Routledge

Bueger, C. (2014) 'Pathways to practice: Praxiography and international politics', *European Political Science Review*, 6(3): 383–406

Bueger, C. and Gadinger, F. (2015) 'The play of international practice', *International Studies Quarterly*, 59(3): 449–60

Buttny, R. (1993) *Social Accountability in Communication*, London, Sage

Buzan, B. (2001) 'The English School: An underexploited resource in IR', *Review of International Studies*, 27(3): 477–8

Campbell, C. T. and Futák-Campbell, B. (forthcoming) '"I thought this is like magic": A discursive study on the ways patients marginalise homeopathy in talk', *Journal of Applied Linguistics and Professional Practice*.

Campbell, D. (1996) 'Political prosaics, transversal politics, and the anarchical world', in M. J. Shapiro and Alker, H. R. (eds), *Challenging Boundaries: Global Flows, Territorial Identities*, Minneapolis MN, University of Minnesota Press, pp. 7–32

Campbell, D. (1998) *Writing Security: United States Foreign Policy and the Politics of Identity*, Minneapolis, University of Minnesota Press

Carr, E. H. ([1939] 1968) *The Twenty Years Crisis, 1919–1939: An Introduction to the Study of International Relations*, London, Macmillan

Carta, C. (2014) 'From the "magnificent castle" to the brutish state of nature: Use of metaphors and the analysis of the EU's international discourse', in C. Carta and J.-F. Morin (eds), *EU Foreign Policy through the Lens of Discourse Analysis: Making Sense of Diversity*, Farnham, Ashgate

Carta, C. and Morin, J.-F. (2014) 'Struggling over meanings: Discourses on EU's international presence', *Cooperation and Conflict*, 49(3): 295–314

Castiglione, D. (1996) 'The political theory of the constitution', in R. Bellamy and D. Castiglione (eds), *Constitutionalism in Transformation: European and Theoretical Perspectives*, Cambridge, Blackwell, pp. 6–23

Cederman, L. E. (2001) *Constructing Europe's Identity: The External Dimension*, Boulder, CO, Lynne Rienner

Checkel, J. T. and Katzenstein, P. J. (2009) *European Identity*, Cambridge, Cambridge University Press

Christiansen, T. (1997) 'Legitimacy dilemmas of supranational governance: The European Commission between accountability and independence', in N. Nentwich and A. Weale (eds), *Political Theory and the European Union*, London, Routledge

Clayman, S. E. (1992) 'Footing in the achievement of neutrality: The case of news interview discourse', in P. Drew and J. Heritage (eds), *Talk at Work*, Cambridge, Cambridge University Press

Clift, R. (2001) 'Meaning in interaction: The case of actually', *Language*, 77(2): 245–291

Connolly, W. E. (2002) *Identity/Difference: Democratic Negotiations of Political Paradox*, Minneapolis MN, University of Minnesota Press

Craig, P. and de Búrca, G. (2015) *EU Law: Text, Cases, and Material*, Oxford, Oxford University Press

Damro, C. (2001) 'Building an international identity: the EU and extraterritorial competition policy', *Journal of European Public Policy*, 8(2): 208–26

Dannreuther, R. (2004) *European Union Foreign and Security Policy: Towards a Neighbourhood Strategy*, London, Routledge

Davies, B. and Harré, R. (1990) 'Positioning: The discursive production of selves', *Journal for the Theory of Social Behaviour*, 20: 43–63

Der Derian, J. and Shapiro, M. J. (1989) *International/intertextual Relations: Postmodern Readings of World Politic*, Lexington, Lexington Books

Derrida, J. (1978) *Writing and Difference*, London, Routledge

Derrida, J. (1992) *The Other Heading: Reflections on Today's Europe*, Indianapolis, Indiana University Press

Dickerson, P. (1997) ' "It's not just me who's saying this ..." The deployment of cited others in television political discourse', *British Journal of Social Psychology*, 36: 33–48

Diez, T. (2005) 'Constructing the self and changing others: Reconsidering "normative power Europe" ', *Millennium Journal of International Studies*, 33: 613–36

Drew, P. (1984) 'Speakers' reportings in invitation sequences', in J. M. Atkinson and J. Heritage (eds), *Structures of Social Action: Studies in Conversation Analysis*, Cambridge, Cambridge University Press, pp. 129–51

Drew, P. (1990) 'Strategies in the contest between lawyer and witness in cross-examination', in J. Levi and A. Walker (eds), *Language in the Judicial Process*, New York, Plenum

Drew, P. (1998) 'Complaints about transgressions and misconduct', *Research on Language and Social Interaction*, 31: 295–325

Drew, P. and Holt, E. (1988) 'Complainable matters: The use of idiomatic expressions in making complaints', *Social Problems*, 35: 501–20

Doty, R. L. (1993) 'Foreign policy as social construction: A post-positivist analysis of US counterinsurgency policy in the Philippines', *International Studies Quarterly*, 37(3): 297–320

Doty, R. L. (1996) *Imperial Encounters: Patterns of Representation in North–South Relations*, Minneapolis MN, University of Minnesota Press

Duchêne, F. (1972) 'Europe's role in world peace', in R. Maynev (ed.), *Europe Tomorrow: Sixteen Europeans Look Ahead*, London, Fontana

Dunne, T. (2008) 'Good citizen Europe', *International Affairs*, 84(1): 15

Duvall, R. and Chowdhury, A. (2011) 'Practices of theory', in E. Adler and V. Pouliot (eds), *International Practices*, Cambridge, Cambridge University Press

Edwards, D. (1997) *Discourse and Cognition*, London, Sage

Edwards, D. (1999) 'Emotion discourse', *Culture & Psychology*, 5(3): 271–91

Edwards, D. (2000) 'Extreme case formulations: Softeners, investment, and doing nonliteral', *Research on Language and Social Interaction*, 33: 347–73

Edwards, D. (2005) 'Moaning, whinging and laughing: The subjective side of complaints', *Discourse Studies*, 7(1): 5–29

Edwards, D. (2007) 'Managing subjectivity in talk', A. Hepburn and S. Wiggins (eds), *Discursive Research in Practice: New Approaches to Psychology and Interaction*, Cambridge, Cambridge University Press, pp. 31–49

Edwards, D. and Fasulo, A. (2006) ' "To be honest": Sequential uses of honesty phrases in talk-in-interaction', *Research on Language and Social Interaction*, 39(4): 343–76

Edwards, D. and Potter, J. (1992) *Discursive Psychology*, London, Sage

Eeckhout, P. (2004) *External Relations of the European Union: Legal and Constitutional Foundations*, Oxford, Oxford University Press

Eglin, P. and Hester, S. (1999) '"You're all a bunch of feminists": Categorization and the politics of terror in the Montreal massacre', *Human Studies*, 22: 253–72

EU HR/VP (2016) 'Shared vision, common action: A stronger Europe. A global strategy for the EU's foreign and security policy', European Commission, https://europa.eu/globalstrategy/sites/globalstrategy/files/eugs_review_web.pdf

Fierke, K. M. and Wiener, A. (1999) 'Constructing institutional interests: EU and NATO enlargement', *Journal of European Public Policy*, 6(5): 721–42

Foucault, M. (1980) *Power/Knowledge: Selected Interviews and Other Writings, 1972–1977*, Brighton, Harvester Press

Freitag-Wirminghaus, R. (2008) 'Prospects for Armenia and Azerbaijan between Eurasia and the Middle East', in D. Hamilton and G. Mangott (eds), *The Wider Black Sea Region in the 21st Century: Strategic, Economic and Energy Perspectives*, Washington, DC, Center for Transatlantic Relations

Friis, L. (1998) 'The end of the beginning of eastern enlargement – Luxembourg Summit and agenda-setting', *European Integration Online Papers*, 2(7), http://eiop.or.at/eiop/texte/1998–007.htm

Garfinkel, H. (1967) 'Practical sociological reasoning: Some features of the work in the Los Angeles Suicide Prevention Center', E. S. Shneidman (ed.), *Essays in Self-destruction*, New York, Science House

Garfinkel, H. (1974) 'On the origins of the term "ethnomethodology"', in R. Turner (ed.), *Ethnomethodology*, Harmondsworth, Penguin

Gergen, K. J. and Davis, K. E. (1985) *The Social Construction of the Person*, New York, Springer-Verlag

Giddens, A. (1991) *Modernity and Self-Identity*, Cambridge, Polity Press

Goffman, E. (1959) *The Presentation of Self in Everyday Life*, London, Allen Lane

Goffman, E. (1979) 'Footing', *Semiotica*, 25: 1–29 [reprinted in E. Goffman, *Forms of Talk*, Oxford, Blackwell, 1981]

Graziano, P. and Vink, M. P. (2006) *Europeanization – New Research Agendas*, Basingstoke, Palgrave Macmillan

Habermas, J. (2006a) 'Political communication in media society: Does democracy still enjoy an epistemic dimension? The impact of normative theory on empirical research', *Communication Theory*, 16(4): 411–26

Habermas J. (2006b) 'Religion in the public sphere', *European Journal of Philosophy*, 14(1): 1–25

Hansen, L. (2006) *Security as Practice: Discourse Analysis and the Bosnian War*, London, Routledge

Hansen, L. (2011) 'Performing practices: A poststructuralist analysis of the Muhammad cartoon crisis', in E. Adler and V. Pouliot (eds), *International Practices*, Cambridge, Cambridge University Press, pp. 280–309

Harmsen, R. and Wilson, T. M. (2000) *Europeanization: Institutions, Identities and Citizenship*, Amsterdam, Rodopi

Have, P. ten (1999) 'Methodological issues in conversation analysis', *Bulletin de méthodologie sociologique*, 27: 23–51

Have, P. ten (2002) 'The notion of member is the heart of the matter: On the role of membership knowledge in ethnomethodological inquiry', *Forum: Qualitative Social Research*, 3(2), www.qualitative-research.net/index.php/fqs/article/view/834

Heidegger, M. (1962) *Being and Time*, John Macquarrie and Edward Robinson (trans.), New York, Harper & Row

Hepburn, A. and Potter, J. (2003) 'Discourse analytic practice', in C. Seale, D. Silverman, J. Gubrium, and G. Gobo (eds), *Qualitative Research Practice*, London, Sage, pp. 180–96

Heritage, J. (1984) *Garfinkel and Ethnomethodology*, Cambridge, Polity Press

Heritage, J. and Greatbatch, D. (1986) 'Generating applause: A study of rhetoric and response in party political conferences', *American Sociology Review*, 92: 110–57

Heritage, J. and Greatbatch, D. (1991) 'On the institutional character of institutional talk: The case of news interviews', in D. Boden and D. Zimmerman (eds), *Talk and Social Structure*, Cambridge, Polity Press, pp. 97–173

Heritage, J. and Lindstrom, A. (1998) 'Motherhood, medicine and morality: Scenes from a medical encounter', *Research on Language and Social Interaction*, 31(3–4): 397–438

Heritage, J. and Raymond, G. (2005) 'The terms of agreement> indexing epistemic authority and subordination in assessment sequences', *Social Psychology Quarterly*, 68: 15–38

Herrmann, R. K., Risse, T., and Brewer, M. B. (2004) *Transnational Identities: Becoming European in the EU*, New York, Rowman & Littlefield

Hester, S. and Eglin, P. (1997) *Culture in Action: Studies in Membership Categorization Analysis*, Washington, DC, University Press of America

Hewitt, J. P. and Stokes, R. (1975) 'Disclaimers', *American Sociological Review*, 40(1): 1–11

Hill, C. (1990) 'European foreign policy: Power bloc, civilian model – or flop?', in R. Reinhardt (ed.), *The Evolution of an International Actor*, Boulder, CO, Westview Press

Hill, C. (1993) 'The capability–expectation gap, or conceptualizing Europe's international role', *Journal of Common Market Studies*, 31(3): 305–28

Hillion, C. (2007) 'Mapping out the new contractual relations between the European Union and its neighbours: Learning from the EU–Ukraine "Enhanced Agreement"', *European Foreign Affairs Review*, 12: 169–182

Hoffmann, S. (1995) 'The crisis of liberal internationalism', *Foreign Policy*, 98: 159–77

Hooghe, E. and Marks, G. (2007) 'Sources of Euroscepticism', *Acta Politica*, 42(2): 119–27

Hurrell, A. (2002) 'Norms and ethics in International Relations', in W. Carlsnaes, T. Risse, and B. A. Simmons (eds), *Handbook of International Relations*, London, Sage

Hutchby, I. and Wooffitt, R. (1998) *Conversation Analysis*, Cambridge, Polity Press

Hyde-Price, A. (2008) 'A "tragic actor"? A realist perspective on "ethical power Europe"', *International Affairs*, 84(1): 29–44

Jefferson, G. (1974) 'Error correction as an interactional resource in language', *Society*, 3(2): 181–99

Jefferson, G. (1990) 'List construction as a task and interactional resource', in G. Psathas (ed.), *Interactional Competence*, Washington, DC, University Press of America, pp. 122–43

Jefferson, G. (1994) 'On the organization of laughter in talk about troubles', in J. M. Atkinson and J. C. Heritage (eds), *Structures of Social Action: Studies in Conversation Analysis*, Cambridge, Cambridge University Press, pp. 346–69

Jefferson, G. (2004) 'A note on laughter in "male–female" interaction', *Discourse Studies*, 6(1): 117–33

Johnston, A. I. (2001) 'Treating institutions as social environments', *International Studies Quarterly*, 45(4): 487–515

Kant, I. ([1795] 1983) 'Perceptual peace: A philosophical sketch', in H. S. Reiss (ed.), *Kant's Political Writings*, Cambridge, Cambridge University Press

Kassenova, N. (2009) 'Kazakhstan and the South Caucasus corridor in the wake of the Georgia–Russia War', *EUCAM EU–Central Asia Monitoring*, no. 3, http://aei.pitt.edu/11079/1/1786[1].pdf

Katzenstein, P. (1996) 'Introduction: Alternative perspectives on national security', in P. Katzenstein (ed.), *The Culture of National Security*, New York, Columbia University Press

Katzenstein, P. (1997) *Tamed Power: Germany in Europe*, Ithaca, Cornell University Press

Knill, C. (2001) *The Europeanisation of National Administrations: Patterns of Institutional Change and Persistence*, Cambridge, Cambridge University Press

Kowert, P. and Legro, J. (1996) 'Norm, identity and their limits: A theoretical reprise', in Katzenstein, P. J. (ed.), *The Culture of National Security: Norms and Identity in World Politics*, New York, Columbia University Press, pp. 451–97

Kratochwil, F. (2011) 'Making sense of "international practices"', in E. Adler and V. Pouliot (eds), *International Practices*, Cambridge, Cambridge University Press, pp. 36–60

Kristeva, J. (1991) *Strangers to Ourselves*, New York, Columbia University Press

Kristeva, J. (2000) 'Europe divided: politics, ethics, religion', in *Crisis of the European Subject*, New York, Other Press, pp. 111–62

Laffan, B. (2001) 'The European Union polity: A union of regulative, normative and cognitive pillars', *Journal of European Public Policy*, 8(5): 709–27

Laffan, B., O'Donnell, R. and Smith, M. H. (1999) *Europe's Experimental Union Rethinking Integration*, London, Routledge

Larsen, H. (1997) *Foreign Policy and Discourse Analysis: France, Britain and Europe*, London, Routledge

Larsen, H. (2000) 'Danish CFSP policy in the post-Cold War period: Continuity or change?', *Cooperation and Conflict*, 35(1): 37–63

Larsen, H. (2004) 'Discourse analysis in the study of European foreign policy', in B. Tonra and T. Christiansen (eds) *Rethinking European Union Foreign Policy*, Manchester, Manchester University Press, pp. 62–80

Lee, D. (1987) 'The semantics of just', *Journal of Pragmatics*, 11: 377–98

Legro, J. W. (1997) 'Which norms matter? Revisiting the "failure" of internationalism', *International Organization*, 51(1): 31–63

Leonard, M. (2005) *Why Europe Will Run the 21st Century*, London, Fourth Estate Ltd

Lequesne, C. (2015) 'EU foreign policy through the lens of practice theory: A different approach to the European External Action Service', *Cooperation and Conflict*, 47: 5–13

Levinson, S. C. (1983) *Pragmatics*, Cambridge, Cambridge University

Livingston, E. (1987) *Making Sense of Ethnomethodology*, London, Routledge.

Lock, T. (2015) *The European Court of Justice and International Courts*, Oxford, Oxford University Press

Lucarelli, S. (2006) 'Introduction', in S. Lucarelli and I. Manners (eds), *Values and Principles in European Union Foreign Policy*, Abingdon: Routledge, pp. 1–18

Lucarelli, S. and Manners, I. (2006) *Values and Principles in European Union Foreign Policy*, Abingdon, Routledge

Lynch, M. (2001) 'Ethnomethodology and the logic of practice', in T. Schatzski, E. Knorr Cetina, and E. von Savigny (eds), *The Practice Turn in Contemporary Theory*, London, Routledge, pp. 131–48

Lynch, M., Livingston, E. and Garfinkel, H. (1983) 'Temporal order in laboratory life', in K. D. Knorr-Cetina and M. Mulkay (eds), *Science Observed: Perspectives on the Social Study of Science*, London, Sage

McCourt, D. (2016) 'Practice theory and relationalism as the new constructivism', *International Studies Quarterly*, 60(3): 475–85

McKinlay, A. and Dunnett, A. (1998) 'How gun-owner accomplish being deadly average', in C. Antaki and S. Widdicombe (eds), *Identities in Talk*, London, Sage, pp. 34–51

Makarychev, A. S. (2008) 'Rebranding Russia: Norms, politics and power', in N. Tocci (ed.), *Who Is a Normative Foreign Policy Actor? The European Union and Its Global Partners*, Brussels, Centre for European Policy Studies, www.ceps.eu

Manners, I. (2002) 'Normative power Europe: A contradiction in terms?', *Journal of Common Market Studies*, 40(2): 235–58

Manners, I. (2013) 'Assessing the decennial, reassessing the global: Understanding European Union normative power in global politics', *Cooperation and Conflict*, 48(2): 304–29

Manners, I. and Whitman, R. (2003) 'The "difference engine": Constructing and representing the international identity of the European Union', *Journal of European Public Policy*, 10(3): 380–404

March, J. G. and Olsen, J. P. (1989) *Rediscovering Institutions*, New York: Free Press

March, J. G. and Olsen, J. P. (2004) 'The logic of appropriateness', Arena Working Papers WP04/09, www.arena.uio.no/publications/wp04_9.pdf

Maull, H. W. (2005) 'Europe and the new balance of global order', *International Affairs*, 81(4): 778

Mayer, H. (2008) 'Is it still called "Chinese whispers"? The EU's rhetoric and action as a responsible global institution', *International Affairs*, 84(1): 61–79

Maynard, D. W. (1980) 'Placement of topic changes in conversation', *Semiotica*, 30(3–4): 263–90

Mendez, M. (2007) 'Note on cases C-317 and 318/04 *European Parliament* v. *Council (PNR)* [2006] European Court Report (ECR) I-4721', *European Constitutional Law Review*, 3: 127–47

Meuser, M. and Nagel, U. (2002) 'Expertineninterviews – vielfach erprobt, wenig bedacht. Ein Beitrag zur qualitativen Methodendiskussion', in A. Bogner, B., Littig, and W. Menz (eds), *Das Experteninterview*, VS Verlag, Wiesbaden, pp. 71–95

Mediamax (2006) 'Weekly analytical report: Armenia and the Black Sea: Geography or politics? 10 June

Melander, E. (2001) 'The Nagorno–Karabakh conflict revisited: Was the war inevitable?', n *Journal of Cold War Studies*, 3(2): 48–75

Milliken, J. (1999) 'Intervention and identity: Reconstructing the West in Korea', in J. Weldes, M., Laffey, H., Gusterson, and R. Duvall (eds) *Cultures of Insecurity: States, Communities, and the Production of Danger*, Minneapolis MN, University of Minnesota Press, pp. 91–118

Milliken, J. (2001) 'Discourse Study: Bringing Rigor to Critical Theory', in K. M. Fierke and K. E. Jørgensen (eds), *Constructing International Relations: The Next Generation*, London, M.E. Sharpe, pp. 136–59

Moravcsik, A. (1997) 'Taking preferences seriously: A liberal theory of international politics', *International Organization*, 51(4): 513–53

Morgenthau, H. ([1948] 1993) *Politics Among Nations: The Struggle for Power and Peace*, New York, Knopf

Morris, R. T. (1956) 'A typology of norms', *American Sociological Review*, 21(5): 610–13

Mueller, H. (2001) 'International Relations as communicative action', in K. M. Fierke and K. E. Jørgensen (eds), *Constructing International Relations: The Next Generation*, London, M.E. Sharpe, pp. 160–78

Mueller, H. (2004) 'Arguing, bargaining, and all that. Reflections on the relationship of communicative action and rationalist theory in analysing international negotiation', *European Journal of International Relations*, 10(3): 395–495

Mulkay, M. (1984) 'The scientist talks back: A one act play, with a moral, about replication in science and reflexivity in sociology', *Social Studies of Science*, 14: 265–82

Neumann, I. B. (1995) *Russia and the Idea of Europe: A Study in Identity and International Relations (1800–1994)*, London, Routledge

Neumann, I. B. (1998) *Uses of the Other: 'The East' in European Identity Formation*, Borderlines Series, 9. Minneapolis, University of Minnesota Press

Neumann, I. B. (2016) *Russia and the Idea of Europe: A Study in Identity and International Relations (1800–1994)*, 2nd edn, London, Routledge

Nye, J. S. (1990) 'Soft power', *Foreign Policy*, 80: 153–71, www.jstor.org/stable/1148580?origin=JSTOR-pdf&seq=1#page_scan_tab_contents

Olsen, J. P. (2002) 'The many faces of Europeanization', *Journal of Common Market Studies*, 40(5): 921–52

Peace, M. (2004) 'Collective identity: The Greek case', in W. Carlsnaes, H. Sjursen, and B. White (eds), *Contemporary European Foreign Policy*, London, Sage, pp. 127–38

Pomerantz, A. (1978) 'Attributions of responsibility: Blamings', *Sociology*, 12: 115–21

Pomerantz, A. (1984) 'Agreeing and disagreeing with assessments: Some features of preferred/dispreferred turn-shapes', in J. M. Atkinson and J. Heritage (eds), *Structures of Social Action: Studies in Conversation Analysis*, Cambridge, Cambridge University Press, pp. 57–101

Pomerantz, A. (1988/89) 'Constructing scepticism: Four devices used to engender the audience's skepticism', *Research on Language and Social Interaction*, 22: 293–314

Potter, J. (1996) *Representing Reality: Discourse, Rhetoric and Social Construction*, London, Sage

Potter, J. (2002) 'Two kinds of natural', *Discourse Studies*, 4(4): 539–42

Potter, J. (2003) 'Discursive psychology: Between method and paradigm', *Discourse & Society*, 14: 783–94

Potter, J. (2004) 'Discourse Analysis as a way of analysing naturally occurring talk', in D. Silverman (ed.), *Qualitative Research: Theory, Method and Practice*, London, Sage, pp. 200–21

Potter, J. and Edwards, D. (1990) 'Nigel Lawson's tent: Discourse analysis, attribution theory and the social psychology of fact', *European Journal of Social Psychology*, 20(3): 24–40

Potter, J. and Hepburn, A. (2005) 'Qualitative interviews in psychology: Problems and possibilities in qualitative research', *Psychology*, 2: 281–307

Potter, J. and Wetherell, M. (1987) *Discourse and Social Psychology: Beyond Attitudes and Behaviour*, London, Sage

Pouliot, V. (2010) *International Security in Practice*, Cambridge, Cambridge University Press

Pouliot, V. and Cornut, J. (2015) 'Practice theory and the study of diplomacy: A research agenda', *Cooperation and Conflict*, 50(3): 297–315

Ringmar, E. (2014) 'The search for dialogue as a hindrance to understanding: Practices as interparadigmatic research program', *International Theory*, 6(1): 1–27

166

Risse, T. (2000) ' "Let's argue!": Communicative action in world politics', *International Organisation*, 54(1): 1–39

Risse, T. (2010) *A Community of Europeans? Transnational Identities and Public Spheres*, Ithaca, Cornell University Press

Rouse, J. (2001) 'Two concepts of practices', in T. Schatzki *et al.* (eds), *The Practice Turn in Contemporary Theory*, New York, Routledge, pp. 189–98

Rumelili, B. (2007) *Constructing Regional Community and Order in Europe and Southeast Asia*, Basingstoke, Palgrave

Sacks, H. (1972) 'An initial investigation of the usability of conversational data for doing sociology', in D. Sudnow (ed.), *Studies in Social Interaction*, London, Collier-Macmillan, pp. 31–7

Sacks, H. (1979) 'Hotrodder: A revolutionary category', in G. Psathas (ed.), *Everyday Language: Studies in Ethnomethodology*, New York, Irvington Press, pp. 7–14

Sacks, H. (1984) 'On doing "being ordinary" ', in M. Atkinson and J. Heritage (eds), *Structures of Social Action*, Cambridge, Cambridge University Press

Sacks, H. (1992) *Lectures on Conversation*, ed. G. Jefferson, Oxford, Basil Blackwell

Sacks, H., Schegloff, E. A., and Jefferson, G. (1974) 'A simplest systematics for the organization of turn-taking for conversation', *Language*, 50 (4): 696–735

Schatzki, T. R., Knorr Cetina, K. and von Savigny, E. (2001) *The Practice Turn in Contemporary Theory*, London, Routledge

Schegloff, E. A. (1982) 'Discourse as interactional achievement: Some uses of "uh huh" and other things that come between sentences', in D. Tannen (ed.), *Analyzing Discourse: Text and Talk*, Washington, DC, Georgetown University Press, pp. 71–93

Schegloff, E. A. (1986) 'The routine as achievement', *Human Studies*, 9: 111–51

Schegloff, E. A. (1991) 'Reflections on talk and social structure', in D. Boden and Z. Zimmerman (eds), *Talk and Social Structure*, Cambridge, Polity, pp. 44–70

Schegloff, E. A. (1992) 'In another context', in A. Duranti and C. Goodwin (eds), *Rethinking Context: Language as an Interactive Phenomenon*, Cambridge, Cambridge University Press, pp. 111–204

Schegloff, E. A. (1997) 'Whose text? Whose context?', *Discourse & Society*, 8 (2): 165–87

Schegloff, E. A. (2007) 'A tutorial on membership categorization', *Journal of Pragmatics*, 39: 462–82

Schegloff, E. A. (2009) 'One perspective on conversation analysis, comparative perspectives', in J. Sidnell (ed.), *Conversation Analysis: Comparative Perspective*, Cambridge, Cambridge University Press

Schegloff, E. A., Jefferson, G. and Sacks, H. (1977) 'The preference for self-correction in the organization of repair in conversation', *Language*, 53: 361–82

Schimmelfennig, F. (1997) 'Rhetorisches Handeln in der internationalen Politik', *Zeitschrift für Internationale Beziehungen*, 4(2): 219–54

Schimmelfennig, F. (2001) 'The Community trap: Liberal norms, rhetorical action, and the eastern enlargement of the European Union', *International Organization*, 55(1): 47–80

Schimmelfennig, F. and Sedelmeier, U. (2005) *The Europeanization of Central and Eastern Europe*, Ithaca, Cornell University Press

Schmidt, V. A. (2007) 'Trapped by their ideas: French elites' discourses of European integration and globalisation', *Journal of European Public Policy*, 14(7): 992–1009

Schmidt, V. A. (2014) 'EU leaders' ideas and discourse in the eurozone crisis: A discursive institutionalist analysis', in C. Carta and J.-F. Morin (eds), *EU Foreign Policy through the Lens of Discourse Analysis: Making Sense of Diversity*, Farnham, Ashgate

Searle, J. R. (1995) *The Construction of Social Reality*, London, Allen Lane

Sedelmeier, U. (1998) 'The European Union's Association Policy towards the countries of Central and Eastern Europe: Collective EU identity and policy paradigms in a composite policy', Ph.D. thesis, University of Sussex

Sedelmeier, U. (2001) 'Eastern enlargement: Risk, rationality, and role-compliance', in M. G. Cowles and M. Smith (eds), *The State of the European Union*: Vol. 5 *Risk, Reform, Resistance, and Revival*, Oxford, Oxford University Press, pp. 164–85

Sedelmeier, U. (2002) 'Sectoral dynamics of EU eastern enlargement: Advocacy, access and alliances in a composite policy', *Journal of European Public Policy*, 9(4): 627–49

Sedelmeier, U. (2003) 'EU enlargement, identity, and the analysis of European foreign policy: Identity formation through policy practice', in Robert Schuman Centre working paper, European University Institute

Sedelmeier, U. (2004) 'Identity and European Foreign Policy', in Walter Carlsnaes, Helene Sjursen, and Brian White (eds), *European Foreign Policy Today*, London, Sage, pp. 123–40

Sending, O. J. (2002) 'Constitution, choice and change: Problems with the "logic of appropriateness" and its use in constructivist theory', *European Journal of International Relations*, 8(4) 443–70

Shapiro, M. (1988) *The Politics of Representation: Writing Practices in Biography, Photography and Policy Analysis*, Madison, WI, University of Wisconsin Press

Shapiro, M. (1989) 'Textualizing global politics', in J. Der Derian and M. Shapiro (eds), *International/Intertextual Relations: Postmodern Readings of World Politics*, Lexington, Lexington Books

Shelley, L. (2004) 'Unholy trinity: Transnational crime, corruption, and terrorism', *Brown Journal of World Affairs*, 11(2): 101–10

Shotter, J. (1993) *Cultural Politics of Everyday Life: Social Constructionism, Rhetoric and Knowing of the Third Kind*, Milton Keynes, Open University Press

Silverman, D. (1985) *Qualitative Methodology and Sociology: Describing the Social World*, Aldershot, Gower

Sjursen, H. (2002) 'Why expand? The question of legitimacy and justification in the EU's enlargement policy', *Journal of Common Market Studies*, 40(3): 491–513

Smith, D. (1978) 'K is mentally ill: The anatomy of a factual account', *Sociology*, 12: 23–53

Smith, Karen E. (2002) 'Conceptualising the EU's international identity: *sui generis* or following the latest trends?', paper presented at the ECPR European Union Politics Conference, Bordeaux

Smith, M. H. (2000) 'Negotiating new Europes: The roles of the European Union', *Journal of European Public Policy*, 7(5): 806–22

Sneijder, P. and te Molder, H. F. M. (2005) 'Health should not have to be a problem: Talking health and accountability in an internet forum on veganism', *Journal of Health Psychology*, 9(4): 599–616

Soetendorp, B. (1994) 'The evolution of the EC/EU as a single foreign policy actor', Walter Carlsnaes, Helene Sjursen, and Brian White (eds), *European Foreign Policy Today*, London, Sage, pp. 103–19

Speer, S. (2002) ' "Natural" and "contrived" data: A sustainable distinction?', *Discourse Studies*, 4(4): 511–25

Stone, A. (1994) 'What is a supranational constitution? An essay in International Relations theory', *Review of Politics*, 55: 444–71

Szczerbiak, A. and Taggart, P. (2008) *Opposing Europe?: The Comparative Party Politics of Euroscepticism*: Volume 2: Comparative and Theoretical Perspectives, Oxford, Oxford University Press

Szczerbiak, A. and Taggart, P. (2013) 'Coming in from the cold? Euroscepticism, government participation and party positions on Europe', *Journal of Common Market Studies*, 51(1): 17–37 [special issue: 'Confronting Euroscepticism']

Telo, M. (2001) *European Union and New Regionalism: Regional Actors and Global Governance in a Post-Hegemonic Era*, Aldershot, Ashgate

Tetlock, P. E. and Belkin, A. (1996) *Counterfactual Thought Experiments in World Politics: Logical, Methodological, and Psychological Perspectives*, Princeton, Princeton University Press

Tonra, B. (2001) *The Europeanisation of National Foreign Policy: Dutch, Danish and Irish Foreign Policy in the European Union*, Farnham, Ashgate

Tonra, B. and Christiansen, T. (2004) *Rethinking European Union Foreign Policy*, Manchester, Manchester University Press

Tully, J. (2002) 'The unfreedom of the moderns in comparison to their ideals of constitutionalism and democracy', *Modern Law Review*, 65(2): 204–28

Turner, S. (1994) *The Social Theory of Practices: Tradition, Tacit Knowledge, and Presuppositions*, Cambridge: Polity Press; Chicago: University of Chicago Press

Ulbert, C. and Risse, T. (2005) 'Deliberately changing the discourse: What does make arguing effective?', *Acta Politica*, 40(3): 351–67

Watson, D. R. (1978) 'Categorisation, authorisation and blame negotiation in conversation', *Sociology*, 12: 105–13

Watson, D. R. (1997) 'Some general reflections on "categorisation" and "sequence" ', in S. Hester and P. Eglin (eds), *Culture in Action: Studies in Membership Categorization Analysis*, Washington, DC, University Press of America

Weiler, J. (1999) *The Constitution of Europe*, Cambridge, Cambridge University Press

Wendt, A. (1995) 'Constructing international politics', *International Security*, 20(1): 71–81

Wessel, R. (2006) 'The multilevel constitution of European foreign relations', in N. Tsagourias (ed.), *Transnational Constitutionalism: International and European Models*, Cambridge, Cambridge University Press

Whitman, R. G. (1997) 'The international identity of the EU: Instruments as identity', in A. Landau and R. G. Whitman (eds), *Rethinking the European Union: Institutions, Interests and Identities*, Basingstoke, Macmillan, pp. 54–71

Widdicombe, S. and Wooffitt, R. (1995) *The Language of Youth Subcultures: Social identity in Action*, Hertfordshire, Harvester Wheatsheaf

Wiener, A. (2007) 'The dual quality of norms and governance beyond the state: Sociological and normative approaches to "interaction" ', *Critical Review of International Social and Political Philosophy*, 10(1): 47–69

Wight, M. (1966) 'Why is there no international theory?', in M. Wight and H. Butterfield (eds), *Diplomatic Investigations*, London, Allen & Unwin, pp. 17–34

Wittgenstein, L. (1953) *Philosophical Investigations*, Oxford, Blackwell

Wittgenstein, L. (1958) *The Blue and Brown Books*, Oxford, Blackwell

Wodak, R. and Weiss, G. (2001) '"We are different than the Americans and the Japanese!" A critical discourse analysis of decision-making in European Union meetings about employment policies', in E. Weigand and M. Dascal (eds), *Negotiation and Power in Dialogic Interactions*, Amsterdam, Benjamins

Wodak, R. and Weiss, G. (2005) 'Analyzing European Union discourse: Theories and applications', in R. Wodak and P. Chilton (eds), *A New Agenda in (Critical) Discourse Analysis: Theory, Methodology and Interdisciplinarity*, Amsterdam, Benjamins

Wong, R. (2007) 'Foreign policy in Graziano', in P. and Vink, M. P. (eds), *Europeanization – New Research Agendas*, Basingstoke, Palgrave Macmillan

Wooffitt, R. (1991) '"I was just doing X ... when Y": Some inferential properties of a device in accounts of paranormal experiences', *Text*, 11: 267–88

Wooffitt, R. (2005) *Conversation Analysis and Discourse Analysis – A Comparative and Critical Introduction*, London, Sage

Wooffitt, R. and Widdicombe, S. (2006) 'Interaction in interviews', in P. Drew and D. Weinberg (ed.), *Talk and Interaction in Social Research Methods*, London, Sage

Žižek, S. (2006) *The Universal Exception: Selected Writings*, vol. 2, ed. R. Butler and S. Stephens, London & New York, Continuum

Index